M000197190

CAPTURED FIRE
The New Daily Homilies
Seasonal and Sanctoral - Year One

Visit our web site at
www.albahouse.org
(for orders www.stpauls.us)

or call 1-800-343-2522 (ALBA)
and request current catalog

Captured Fire

The New Daily Homilies

Seasonal and Sanctoral - Year One

S. JOSEPH KREMPA

ST PAULS

Library of Congress Cataloging-in-Publication Data

Krempa, S. Joseph.
Captured fire: the new daily homilies / by Stanley J. Krempa.
   p. cm.
  ISBN-13: 978-0-8189-1288-7 (v. 1)
  ISBN-13: 978-0-8189-1289-4 (v. 2)
  ISBN-10: 0-8189-1288-X (v. 1)
  ISBN-10: 0-8189-1289-8 (v. 2)
1. Catholic Church—Sermons. 2. Sermons, American I. Title.
  BX1756.K782C36 2008
  252'.6—dc22
                      2008035227

Produced and designed in the United States of America by the
Fathers and Brothers of the Society of St. Paul,
2187 Victory Boulevard, Staten Island, New York 10314-6603
as part of their communications apostolate.

ISBN-10: 0-8189-1288-X (v. 1)
ISBN 10: 0-8189-1289-8 (v. 2)
ISBN-13: 978-0-8189-1288-7 (v. 1)
SBN-13: 978-0-8189-1289-4 (v. 2)
Two-Volume Set: ISBN 10: 0-8189-1290-1
Two-Volume Set: ISBN 13: 978-0-8189-1290-0

© Copyright 2008 by the Society of St. Paul / Alba House

Printing Information:

Current Printing - first digit   1 2 3 4 5 6 7 8 9 10

Year of Current Printing - first year shown

2008 2009 2010 2011 2012 2013 2014 2015 2016 2017

Table of Contents
Seasonal Homilies

Sanctoral Cycle

Season of Advent

MONDAY OF THE FIRST WEEK OF ADVENT
Isaiah 2:1-5; Matthew 8:5-11

Advent, if we really keep it as Advent, is a wonderfully sublime season of the Church year because it carries within it the "grace of beginning again." Advent is not just a time to remember the ancient yearning of old Israel for a Redeemer. It is also very contemporary.

Each year, we face new challenges and are faced with a new aspect of our life's mission as well as the need of new graces. In Advent, we use old Israel's prayers of expectation to express the needs we have today.

Maybe we are like the ailing boy for whom the centurion prays in today's Gospel reading. Some of us may need healing in our body. All of us, however, need healing in our soul. Many of us carry within us interior wounds and scars of the past year and now seek to be made whole.

Maybe we are like the Gospel centurion praying for people in our personal life or in public life. Many people we know have lost their way and need the strength and wisdom to return as well as the gift of being faithful in an unfaithful time.

Maybe we are like the loyal remnant Isaiah describes who in the middle of vast cultural corruption are called to be "the cloud by day or the fire by night" to show people another way to live. We can be the "people of the mountain" to whom others can come to rediscover the way and word of the Lord.

It is helpful to identify during this first week of Advent the graces we need during this season and make them the focus of our prayer and reflection. Seeking the special gift from the Lord that we need at this point in our life will make our Advent unique and productive. It will also provide a strong counterweight to the commercial tsunami that usually swamps the quiet spirituality of this season.

We can also pray that the Lord will give us the grace to recognize His response when it comes.

Advent is not just about what God has done in the past but about what God can do in our world and in our life today.

dle "coming," He is our strength for living. The Eucharist has been called "esca viatorum," food for the journey and food for travelers on the road to heaven.

As we prepare to celebrate Christ's unique birth in Bethlehem at Christmas, we can try to appreciate the abiding, Emmanuel presence of Christ in the Eucharist and in the Mass. Here, Jesus still teaches. Here, Jesus still heals. Here, Jesus still gives hope. Here, Jesus is food for our life's most serious and important journey, the journey to heaven.

The Mass is the deepest of many ways that Jesus continues to be Emmanuel, God with us, all year long.

THURSDAY OF THE FIRST WEEK OF ADVENT
Isaiah 26:1-6; Matthew 7:21, 24-27

In today's Gospel, the Lord speaks of two houses. One is built on sand and the other on rock. In good weather, they both look alike. In fact, the one built on sand might even appear more spectacular, as do many seashore homes today.

The Lord warns us, however, that good weather does not last. Storms with their rains, floods and winds will come to all of us. It is not the fair weather but the storm that will reveal the strength of the foundation.

In the face of the storms that will inevitably come our way, the only question is whether we have built on sand or on rock. Have we spent our lives and resources focused on foundation or façade?

From where do we derive strength for living? Can wealth unite a fragmented and distrusting family or accelerate its division? Can gadgets and gifts help a person deal with terminal illness in any deep way or distract from its truth? Can upward mobility aid a person trapped by addiction or enable it? Can passing relationships in our life substitute for the abiding relationship we have with Jesus Christ?

We can widen our screen. Is a nation's strength found only in its military or economic muscle? Is it not rather found in the quality of its family life, its respect for human life, its quest for justice as well as the character of its citizens?

Isaiah's strong nation of "firm purpose" is strong because it is firm not only in the strength of its conviction. Lots of people have strong but destructive convictions. Its strength comes from the rightness of its goal, from living in the way of the Lord. The same is true of us.

Is our personal life built on anything deeper than material accumulation or cultivation of image? A façade may impress but it cannot give support because a building, however beautiful, is only as strong as its foundation.

Advent calls us to rebuild our lives on the mystery of Jesus Christ. Through Baptism, He is part of our life and we are part of His life today. God's grace and purpose are embedded in everything that happens to us.

Our embrace of that truth is strength in any storm.

FRIDAY OF THE FIRST WEEK OF ADVENT
Isaiah 19:17-24; Matthew 9:27-31

Jesus' instruction to His followers to remain silent about this miracle might seem puzzling to us. There has been a great deal of reflection over the centuries about the meaning of this caution from Jesus.

At the end of Matthew's Gospel, in contrast, the Lord sends His Apostles to tell the whole world about the Good News.

Perhaps these two individuals were not yet ready to become evangelists. Hopefully, their witnessing the extraordinary grace of this cure will prepare them to become disciples. But they may not yet have been ready to proclaim the Good News because one miracle does not an evangelist make. Before we begin an outreach to others, we need to secure and mature our faith by grafting the teaching of the whole Gospel onto our own life.

We are not called to communicate temporary enthusiasms but to share our experience of the Lord. Knowledge of the Lord grows most deeply when there are few miracles, when religious feelings do not easily percolate and when consolations are not profuse. Those are not times of barrenness but of growth deeper than that of feelings as the Lord's call to conversion really takes deep and silent root in our lives.

A healthy and strong spiritual life needs not only spring and summer. It needs autumn and winter where the energy of new life is strengthened and stored.

Only when we have experienced the charity of Holy Thursdays, the sufferings of Good Fridays and the desolation of Holy Saturdays in our life are we ready to go out and give the Good News of Easter to others.

Isaiah says that in the Day of the Lord, the spiritually immature will acquire understanding and people of constant complaint will be willing to listen to voices other than their own.

When these dispositions start to occur in our life, then we too are ready to move from being disciples of the Lord to becoming evangelists.

Serious evangelism needs not only enthusiasm but also maturity, light as well as fire. The good news we share with others must first be deeply rooted in our own life.

Abundant fruits need deep roots.

SATURDAY OF THE FIRST WEEK OF ADVENT
Isaiah 30:19-21, 23-26; Matthew 9:35-10:1, 6-8

We have in today's Gospel a traditional reading about vocations. We always need to ask the Lord for more laborers. But we should not forget what the Lord is telling us about the harvest.

The harvest is all around us. We all know men and women ready to open their hearts to the truth of Christ, willing to give of their substance to the advance of God's rule here on earth.

Unscrupulous people who appeal to this good will for selfish and dark reasons can, however, manipulate them. The harvest can be squandered by laborers who are incompetent or darkly motivated.

But, the harvest is still there. The yearning for truth, the search for light, the quest for deep community are all still present in the human race. Consider, for example, the billions of dollars given each year to charities of all sorts. Consider the search for saving truth that fuels the market for intellectual fads and ersatz religiosity. Consider the quest for the supernatural displayed by the advertisements that fill the tabloid newspapers.

Beneath the surface selfishness that our culture fuels, there remains a deep goodness within people, a "deep down freshness" that we call the image of God. It can be damaged, defaced or deformed but it cannot be completely destroyed. The flame may be little more than a "pilot light" but it still burns.

Within every person, beneath the defenses, the fears, the accumulated hurts and the surface cynicism, deep within is the image of God, like a light ready to be sparked into flame, a seed to be coaxed into growth.

That takes work, time and patience by the Lord's disciples. That is why they are called "laborers."

We should pray for vocations. Still, the Lord's teaching remains a source of strength and confident hope for us. The laborers may be few but the harvest can still be huge!

MONDAY OF THE SECOND WEEK OF ADVENT
Isaiah 35:1-10; Luke 5:17-26

One detail of today's Gospel reading stands out at this time of year. It is the care and faith of the sick man's friends.

It is significant that all the Gospel accounts mention the faith of the friends who bring him before Jesus. They were willing to break down any barrier, even the tiles of the roof, to bring him before the Lord.

How far are we willing to go to bring people to Christ? What barriers are we ready to overcome to present people to Jesus? We may not face the barriers of a crowded room but the more formidable ones of popular prejudice, past resentments and current indifference.

Through prayer, of course, we can bring people before the Lord. This season of Advent is a splendid opportunity to gather in our prayer all the people we like and the people we don't like who are in need of God's grace. We can pray for the physical healing they may need, the spiritual cleansing they may require or the grace of the Holy Spirit to enable them to reorient their lives toward Christ.

Prayer for others not only helps them but also enlarges us. We all need the grace of the Holy Spirit to make that journey on the "salvation road," which Isaiah describes in today's first reading. Many people have been detoured from that road to Christ. Some have been sidelined along the road because of illness or spiritual weariness. Others may have lost their way.

We can all take some concrete steps to invite others to Christ and His Church. We all can be like people who stop to help those who are disabled on the side of the road. Our invitation can be a vehicle to help them back on their journey to the Lord.

Advent is a grace-filled time to help others back on the road to Christ. As Isaiah says in today's first reading, we all have a journey to make. We all need help along the way. Prayer can help others rise and walk again toward Christ.

TUESDAY OF THE SECOND WEEK OF ADVENT
Isaiah 40:1-11; Matthew 18:12-14

They say that sheep get lost... easily! That is a fact of the shepherd's life. Yet, the missing stray stays on the shepherd's mind so much that he leaves the others to search for that one sheep. It is much like a parent with many children whose attention is fixed on the one who is ill.

The Good News of the Gospel is not that the lost one can find the way home, or that those who have drifted or gone away can discover a road map back. It is that the shepherd is out searching, seeking, looking and finding in all kinds of ways.

What we celebrate at Christmas is not the fact that God let Himself be rediscovered by the human race, but that He came in search of His people, a divine quest that is recounted throughout the Old Testament. Finally, God Himself entered human history to heal it from within.

The human race needed more than a pardon from above, a kind of cosmic absolution. It needed healing and restoration from the inside. The wounded heart of the human race did not need a bandage, it needed surgery. It needed not only a diagnosis but a transfusion. So, the shepherd became one of the sheep. God took on human nature to become the new "Adam" of a fresh, healed and restored creation and to lead the flock in a way they could understand, by word and example.

It is Isaiah's prophecy come true. The Lord is leading His people back from exile, "leading the sheep with care." This is the mystery and majesty of the Incarnation as well as its drama and drive.

Christmas celebrates the fact that God embraced our life so that we might share His life once more.

We have all strayed in different ways. The shepherd is calling us back in many ways, sometimes in ways and through intermediaries we least expect.

This Advent let yourself be found once again.

WEDNESDAY OF THE SECOND WEEK OF ADVENT
Isaiah 40:25-31; Matthew 11:28-30

A yoke is a collar that fits on the shoulders to help a person carry a load. There are good yokes and bad yokes.

Bad yokes are no laughing matter. If they fit poorly and do not distribute the weight properly, they can increase the load and even break our backs. A good yoke, on the other hand, fits well and spreads out the weight through leverage so we can lift a burden several times our own weight.

Jesus' yoke is easy to wear because it fits perfectly. His grace complements and enhances our nature; it does not add to our burden.

11

The temptation in reading this particular Gospel passage is to interpret it as a quantitative comparison of Jesus' directives with Old Testament regulations. Instead, the Lord is speaking about helping us manage the troubles of life.

Jesus not only gave a message for healthy and holy living. He also helps us carry the burdens that come our way. As Isaiah predicted, "He gives strength to the fainting, they will soar with eagle's wings." This is a dramatic image that drives home the heart of what Jesus is giving us – the Holy Spirit Who is, in a contemporary image, the "wind beneath our wings."

Our faith and our Church are not intended to be additional obligations added to work, social responsibilities and school activities. They are the levers that help us carry the rest. Our faith and life within the Church provide the framework, the yoke or handle that helps us see purpose, direction and mission in everything we do and in everything that occurs in our life. We wear glasses not just to see the glasses but beyond them. Faith provides the "glasses" that help us see everything else clearly.

Our Faith should not add to our burdens but give us the purpose and power to carry any load.

THURSDAY OF THE SECOND WEEK OF ADVENT
Isaiah 41:13-20; Matthew 11:11-15

"Worm, Jacob!" "Maggot, Israel!" "The kingdom taken by force!" These are strong and striking images used in today's readings that speak of truths that are experienced in every life.

Isaiah is speaking to a nation that was despised and considered inconsequential in the world politics of its time. Yet, these are the very people the Lord will raise up to be a blade, strong and gleaming, to cut the harvest. The Lord will take Israel's barrenness and bring forth abundance and vitality.

As with old Israel, our failures, mistakes and sins do not have to be the end of the story.

If we have sinned, that does not mean that the story of grace in our life is over.

If we have failed the Lord, that doesn't mean that the power of our Baptism is exhausted.

If we have drifted far from the Lord, that does not mean that there is no way back.

If we have abandoned Christ, that does not mean that the Lord has abandoned us.

If, at times, we feel like a worm, God can still make of us something splendid but that takes our cooperation.

The Kingdom of God in our life does not grow naturally or easily. There is no "golden parachute" by which we can easily fall into the Kingdom of God. It takes effort, zeal, a wrenching from our old ways, all part of the "violence" to which Jesus refers in today's Gospel.

The Lord's words about violence and the Kingdom can be variously interpreted. But, one truth is clear. The spiritual growth of the Kingdom doesn't just happen by adding water, even baptismal water. It requires not "microwave spirituality" but the hard, serious and long work of conversion and renewing our honest participation in the Church's life.

We cannot stop physical decline. That happens to all of us. But spiritual rebirth is always possible. God can always restore the "joy of our youth."

FRIDAY OF THE SECOND WEEK OF ADVENT
Isaiah 48:17-19; Matthew 11:16-19

Many people in Jesus' time claimed to be eager for the Kingdom of God. Yet, they rejected the preaching of John and the message of Jesus. In today's Gospel reading, the Lord compares them to children who were constantly dissatisfied in doing what they were being asked to do. Here, Jesus is speaking about the people of His generation and people of every generation.

The people refused John the Baptist's call to repentance because they considered him too severe, too conservative. They refused Jesus' call to reform and live the Kingdom life because He was too tolerant, too "progressive" for them.

The same thing happens today. Many people claim that they want God to come into their life but they want God only on their own terms.

They do not want their relationship with God to affect the way they spend money.

They do not want their relationship with God to impact their sexual activity.

They do not want their relationship with God to interfere with their business life.

They do not want their relationship with God to curtail the way they treat others.

They want the Church to "be there" for them but they do not have time to "be there" for the Church.

The excuses are many. The parish may be too conservative or too liberal; there is too much music or too little music; there is too much talk of politics in the pulpit or the sermons do not address the issues of the day; the bishop should speak out on certain things or the bishop is speaking out on too many things. These are all ways of evading commitment. Yet, without commitment to the Lord, none of the great spiritual things of which Scripture speaks will ever happen in our life.

The Lord says through Isaiah, "I teach you what is for your good." To follow the Gospel is to move toward spiritual vitality but the avenue to that new life is through the Gospel. God will not be a real part of our lives unless we follow on His terms and not on our own.

The Gospel is not a seasonal game for us to play at our leisure. It is the road to salvation, inner peace and eternal life. Take away the Gospel and life itself becomes only a game of short-term winners and losers. The Gospel gives our life an eternal meaning as the Creator God intended.

SATURDAY OF THE SECOND WEEK OF ADVENT
Sirach 48:1-4, 9-11; Matthew 17: 9, 10-13

Our readings today focus on a major figure in Old Testament history and Jewish lore, Elijah the prophet. Called by God to summon a people back to the true God, Elijah worked wonders that sought to recapture the people's appreciation of God's saving power on their behalf.

The Old Testament does not record Elijah's death but portrays him as going into the heavens in a chariot of fire only to return before the time of the Messiah. Jewish tradition has looked to the coming of Elijah to usher in the Messiah and a time of peace and unity. Those end times would bring a solution to all mysteries of life.

To this day among some Jewish people a difficult question of faith is said to find a solution "when Elijah comes." The fifth cup of wine at the Passover Seder is blessed in honor of Elijah. At a Jewish child's circumcision, a chair is left unoccupied for the invisible presence of Elijah. Jewish legend says that Elijah roams the world today in various disguises continuing to do good and to prepare people for the Messiah.

The Lord tells the Apostles that John the Baptist fulfilled Elijah's role in announcing Jesus' coming. For us, John the Baptist's message within the Advent season continues his role as our Elijah calling us to reform and preparation.

The Messiah is now among us. The challenge facing us today is not that of chronological waiting for the Christ but of opening our lives now to His message and His grace in order to experience the beginning of the Kingdom in our life.

Backsliding was as common in the Old Testament as it is today. That is why prophets such as Elijah were constantly needed to call the people back to the Lord. We too can slide away from the Lord in small ways that generate a "snowball" effect. Few people abandon the Lord in one dramatic act. Departure from the Lord most often happens gradually. Just as water doesn't evaporate suddenly, so our loyalty to Christ can gradually diminish.

Advent is very much an "Elijah season" that challenges us

and fills us with the hope that the Lord will renew His presence in our life.

Elijah called down fire from heaven against the pagan priests. Advent, our "Elijah season" seeks to ignite the fire within us.

MONDAY OF THE THIRD WEEK OF ADVENT
Numbers 24:2-7, 15-17; Matthew 21:23-27

The account of Balaam in today's first reading is an unusual little story with a huge import. Balaam was a free-lance "sorcerer" who was hired to place a curse upon Israel.

Four times he looked out on Israel and was unable to curse but was instead compelled to bless Israel.

Four times he looked out and saw a different dimension of the mission of Israel and of the Messiah.

Four times he beheld a powerful truth about the Messiah's reign.

Today's first reading combines the final two prophecies of Balaam about the Messiah concerning His might and His light.

"His royalty shall be exalted..." exclaims Balaam. The Kingdom of Christ does not know national boundaries or term limits. Military might or economic power does not extend it. It is composed of all those who embrace the teaching of Jesus Christ. It grows not through coercion but through the grace of Christ's Death and Resurrection. It lives not in a particular latitude but in the hearts, minds and souls of Christians everywhere.

"A star will advance...," says Balaam as well. Christ comes as guiding light not to spiritual dilettantes as those in today's Gospel reading but to people who are on a serious quest. In a world of so much artificial and temporary light, Christ is the true light.

Might and light – glimpses of the Messiah that Balaam saw from afar, "beholding him though not near."

The spiritual might and light of Christ's Kingdom show themselves particularly in times of cultural crisis when people do not know where to turn or upon whom to rely. Light shows best in darkness.

What Balaam saw from afar was a glimpse of the Lord's Kingdom dwelling among us now.

What he could only glimpse and bless from the mountaintop, we can inhabit by grace. The Kingdom of Christ, source of spiritual might and light for each of us, is growing and alive within His Church.

TUESDAY OF THE THIRD WEEK OF ADVENT
Zephaniah 3:1-2, 9-13; Matthew 21:28-32

"Actions speak louder than words." That is certainly one point we can draw from the Lord's parable.

There is, however, a deeper point here that is profoundly challenging to each of us and takes us into the dynamics of conversion.

In the parable's terms, both sons were honest. One said, "I will" and the other said, "I won't."

The crux of the parable is in what happened later. They changed and the same can happen to us.

Our "no" can become a "yes." More troubling, however, is the fact that our "yes" can become a "no."

In a marriage, in the religious life, in our daily Christian life, slowly, almost imperceptibly, our words can stop matching our actions. Soon, all we have are words. The substance of the Christian life is gone. Our rhetorical "yes" uttered in a time of great fervor has become an experiential "no."

The reverse is also true. Our initial "no" can become a "yes." People who refuse the Lord, who decide to depart from life within the Church find themselves slowly beginning to live the Gospel once again, praying occasionally and then once more joining the community of faith. Their "no" can become a "yes."

We all need to carefully attend to the stirrings of sin in our life to make sure that our "yes" remains a "yes."

This parable is not only about the history of salvation when the Gospel was refused by the religious elite of Jesus' time but accepted by sinners who knew their need of salvation. It is also about the story of every soul.

The Lord calls us to work in the vineyard. In church, we say "yes" every Sunday. But what are we really saying in the actions of our life later on?

Is our "yes" becoming a "no"?

WEDNESDAY OF THE THIRD WEEK OF ADVENT
Isaiah 45:6-8, 18, 21-25; Luke 7:18-23

The art and science of translation are very much in the news these days. It seems that everyone has an opinion about translation: accuracy vs. intelligibility, elegance vs. precision.

In today's first reading, the prophet Isaiah describes the Day of the Lord as the time when justice descends from heaven and salvation springs out of the earth. St. Jerome, in his Vulgate translation, gives a directly Messianic focus to this verse when he renders Isaiah's description of the Day of the Lord as the time when the "Just One descends from heaven and the Savior springs forth from the earth."

In his version, St. Jerome captures the magnificence of the Incarnation as the Second Person of the Trinity descends into the womb of Mary and she brings forth the Savior.

The Savior comes to us today so we can project to others His saving power. The signs of the Messiah's presence that Jesus enumerates in today's Gospel need to be made present for every generation.

Today there is a blindness to truth and human dignity. Today there is an inability to walk with the poor and with unpopular minorities. Today, there is a new kind of leprosy in diseases that carry a social stigma. Today, there is a deafness that refuses to hear the cries of the poor and lonely. Today, there is a spiritual dying by people in sin and despair. Today, there is poverty in people from the lack of the spiritual goods of faith, hope and charity.

We are called to bring forth the Savior to people around us so that the blind people we know can see, the lame today can walk, today's lepers can be cleansed of isolation, the deaf among us can hear, the dead we know can be brought to life and the poor around us can see the Church as good news in their lives.

The Just One has come; the Savior has come forth. It is our task to be His instruments in our world. That is the Advent challenge to every Christian and to every generation.

THURSDAY OF THE THIRD WEEK OF ADVENT
Isaiah 54:1-10; Luke 7:24-30

Isaiah's call to Israel to "enlarge her tent" to accommodate all her spiritual children who will come to her reminds us of the crowds that will fill our churches at Christmas. If such numbers came on a weekly basis, virtually every parish would have to initiate a capital campaign to double the size of its building.

Why do the people come? Do they come simply for the music? Do they come for the solemn rituals? Do they come for nostalgia or to hear the self help messages they hear on television every day? Like the people who crowded the desert to hear John the Baptist, most people come to hear the Word of truth, redemption and hope. Every Christmas is an opportunity for the Church to present once more the ancient message that every generation needs to hear. It is the message not of condemnation but of new life that can be ours in Christ. It is a message not of judgment but of reconciliation. It is a message not of nostalgia but of hope.

The liturgical surroundings of Christmas are something to which we all look forward. They evoke tradition, beauty and solemnity. But the center of Christmas past, Christmas present and Christmas future remains the hope of new life. We should never forget that Christmas is not only about the Christmas season but also about the transformation that can be ours in Christ.

It was the hope of new life that drew people to hear John the Baptist. It is this hope that brings so many people to church at Christmas. Our Christmas celebrations at home or in church

19

should be like John the Baptist in pointing the way to Christ, inviting people to experience Christ's power and grace.

As we approach Christmas, it is important that we examine whether our Advent and Christmas celebrations speak in some way to others of our faith in Christ, whether they point to Christ. It is very easy for the activities of this season to become separated from Christ, like the amputation of a limb from the body or a branch from the vine. That is the special danger of this season more so than that of Easter.

Let us take care that our Advent and Christmas traditions speak of Christ and the message of salvation for each of us. Christmas is not simply a holiday season. It is about the birth of Christ into the world two thousand years ago in Bethlehem and in our lives today.

FRIDAY OF THE THIRD WEEK OF ADVENT
Isaiah 56:1-3, 6-8; John 5:33-36

The Lord gives a magnificent testimony to John the Baptist when He calls him a "burning and shining lamp." During his ministry, John the Baptist drew huge crowds and received the popular acclaim of the people. He was a spiritual "rock star."

John worked hard, prayed hard and preached hard. He lived a life of penance and witness to the coming Messiah. Then came a time for that role to end when Jesus came forward. John went offstage and Jesus came to the center.

It is not easy to go into the shadows after a time in the spotlight. If we live long enough, however, that will happen to all of us. We leave our jobs, vacate our positions or we retire. It is then time for someone else to take our place. Our children meet their future spouse and we have to let them go to start a family of their own. What we were given to do is done and we hope we did it well. Now, someone else will take over and our way may not be theirs. It is hard to let go.

The larger question for us is whether the work site, the parish, the neighborhood and the family are better because we were there. Are people stronger and more Christ-centered because they have known us? Have we been "burning and shining" lamps to others?

Jesus says in today's Gospel reading that He will give a greater testimony than John did in the works He will do. One of Jesus' works will be His Church. Will the Church be that "bright and shining lamp" that will bring all people to the Lord? We can apply this question not only to the universal Church but also to our parish church.

Are we the "bright and shining lamp" that will draw people to the light of Christ? Do we have an open door to all those who are seeking the light? Are we a welcoming community where people can touch the spirit of Christ? Are we a place not only of electrical light but also of spiritual light which is light for the mind, the heart and the soul?

The Advent season is a time for the Church to renew itself as a "house of prayer" for all people. Anyone willing to embrace the Catholic way of life should find in us a place of welcome, a place of peace and a place of fellowship.

Advent is a time to refresh our faith. It is also a time to renew our parish to be that "bright and shining lamp" in whose preaching and life people can discover Christ.

DECEMBER 17 – LATE ADVENT WEEKDAY
Genesis 49:2, 8-10; Matthew 1:1-17

This lengthy Gospel reading looks like a family tree, but it is much more than that.

Often we have to look to the past to understand the present. To comprehend modern day America, we need to appreciate the impact of the Civil War, the Great Depression, the two World Wars as well as recent political history. In the same way, the uniqueness of each parish community is partially explained by its past.

To understand the significance of Jesus Christ as the fulfillment of the promises of God to Abraham, Isaac and Jacob, we need to see the history that He completes. Woven like threads through the story of God's people is the recurring failure to be the people God intended as well as God's abiding faithfulness to His covenant.

Each of the names in Matthew's catalogue expresses a piece of that story. Each is a stone in the mosaic that is fulfilled in Jesus Christ.

We are accustomed to reflecting upon the wisdom of God shown in the work of creation. Matthew's catalogue teaches us that the wisdom of God is also at work in God's re-creation of the human race as well. We call it providence.

From the tragedies and failures of the human story, God's wisdom fashioned and continues to fashion a redeeming history. Alongside the cruelty, sin and brutality that punctuate the Old Testament with the rhythm of a metronome, there is the patient providence of God leading His people to new birth.

Are we willing to see the same wisdom of God present in our life? Each of us can look at people who, for better or worse, have influenced the person we have become. We all carry scars and bruises from others.

But, we have also been loved. Inserted within our life as well is the renewing grace of Baptism. That abiding mark of Christ is also a factor in our life. The wisdom of God is present not only in our creation but in our re-creation as well.

Whatever our personal past may be, we can still make it into a story of redeeming grace.

DECEMBER 18 – LATE ADVENT WEEKDAY
Jeremiah 23:5-8; Matthew 1:18-24

This Gospel reading gives us an opportunity to dwell upon Joseph, the husband of Mary. It shows the dignity of the man as well as his genuine love for Mary.

To understand the reason for Joseph's reluctance to expose Mary to the legal trial prescribed for women suspected of infidelity, we have only to read chapter five in the Old Testament Book of Numbers. This portion of that ancient legal code requires a "trial by ordeal" for a woman suspected of being unfaithful. Joseph wanted to preserve Mary from that humiliation.

Then, of course, the angel assured him that Mary's child was a child of miracle and promise. Joseph's dignity in all this is admirable.

We do not have a single word of his recorded in the Gospels. Yet, as Pope John Paul II once said of him, Joseph's way was not the way of words but the way of action.

We all know people like that. They are not verbally eloquent but like Joseph, they are available, reliable, loving and strong. Too often, Joseph gets short shrift in our reflection as though he became part of Mary's life simply to complete the nativity scene.

But, as the Holy Father remarked, his love for Mary was real. He was very much her husband and very much a part of her life.

Although he did not express his love physically, Joseph shows that there are many ways that love can be shown.

There are all kinds of ways that a spouse can be cherished and affirmed. Joseph models that richer love for us.

There are all kinds of ways that a family must be protected and kept together. Joseph exhibits that more spacious love for us.

There are all sorts of ways that a father can convey strength to the family. Joseph is an example of that wider love for us.

Justice without love is blind. Love without justice is bland. Joseph was indeed a man of justice, blending fairness and generous love.

We should try to do so as well.

In both of today's readings we see God restoring life-giving power to the sterile.

In the Old Testament, few disabilities were considered to be as tragic as sterility. If a woman was unable to have children, she was seen to have lost her chance for a kind of genetic immortality and was perceived to have failed the nation. In the Old Testament, the transmission of life gave one's time on earth purpose and meaning. Fertility not only obeyed the Creator God's command to multiply, it also implemented God's promise to Abraham to make his posterity as countless as the sands.

It was a sign of God's generosity and blessing that, in their old age, the mothers of Samson and John the Baptist were both given life-giving power once more. The conceptions were natural. The miracle was that God revived the fertility of these women, which seemed to be spent.

The message for us in all this is, of course, more than two cases of miraculous biological revival. There are many ways of being sterile. There are, as well, many ways of being fruitful.

Sometimes the word "generativity" is used. It means being able to transmit vitality, inspiration, enthusiasm, knowledge, wisdom and strength to others even though a person might be long past the age of biological conception.

The real sterility in human life is the self-absorption that makes a person spiritually stagnant, when nothing of us flows out to others. The real fertility, on the other hand, is to share our talents and our selves with others. There is no age barrier to this kind of life-giving power.

The measure of our fruitfulness is not the number of children we have but the number of lives we touch.

DECEMBER 20 – LATE ADVENT WEEKDAY
Isaiah 7:10-14; Luke 1:26-38

There are several deep analyses of this Gospel passage. But after we have finished reading all of them, one simple and strong fact stands out: Mary said, "Yes!" That moment was the start of a new creation.

She said "Yes" to God. So often, we can become so wrapped up in reflection on doctrine, the examination of Church life and policy as well as proposals to improve parish life that these can easily become a substitute for the actual surrender of our lives to the Gospel.

She said "Yes" to God.

Are we using substitutes for submission?

Do we use the Sacrament of Reconciliation as a substitute for the reconciliations we have yet to achieve outside the confessional?

Do we use our Holy Communion as a substitute for the communion with our brothers and sisters that needs to be fostered when Mass is over?

Do we substitute our study of the Word of God for our submission to its demands in our daily life?

Mary said "Yes" to God. Let's be very clear about what is occurring at this moment. Mary is not simply acknowledging God's power. She is submitting to a mysterious, solemn, dramatic rearrangement of her life. She did not see all the implications of her surrender to God's will. Yet she submits and "walks by faith."

Are we willing to risk our life as the Gospel teaches? Most people are not. Many are more willing to analyze the Gospel than to submit to it.

The new creation in Christ is born not from theoretical agreement with the Gospel but from surrender to it.

Mary said "Yes" to God. Will we?

DECEMBER 21 – LATE ADVENT WEEKDAY
Song of Songs 2:8-14; Luke 1:39-45

In this familiar Visitation scene from today's Gospel reading, Elizabeth is filled with the Holy Spirit and given the gift of four prophetic utterances that signal four powerful threads of future devotion to Mary in the Church's life.

Elizabeth's words are spoken not simply for Mary's information but are really being proclaimed to all of us.

Elizabeth speaks of the blessedness of Mary and the fruit of her womb. These words will be incorporated centuries later in the "Hail Mary," the beginnings of a cascade of prayer and chain of praise that will be given to Mary, the mother of Jesus, through the centuries in the Rosary.

Elizabeth speaks of the wonder of Mary's coming to her. It remains a marvel that Mary not only has come to Christ's people in her great interventions and apparitions throughout history but also to each of us as we seek her guidance and intercession in our lives.

Elizabeth's remark on the baby's leaping in her womb for joy speaks to the power of Mary's intercession with her Son to activate the grace of our Baptism and all the sacramental graces given us in our life.

Lastly, Elizabeth's "beatitude" about Mary reminds us of Mary's trust in God's Word, a trust that we all very much need in our lives today.

Here, in the very springtime of our redemption, the Holy Spirit moves Elizabeth to speak words that describe the features of Marian spirituality for centuries to come: devotion to Mary, reliance on Mary's presence in our life, the power of her intercession to ignite Christ's graces inside us and her example of trust in God's Word.

Elizabeth's inspired words teach us that Mary's role in the story of salvation was not completed with her giving birth to Jesus. Now, she helps us experience His birth in our life.

DECEMBER 22 – LATE ADVENT WEEKDAY
I Samuel 1:24-28; Luke 1:46-56

Today's Gospel records the "Magnificat," Mary's song of praise that is sung or recited every day of the year as part of the Church's evening prayer.

In this canticle, Mary celebrates and praises God for what He has done in her life. "God, who is mighty, has done great things for me." Mary accepted God's mysterious mission for her life and through her cooperation with the Father's will, the redemption of the world, the "great thing" was begun.

Mary's song continues, however, to teach that the intervention and providence of God do not end with herself. "His mercy is from age to age..." on all those who revere Him. All who submit themselves to God's will as it is given to us in Scripture and Tradition will experience salvation and will also become conscious instruments of His saving grace to others.

As we approach Christmas this year, a question for us to examine is the effect on others of the Lord's coming to us.

The Lord's coming to Mary brought redemption to the world. Whatever spiritual light we experience this Christmas is not only for ourselves but also for others. We are called to be light not only for our own house but to illuminate the way for others.

Through the generations since Mary first sang the Magnificat, she has reflected and shared her love for her Son and His grace with others.

Our devotion to Mary should not end with admiring Mary but in trying to do as she did. We are called to be, as Mary was and is today, "lanterns of Christ."

That is how we can "magnify the Lord" today.

Both of our readings seem to contradict the popular spirit of the season we are about to celebrate.

The Gospel tells us that fear came upon the people in the area as they wondered who this extraordinary child named John will be. Then we have the striking words used by the prophet Malachi to describe both the Messiah and the one who will usher him in.

Malachi pictures the Messiah as one who will refine, cleanse and clarify. He wonders whether anyone will remain standing and innocent at the Lord's coming. So, a great prophet who will urge reconciliation among people will have to precede the Messiah's arrival.

Maybe we have domesticated Christmas a bit too much. It has become a season of warmth, charm and cheer. We certainly need that in our life. But we also need something deeper than that.

The One Whose birth we are about to celebrate comes with refining judgment to distinguish true joy from its counterfeits. He will speak God's Word to cleanse the soul and mind from the false clichés that influence us. He will speak clarifying truth about how we are to live if we are to have eternal life. At its core, the Gospel of Jesus Christ is not a message of seasonal cheer but a cleansing, clarifying challenge to deep life, which we can either accept or reject.

To prepare us to encounter the Lord, John the Baptist was sent not just to the people of Judea 2000 years ago but, through the liturgy, to people of every age. He calls us to prepare for a great coming of God into our life.

For all the delicacy and charm of this time of year, the Incarnation is profoundly serious business. It carries awesome implications of life and death for all of us.

In Jesus, the way to life, eternal life, is now wide open. But first, there is a journey we have to make. It is a journey not in miles but in repentance to enable us "to recover by penance what we have lost by sin." Maybe we still have some spiritual traveling to do.

John the Baptist, Malachi's "messenger" and Christ's usher, will guide us.

December 24 – Late Advent Weekday
2 Samuel 7:1-5, 8-11, 16; Luke 1:67-79

Zechariah chants a great hymn of God's deliverance. It is called in Latin the "Benedictus" and is part of the Church's Morning Prayer each day. He sings of God's faithfulness in fulfilling His promises.

The seed of this fulfillment is planted in the family line of David and finally bursts to life in Jesus Christ.

Only toward the end of this canticle does Zechariah sing of John's great mission to prepare a path for the Lord. Maybe this is our mission today.

We cannot redeem someone but we can show the way to the Redeemer.

We cannot forgive someone's sins but we can show the way to One Who forgives.

We cannot save someone but we can show the way to the Savior.

We cannot implant peace into another's heart but we can show the way to One Who is our peace.

We cannot impart meaning to another's life but we can show the way to One Who can.

We cannot grant eternal life to another but we can show the way to One Who is Life.

Perhaps our most significant role in other people's lives is not to lead their life for them. We cannot do that and might do great damage if we try.

But we can show them the way to the Lord Who, long after

we are gone, will be their abiding friend and Savior for the rest of their days.

There is a wonderful Hispanic custom of "luminarias" at Christmas time. These are lights that are placed along a road leading to the church. Each of us can be one of those "luminarias" that can lead others to Christ.

The greatest gift we can give another is to be a John the Baptist for them and illumine their way to Christ.

Christmas Season

(December 26, 27, 28 – see Sanctoral section)

DECEMBER 29 – FIFTH DAY IN THE OCTAVE OF CHRISTMAS
1 John 2:3-11; Luke 2:22-35

In today's Gospel, the old man Simeon sees the centuries-old promise to the Hebrew people come true in his own arms. In Jesus, the age-old love and care of God now dwells among us. As the preface for the Christmas Mass states, "in Him, we see our God made visible."

In Christ, the love of God came to life as He enters our world to recreate and renew all that was lost by sin.

That work of Jesus continues in the Church as the truth of Christ is brought to each generation to show its life-giving and saving power.

John the Apostle underscores this truth when, to a community facing the distress of schism, he writes about the importance of loving one another as the measure of our spiritual honesty. We truly know Christ if we try to live like Him.

John then remarks that this commandment of love is an old one, from the Book of Leviticus. Yet, "loving our neighbor as ourselves" is not necessarily benign because we can have a self-destructive love for ourselves. St. John calls us to love others as Christ loves us. In Jesus, St. John continues, love is given fresh power and expression.

"Loving one another" is a phrase of which we can all tire very easily. Yet, we never tire of seeing it put into action. The crucifix, the caring heart, the loyal friend, the self-sacrificing spouse are always striking and never lose their vivid power to impress and to provoke imitation.

We can grow weary of words. But when these words become flesh in human life, they acquire convincing and irresistible power.

Jesus did not establish the Church only to talk about light but to be light. When we behave as the Light of Christ, the world will always stop, always look and even listen!

33

DECEMBER 30 – SIXTH DAY IN THE OCTAVE OF CHRISTMAS
1 John 2: 12-17; Luke 2: 36-40

Three generations come together in the Temple at this moment. Each is graced by God in a different way.

Anna, the elderly seer, is enabled to view the Messiah, to see her prayers of longing fulfilled as she speaks from the experience of her years about the marvelous ways of God.

The young couple, Mary and Joseph, come to dedicate the Child and are given the blessing of God as they begin their years of parenting.

The infant Jesus is placed before the altar of God initiating an entire life that will be lived as a sacrifice to the Father.

Three generations and three moments of grace.

In today's first reading, St. John also addresses three generations of Christians – children, young adults and mature adults – about the enticements of the world and their commitment to Christ. Each stage of life has its own temptations that lure us away from the Lord as well as its own call to be faithful.

The message of Christmas isn't just for children. Whatever our age, we always need to be reminded of God's love for us and of the strength He gives us to follow Him as well as the graces that will follow.

When we are young, we are in the season of spiritual hopes and dreams. That is an important part of our life.

Our young adult years make up the time of spiritual sorting and discernment to find that special way we are called to follow.

Our senior years are the years of perspective, gathering and review. In these later years, the ways of God may start to become a bit clearer for us.

Christmas reminds us that the Lord comes to us with new power whatever our age may be.

In every period of our life, the love and call of God are always fresh and vigorous.

December 31 – Seventh Day in the Octave of Christmas
1 John 2:18-21; John 1:1-18

In a very stark first reading, St. John writes that it is now the final hour. Yet, these words were written two thousand years ago. The "final hour" of history is not necessarily the only decisive one.

Is there any period in human history or in human life that is unimportant? When we study history, certain years and ages are emphasized as especially significant. But in the course of human lives, as they are lived day in and day out, no time is trivial.

After all, each day is a day of someone's birth or death, a day of learning or discovery, a day when love in someone's life is born or dies, a day when sin takes hold or is banished, or a day when someone embraces Christ or leaves Him. Each day is a day of growth in grace and is decisive for the Kingdom of God in the life of some individual. At this very moment some individual somewhere is making a commitment to Christ or beginning to abandon that commitment.

It is very easy for us to focus on the final hour of history and forget that each hour is crucial to someone. Like the song, "It's five o'clock somewhere," each hour is a time of light and darkness in some individual's life. Each hour is decisive somewhere in our world.

Whatever the identity of the "anti-Christ" at the end of time, there are figures and movements in our world right now who can just as surely entice us away from Christ.

The point St. John is making is that there are many "anti-Christs," many "phony Christs," and we need to watch not just for the final one but for any individual in our life who can lure us away from Christ. It is not only the ultimate anti-Christ who can lead us to self-destruct. It is not only the final hour of history that is decisive.

But then, there is also the Word present at the creation, made flesh in Jesus and now present to you and me in the life of the Church. We do not have to await the Second Coming of Christ to experience His redemption and saving grace.

In the spiritual life, it is not only beginnings and endings but also every day of our life that is important.

(January 2, 4, 5 – see Sanctoral section)

JANUARY 3
1 John 2:29-3:6; John 1:29-34

Truth does not always come to us after a labored period of study. It can come suddenly as when we get the point of a joke, see a solution to a problem or are hit by a moment of insight about someone or something.

John the Baptist at first did not recognize Jesus as the Messiah. He had prepared, knew the prophecies and spent time in desert prayer. Yet, it took that moment when the heavens opened for him to recognize Jesus of Nazareth as the Lamb of God. The "flash of recognition" is not like the conclusion of a geometric theorem. It is a grace, enabling us to recognize the truth in a convincing and personal manner.

The first reading speaks about the world's not recognizing God's chosen ones. The people of God do not carry identification cards, emit rays or auras of holiness around them. They look like everyone else in appearance, standing in shopping lines, waiting for traffic lights to change, paying their mortgages, and having their cars inspected. But, St. John writes, we can tell who is of Christ from the way they behave. Outward appearance does not necessarily express the inner truth about someone. Lifestyle does.

The full glory of the sons and daughters of God will only be apparent for all to see in the Kingdom. But here on earth we recognize the truth about where someone stands with the Lord largely by examining the way they behave.

It is not religious rhetoric, facility in quoting Scripture, knowledge of theology, traditionalism or liberalism, the garments one wears or a person's position in the Church or parish nor the amount of time spent in prayer that reveals closeness to Christ. It is how a person lives.

John the Apostle gives us a principle that abides: the person who remains in Christ does not sin; the one who sins is not fully abiding in Christ. Closeness to Christ and sinful behavior are in inverse proportion to each other.

36

How do we recognize the grace of Christ in another? We can't see grace, can't touch it, weigh it, hear it or smell it. There is no thermometer to measure grace. We cannot see grace but we can see its effects.

In this world, how we live is the best evidence of how and what we love.

JANUARY 6
1 John 5:5-13; Mark 1:7-11

There was a program in the early days of television called "You Are There." It tried to recreate historical events as seen through modern news reporting. In today's first reading, St. John is doing something similar.

He speaks of Jesus coming in the "water and the blood." At the Jordan River, the Father's voice was heard affirming Jesus as His Son as recounted in today's Gospel reading. Later, on Calvary, the Father spoke through the phenomena of nature affirming the universal redeeming significance of Christ's Death.

Today, for us who were not present at the Jordan River or on Mount Calvary, we have the Holy Spirit that gives the same testimony about Christ. Through the Holy Spirit, "we are there." The Holy Spirit within us from our Baptism gives us the conviction that Jesus is Lord and Savior. St. John says that whoever believes in Jesus has this testimony of the Holy Spirit within. The Spirit, the water and the blood all make the same affirmation and speak the same truth. They are of one accord that Jesus is Lord.

The conviction and assurance of faith is not, however, a conclusion that we draw by ourselves. We come to many conclusions in our life that do not have life-changing power. The gift of faith, however, enables us to entrust our life and our future to Christ and His Gospel. The gift of faith enables us to be strong in the face of failure, spiritually victorious in the face of suffering, and sure of eternal life in the face of death.

At its core, faith is not an idea but a connection. It is as though we are wired for God, but the electricity of grace has to come to us to enable that connection to come alive. When it does, our life lights up and we begin to see clearly. Faith is the "spiritual electricity" that makes the power of our Christian identity come to life. The Christmas season is a chance for us to connect with Christ not as an historical figure or a moralist but as our Savior and Redeemer.

The Gospels show us how Christ taught, healed and saved two thousand years ago and how the Lord teaches, heals and saves today. Now, through the Holy Spirit and the Sacraments, "we are there."

JANUARY 7
1 John 5:14-21; John 2:1-11

Late in the year 2004, archeologists announced that they had found the location of the original town of Cana about 8 miles northwest of Nazareth. It is one of three sites, two in Israel and one in Lebanon that have claimed to be the original Cana where Jesus first "showed His glory." It was a rural town without fortifications which meant that it was not considered a military or strategic stronghold.

There is still some dispute whether this site is the location of the original Cana of the Gospels especially since pilgrims have been going to the other sites for centuries. Whether the exact location of Cana has been found or not, we all have a personal "Cana" in our life.

Cana is the place of Christ's glory, of new possibilities, where Jesus can transform the ordinary into something supernaturally productive. We all have or have had a Cana in our life. We have all had the experience of Jesus' transforming our grieving for the loss of a loved one into gratitude for that person's life. We have all had the experience of a career loss being the occasion for a new turn in our life. We have all had the experience of illness triggering a revision of our priorities.

Cana is much more than a location on a map. It is the experience of the power and glory of Christ. That experience may not be like the generous miracle Jesus works in today's Gospel. The heart of this miracle recounted by John is not that Jesus saved a wedding feast from social disaster. It is the transformation that Jesus can work on anything in our life.

We can identify stages in our journey to a personal Cana. There is the recognition of our need, "They have no wine." This is followed by the call to open ourselves to trustful Gospel living, "Do whatever He tells you." Then we use our capacities to the fullest for Christ, "Fill the jars with water." We will then notice how slowly our talents become magnificently transformed gifts that convey Christ's grace to others, "Draw some out and take it to the headwaiter."

The Christmas season invites us to begin walking the road to Cana. We should seek out our personal Cana. We should expect a Cana in our life. Cana is not simply a site for archeological debate. It is an experience that can be part of every Christian's life.

MONDAY AFTER EPIPHANY
1 John 3:22-4:6; Matthew 4:12-17, 23-25

Many people praise the power of the "marketplace" these days. Even though it is powerful in rooting out economic inefficiencies, the marketplace is not powerful in promoting truth, honesty or morality. Unregulated, the marketplace will race for the most lucrative and least moral common denominator in the media, in the professions, in commerce and in religion.

Discernment in the spiritual marketplace is what St. John addresses in today's first reading as he calls us to test every spirit. The assertions of people who claim to be moved, inspired and guided by the Spirit need to be evaluated. Everyone who quotes the Gospel, the Pope or the saints is not necessarily moved by the Spirit. John gives us a two-pronged test.

The first test asks whether what such teachers tell us is consistent with the Gospel of Jesus Christ, with the truth of His Incarnation and all the affirmations of the Creed. We should be wary of novel interpretations of the Faith of which twenty centuries of Christian experience were unaware.

The second test John suggests is to examine the results of a person's preaching. Does the teaching we are given unify or divide the Church? Does it create an elitist "church within the Church"? Does it strengthen our bonds with the Church's mission and life? Does it make family life stronger and confirm us in our vocations? Does it gather us toward other Christians or segregate us? Does it enhance or diminish our prayer life? Does it guide us to a reading of Scripture or divert us to private revelations, esoteric spiritual writings or locutions? Does it deepen our participation in the parish liturgy or not? Does it draw us to the preacher or to Christ?

The spiritual marketplace these days is like the "Wild West." Just as we have governmental bodies to regulate our food and drugs, our restaurants, our media, our electrical appliances, our lawyers, doctors and businesses, so we should take care about the spiritual material that we consume.

The test of religious material we read or hear is whether it creates a self-righteous clique of Christians or whether it draws us closer to the Church as it is. After all, where the real Church is, there is the real Christ.

TUESDAY AFTER EPIPHANY
1 John 4:7-10; Mark 6:34-44

The Gospel recounts a great and generous miracle from the Lord. It is a miracle not isolated to that mountainside but one that is repeated at every Mass as the Lord feeds us fully and faithfully with His own Self.

Throughout his letters, St. John is preoccupied with love. Our culture is also fascinated by love but in a very different way.

Popular culture emphasizes love as romance, sentiment, passion and infatuation, which are all emotionally driven. It is said, "Love happens." We "fall in love." It is seen as something that virtually invades our life.

St. John's perspective is very different. For him, love is not an emotion but an action, a way we choose to live. When St. John says, "let us love one another" he is not referring to sentiment because emotions are not in our control. He calls us to love as God loves and he highlights three features of God's love as made visible in Jesus Christ.

God sent His only Son. God took the initiative. His love is not a response or a reaction. God's love took the first step across the yawning divide caused by sin and sent His Son. Christian love also takes the first step.

God sent His Son as an offering for our sins. God's love is a sacrificial love captured in every crucifix we have. Christian love is focused not on what it gets but on what it gives.

God sent His Son that we might have life. God's love is a love that heals, redeems and makes whole. Can we say that about our love for others? Does it enlarge others, ennoble them, make them aware of their worth and dignity, and bring them closer to Christ? Or is our love manipulative, petulant, demanding and self-absorbed, designed to make ourselves feel good?

St. John's brief and profound portrait of God's love lets us glimpse a universe different from our common culture. In the world of the Gospel, love acts rather than emotes, it sacrifices rather than acquires, it ennobles rather than treating another as a useful commodity to satisfy our needs.

This kind of love does not happen to us. It is something which, with God's grace, we do.

WEDNESDAY AFTER EPIPHANY
1 John 4:11-18; Mark 6:45-52

St. John writes, "We have come to know and believe in the love God has for us."

Many of us know of God's love for us. The Scriptures teach it; St. John repeats it over and over; the Church preaches it. Our liturgical seasons of Advent and Christmas, Lent and Easter spotlight God's love for us.

We know of God's love for us but do we believe in that

love? Do we trust that love? In times of crisis and fear such as the disciples' experience in today's Gospel reading during the storm, do we believe in God's love for us?

When we face a health crisis, a family crisis, and a financial crisis, do we believe in God's love for us?

When we come to the evening of life and know that we will face the Lord with the full record of our life that He alone fully knows, do we believe in God's love for us?

To assert the truth of God's love is one thing. To trust that His love is an abiding presence and power in our life is another.

If, as St. John writes, perfect love casts out fear, the reverse can happen. Feeding our fears can displace love. Anxiety about some things is normal. But anxiety that fuels the fear that we are alone, abandoned and forsaken by the Lord can cause our faith to atrophy.

Christ is with us in the boat. The continuously burning lamp in front of the tabernacle reminds us that the Lord abides with us even when we are not in church. Time before the tabernacle reminds us that the Lord abides with us even when we are far from the tabernacle. His plan, His providence and His grace are part of our life. Our prayer life, our study, our celebration of the Eucharist should all reinforce our trust in His plan, His providence and His grace.

The truth of the Incarnation is not only that God became flesh in Bethlehem but that the Lord dwells with us now in Word and Sacrament. He is not only part of our life, we are part of His.

THURSDAY AFTER EPIPHANY
1 John 4:19-5:4; Luke 4:14-22

History books are filled with the lives of people who strove to be world conquerors: Alexander the Great, Julius Caesar, Philip of Spain, Napoleon, Adolf Hitler, Joseph Stalin – it is a long list.

St. John writes about our being conquerors because our faith conquers the world, that is, the spirit of the world.

It is very easy for people to be affected, dominated and taken over by the spirit of the world and its cynicism, its materialism or its violence. Faith in Jesus Christ enables us to be victorious over the self-absorbed spirit of the world.

It is easy for people to be affected, dominated, and taken over by events in life such as illness, divorce and problems at work.

Faith in Jesus Christ enables us to be victorious by seeing God's grace and purpose embedded in every event of our life.

The victory of which St. John writes is not military victory, political victory or economic victory but spiritual victory that comes when we are not dominated by events, driven by the spirit of the world, or overcome by tragedy and distress.

We all know heroic people who did not let the tragedy of cancer, the death of a loved one, or the attack by the media on Christian values destroy their faith or their identity as disciples of Jesus. They were conquerors. They had spiritual victory.

No matter what goes on around us, if we are able to retain our values, sustain our faith, and maintain our discipleship of Christ, then we are spiritual conquerors as well. We have overcome the spirit of the world.

Fidelity to Christ is, in the last analysis, the greatest victory of all because it is the only victory that counts.

FRIDAY AFTER EPIPHANY
1 John 5:5-13; Luke 5:12-16

St. John writes about Jesus Christ coming through water and the blood; not just water only but water and blood.

One understanding of these enigmatic words is that Jesus showed Himself to be Messiah not just in His public ministry that began at the Jordan River and continued through His teachings and healing but also in His sacrificial death for us.

Jesus is Messiah through His life and through His death, through water and through the blood.

We can apply this teaching to ourselves. We receive the very life of God, the Holy Spirit, in Baptism but we maintain that life through the sacramental life of the Church, especially the Eucharist. The life of God comes to us not only through the waters of Baptism but also through the blood of the Eucharistic sacrifice.

Making a "decision for Christ" can be a powerful moment for an individual whether that happens on a crusade, a retreat or at a solemn church celebration.

But we need to sustain that decision and commitment through the weekly Sunday Mass. Otherwise, our Baptism can become like a New Year's resolution, easily forgotten and put on hold.

We need the water, the commitment of Baptism, and the blood, the Mass that enables us to renew and sustain that commitment. Baptism makes us holy. The Eucharist keeps us holy.

Our Christian life grows not only through water, but also through water and the blood.

SATURDAY AFTER EPIPHANY
1 John 5:14-21; John 3:22-30

We have the unusual scene in today's Gospel reading of Jesus and John baptizing at the same time, calling people to repentance.

The disciples of John complained that people were leaving him to follow Jesus. John replies, "He's the groom, I'm the best man." Jesus is uniting the human race with God; John simply is preparing the way. Jesus' impact must increase as John decreases in popularity.

That is a splendid way to end the Christmas season.

John's focus on Jesus should be the theme of every Christian, of everyone involved in ministry, and of everyone who works for the Gospel.

The measure of the success of any ministry and really of all work for the Gospel is whether it brings people closer to Jesus

Christ and His Church and away from those idols and deadly sins, which the Apostle John describes.

There is much in our world that is deadly although it may appear alluring and attractive. We need discernment to distinguish what is bringing us closer to Christ or drawing us away from the Lord.

Every program, every relationship, every book we read can be judged by the criterion: "Is this making me a better Christian?" The same can be said of every spiritual director, pastor and bishop. The question is not whether we are followers of a particular personality but whether we are stronger followers of Christ.

If from this Christmas season we can resolve in the coming year to bring one person closer to Christ, to strengthen that person's prayer life, give a better understanding of the Gospel, a more accurate understanding of the Church, then we will continue John's ministry today.

Jesus must increase, we must decrease.

Lenten Season

ASH WEDNESDAY
Joel 2:12-18; 2 Corinthians 5:20-6:2; Matthew 6:1-6, 16-18

Ash Wednesday fills the churches all over the world every year. The ashes of "Ash Wednesday" must be one of the most popular sacramentals in the Church. They remind us of the mortality of the body and the eternity of the soul. The body upon which we lavish so much attention will turn to dust. The soul that we often ignore will live forever. Today is a serious day as it should be. It is not, however, a day of gloom but of hope.

We begin a very powerful season of the Church year, a journey that will take us to Easter in the Church and hopefully in our life as well.

Lent is a great time of Christian and Catholic identity because it is something we all do together. Sometimes we see people on the street today with the ashes on their foreheads and never realized that they were Catholic. As the prophet Joel calls the whole community together to seek the Lord, so we are all called to make the spiritual journey to new life in Christ.

Sometimes we put off our renewal as Catholics to the future, a future that never quite comes. St. Paul writes that now is a grace-filled hour. Now is the time when we can begin to revise and remodel our life. Now is the time for an "extreme makeover," to reverse destructive choices, halt spiritual drift, go back to basics, and refresh our lives in the truth of the Gospel, the grace of the Sacraments and the life of the Church.

In today's Gospel reading, the Lord points to three ancient pathways for our Lent. There is fasting when we give up certain foods. The effort to give up food makes us realize how trapped we are in the self-gratification of a consumer culture. Our economy is fueled by consumption. Fasting is difficult to start but as it becomes easier, we experience a personal liberation. The practice of almsgiving reminds us that we have a responsibility to others. We are part of a spiritual web. The third path is that of reviving in our life the potential of prayer to unify all the sectors of our life around Christ and establish an open line to God.

The season of Lent is a great inheritance from the past. It

probably evokes many memories from our youth. Lent, however, is not about our past but about our future. A serious Lent will help us restore an honesty and clarity about our life and its purpose that we may have forgotten.

Lent is not about our past. It is about our future.

THURSDAY AFTER ASH WEDNESDAY
Deuteronomy 30:15-20; Luke 9:22-25

"What profit to gain the world... and destroy ourselves?" These words have changed the lives of many people through history who were caught up, even swept up, in accumulating things that pass and neglecting the part of us that lasts forever, our soul. These words of Jesus came to them like a "fire bell in the night."

It is not gaining things that is wrong; it is neglecting our soul that is destructive. This can lead to some critical self-examination.

Are we making choices as though this life here is all we have or do we see life here as a pathway to the Lord and to eternal life?

Are we putting the Gospel on the back burner or even in the freezer as we live our life?

Lent is a time to realize once again that the following of Jesus in our daily life is the only road to the real life that lasts. "Map quest" can give us directions to a particular address. The Gospel and the Commandments give us directions to eternal glory.

As Moses says in today's first reading, keeping the Commandments is not slavery. It is true liberation; it is strength; it is life. To disobey the Commandments is not freedom but bondage, moral chaos and living death.

A society where everyone violated the Commandments is not a place any of us would want to be.

Our daily life is where we follow in Jesus' steps. We don't follow Christ only in our mind. We don't follow Jesus only in our heart. We don't follow Jesus only in our prayer life.

If we don't follow Christ in our daily life and in the daily choices we are making, we aren't really following Him at all.

FRIDAY AFTER ASH WEDNESDAY
Isaiah 58:1-9; Matthew 9:14-15

Today, a Friday in Lent, our readings are about fasting, a classic Christian journey through the holy season of Lent.

Fast and abstinence are good for the body and for the soul, especially the soul. Fasting means that we have only one full meal a day. There are two official fast days in the Church year, Ash Wednesday and Good Friday. Abstinence means refraining from certain kinds of food such as meat. We abstain from meat products on all Fridays of Lent. Fasting is about the amount of food we eat while abstinence is about the kinds of food we consume.

Giving up certain foods is a way of reclaiming self-control in our lives. We live in a very self-indulgent culture where priority is given to satisfying all physical cravings. We are urged to take immediate action "when the hungries hit." Fast food stores abound to prevent us from experiencing a few seconds of hunger. Snacks are even available in shopping centers to sustain us while we shop for food.

The deeper vice which all this feeds is the indulging not only of our physical hunger but also of all our emotions and appetites as well.

By fast and abstinence, we make a "declaration of independence" from the hold our consumer culture has on us and regain control not only over our bodies but over our other desires as well.

If the point of fasting were only physical, it would differ little from dieting. The purpose of fasting is spiritual, to help us bring order to our interior life.

During Lent, the difficulty of giving up certain foods shows us how self-indulgent we are, how weak our will is and how we need the spiritual strengthening of God's grace. If we are faithful to our Lenten fast, we will come to Easter not only a little thinner and healthier but also with an inner life more ordered, more at peace, more with Christ.

Giving up food for Lent is not about the body. It's about the soul.

SATURDAY AFTER ASH WEDNESDAY
Isaiah 58:9-14; Luke 5:27-32

This Saturday after Ash Wednesday is the last "introductory" day of Lent. Tomorrow is the first Sunday of Lent.

Lent is a time to renew our lives, to cleanse the obscured face of Christ, to shake off the dust of sin and indifference, and to effect that change to which the Lord calls the Pharisees and us in today's Gospel reading.

The reading from Isaiah suggests a focus for us and a dimension to Lent that we might consider today, which is to renew our observance of Sunday as truly the Lord's Day.

He speaks of the Sabbath as a day of spiritual renewal and revival of the covenant for the people of Israel. Sunday is such a day for us. It includes Sunday Mass, of course, but much more than that. The commandment is to keep the Lord's Day holy – the entire day.

It should be a day for spiritual recuperation and renewal with family and friends. Lent each year is a good time to examine how we are keeping our Christian Sabbath. Is it rest? Is it prayer? Is it renewal? Is it time to dwell on our spiritual priorities or is it just another day?

Sunday is a day to celebrate the Creator's work and to enjoy the fruits of our labors with family and friends. It is the day to attend to God's Word and to the Eucharist. It is the day of the Church to gather with the Body of Christ.

Some people regrettably shrink the spiritual dimension of Sunday only to attendance at Mass and nothing more. But the spiritual potential of Sunday is enormous especially in a society as eccentric as our own where we are drawn in multiple directions away from the bonds of family and friends. Our life can easily become compartmentalized. Sunday is a day to gather with the Church and to unify the scattered strings of our life. It should be different from other days and not simply a "catch-up" day.

Maybe this Lent we can revive our full observance of Sunday and restore its potential to enable us to "ride above the heights of earth" closer to the Lord.

MONDAY OF THE FIRST WEEK OF LENT
Leviticus 19:1-2, 11-18; Matthew 25:31-46

These readings at the beginning of our first full week of Lent provide two powerful searchlights to help us examine our conscience.

The first reading from the Book of Leviticus outlines ways we can harm or damage our neighbor through things we do such as stealing, lying and assault. These are the sins of commission, the active injuries we are inflicting on others, on the community and on the Church.

The Gospel parable from Matthew 25 reminds us of the other great catalogue of sin, the sins of omission.

Those who are condemned in this parable receive judgment not because of anything they did but because they did nothing. They did not cause harm but stood by and did absolutely nothing to alleviate harm already done. A gigantic area of sin, which we seldom explore, is the "continent of apathy."

When we examine our lives, we should note the wrongs we have done, of course. We should also look at the good we have failed to do, the missed opportunities, the inactivity in the face of evil and indifference to the distress of others around us.

At the end of our life, the Lord will assess our fidelity to Him not only by the important things we may have done for Him but also by the good we could have done, but didn't.

Our obituaries will surely recite our accomplishments. The

world will be told what we have achieved. But the Lord alone will know what we could have done but failed to do. That will be our judgment.

Turning that second powerful searchlight into our soul can open a new vista in our spiritual life and be the source of an insightful and even transforming season of Lent this year.

TUESDAY OF THE FIRST WEEK OF LENT
Isaiah 55:10-11; Matthew 6:7-15

In the moment recounted in today's Gospel reading, Jesus teaches His disciples and us how to pray as He did. It is called the "perfect prayer" not primarily in its specific words but as the pattern of all Christian prayer.

The "Our Father" teaches us that the purpose of all prayer should not be a way of doing penance or of manipulating God. Prayer is a way of establishing communion with God – Father, Son and Holy Spirit. Prayer is how we open the window of our life to God's grace and will.

Just as Isaiah says that the rain comes down to produce a harvest, so our opening ourselves to God's Word and grace can produce a harvest of peace, repentance and order within us.

How we Christians should pray is displayed in the Our Father.

We pray to God in the intimacy of a child to a Father. Any prayer that sees God as distant and remote from us may be prayer but it is not Christian prayer.

We pray that God's Kingdom come before all else. Any prayer that tries to manipulate God through the number of times it is recited or the number of its copies left in the church may be prayer but it is not Christian prayer.

We pray for our daily bread. We present to God all the needs and graces we require in our daily life. Any prayer that sees God as disinterested in the details of our life and involved only in grand events may be prayer but it is not Christian prayer.

Finally, we pray for forgiveness as we forgive. St. Augustine called this the "terrifying petition." Any prayer that seeks God's mercy without our own conversion of life may be prayer but it is not Christian prayer.

Many great spiritual masters have suggested that a meditation on the Lord's Prayer, word by word, can yield a magnificent spiritual harvest as well as guide our own personal prayer.

The power of the Lord's Prayer lies not in repeating Jesus' words but in imitating in our prayer life the attitude of prayer it shows.

WEDNESDAY OF THE FIRST WEEK OF LENT
Jonah 3:1-10; Luke 11:29-32

The Book of Jonah is certainly a "whale of a tale." But there is much more to it than three verses about the whale.

The people of Nineveh were traditional enemies of Israel. God calls Jonah to preach repentance to them. Jonah didn't want to go and, in fact, fled in the opposite direction. A whale swallowed him and then ejected him on the shore of the place where God wanted him to be. He realized that one couldn't run from God's will.

He preached the message of repentance in a half-hearted way and, to his astonishment, all the people repented. Jonah's response was disappointment. He had wanted to see fire and brimstone come down from heaven. But, regrettably to Jonah, they repented!

He went up the mountain distressed that they had not been punished. He noticed the next morning that the tree that had given him shade the day before had dried up. He lamented to God that a good tree had been allowed to die. The Lord then tells Jonah that the tree is incidental compared to the punishment Jonah wanted to be inflicted on Nineveh.

We should never close the books on anyone. People change because God's grace can be at work in their lives and we never know when and how they will respond. Like the people of Nineveh, repentance can always happen.

Who needed repentance in this story? The people of Nineveh certainly did but so did Jonah! He was also in need of a change of heart.

We all have some hardening of our spiritual arteries. It is very easy for us to point to wrongdoing elsewhere and miss the failures and rebellion in our own life. The story of Jonah reminds us that we all fall short of the glory of God and we all are in need of the light and grace of repentance.

Lent is not a time to look at the failings in other people's lives and miss the subtle rebellion in our own. It is a time to shine the light into ourselves and see the truth of who we are and what we may have become.

THURSDAY OF THE FIRST WEEK OF LENT
Esther C, 12, 14-16, 23-25; Matthew 7:7-12

Is there such a thing as unanswered prayer? The Lord says not in today's Gospel reading. Yet, our experience seems hard to reconcile with the Lord's assurance here. Or is it?

There is a popular saying to the effect that all prayer is answered even though that answer may be "no." There is a truth to that.

But there is also a larger truth. Jesus says in today's Gospel that the Father is a father Who acts toward us as a father. He does not play games with us or answer our prayers in ways that are destructive to us.

Isn't it our experience, if we are honest, that when the Lord does not answer our prayer as we would prefer that He always gives us the strength and the grace to deal with the situation we sought to change?

That strength and that grace are real and true answers to prayer. It is the Father's wise and loving response to our petitions. We don't possess the range of wisdom to see the full and final effect of our prayers. What we can all discern now, however, is the strength to cope that we have all received.

In the first reading, Esther, a grand heroine of Jewish history, prays for God to give her strength to protect the Jewish people and He does. In this, she is a model for us.

The story of God's response to prayer is one of the great secrets of our world. We so easily notice what appear to be unanswered prayers but fail to notice the billions of answered prayers to which all people can attest.

There is also the untold story of the unseen strength, resilience and power to cope that God always gives to all who turn to Him in their need.

We all know how to pray our need. We also need to pray so we can recognize the shape of God's answer when it comes.

FRIDAY OF THE FIRST WEEK OF LENT
Ezekiel 18:21-28; Matthew 5:20-26

The Lord calls His followers to a more abundant holiness than that of the Scribes and Pharisees.

On the most basic level, there is a discipleship that concentrates on behavior, on what we are doing and saying. This is frequently identified with obedience to the Commandments. This is an important starting point for our following of Christ.

But the "critical mass" of authentic discipleship occurs not on the level of our behavior but on the level of our attitudes. This is the area the Lord addresses in today's Gospel reading.

Attitudes are not incidental. Our angers and resentments do not remain encapsulated in our hearts and minds. They eventually find expression. In fact, left unchecked, they acquire a "snowball effect" as they increase in intensity.

Jesus' practical advice to us is to nip things in the bud. Long before there is any overt expression of animosity to others, we should reconcile while it is easy.

The Lord uses an image from the legal system. It is usually easier to settle than to go to trial because the jury award can be colossal. The same pattern occurs in human life.

Resentments, angers, jealousies can mushroom until they get out of hand and develop a momentum that seems unstoppable.

This Gospel reading calls us to examine our inner life, that secret world of our judgments, attitudes, loves and hates. Because it is private and personal does not mean that it does not have a public effect. It affects our spirituality and our dealings with others.

There are many things in life that we cannot control. The inner world of our loves and hates, however, is a domain that always needs reconquest.

Lent is an ideal time for that.

SATURDAY OF THE FIRST WEEK OF LENT
Deuteronomy 26:16-19; Matthew 5:43-48

Our first full week of Lent ends with a challenge, actually two challenges.

Through the words of Moses, we are challenged to renew our covenant with God as individuals and as a Church. We embrace the Lord as our God by living as He has taught.

God's promise is that if we are faithful to the covenant, we will be a people of glory, a staging ground for the renewal and revival of society under God.

The Gospel reading, in a second challenge, specifies the particular way that we show our following of Christ by loving our enemies. The Lord does not call us to like our enemies but to love them.

This really is a summons to see all individuals through the eyes of Christ. The Lord sees us as children of God, made in God's image, with a dignity and mission that we may have squandered, but which we can still recover.

Unless we see people with the eyes of Christ, it is almost impossible to love them with the love of Christ. When we see individuals only through the eyes of anger, resentment or jealousy, they become distorted. The command of the Lord to love them seems like poetic if not impossible rhetoric.

But when we try to see people as Jesus does, dimensions of their personalities come open to us. Arrogance is seen as a mask for insecurity; anger is exposed as a reaction of fear; brute force is unmasked as the failure of intelligence to resolve conflict.

All this is not apparent on its face but it becomes clear through prayer as we bring our enemies before the Lord as they really are, without idealization, and try to look at them as Jesus does from His cross.

The Lord does not ask us to live in a fantasy world. He asks us to be thoroughly realistic about people around us and then to love them and seek the spiritual good they really need.

MONDAY OF THE SECOND WEEK OF LENT
Daniel 9:4-10; Luke 6:36-38

Today's Gospel reading can be summed up in its last verse that the measure we use for others will be used for us.

There are two reflections we can draw from these words of the Lord.

The first echoes the petition of the Our Father in which we ask forgiveness in the same way that we forgive. We ask the Lord to deal with us as we deal with others. That should make us think twice. So often we seek forgiveness, plan on it, expect it through the confession schedule at church but are unwilling to be forgiving to others.

The second meaning of the Lord's words is the truth of the "ripple effect." If we drop a stone in water, its waves radiate into ever widening circles.

If people see us willing to forgive, they may be willing to forgive others in their life.

If people see us being compassionate, they may be more likely to show consideration to others.

If people see us refraining from snap judgments of others, they may refrain from doing so as well.

We know how it works in reverse. If people see us unwilling to forgive, that may legitimate that kind of behavior to them. If people see us indulging in gossip, that may enable them to rationalize their doing the same.

If we create an environment of deception, eventually we will be deceived.

If we create an environment of suspicion, eventually we will be suspect.

If we create an environment of detraction, eventually we will be the objects of gossip.

This is a potent meditation for the second week of Lent. The measure we use on others will be used on us.

TUESDAY OF THE SECOND WEEK OF LENT
Isaiah 1:10, 16-20; Matthew 23:1-12

Sometimes we take the last sentence of today's Gospel reading about the exalted being humbled and the humble being exalted as a truth about life. Sooner or later, we hope, those who have pushed their way to the top will get their comeuppance and those who have bided their time will receive acknowledgment.

That may or may not be true in daily affairs but it is a universal truth about the spiritual life.

In this Gospel, the Lord addresses true and bogus glory. People who love all the ceremony and badges of ecclesiastical position are not necessarily the truly great people in the Church. A chart that diagrams positions of authority in a corporation is not an accurate reflection of competence, spiritual substance or greatness.

People who genuinely dedicate their lives to the service of

others and the love of God without notice or notoriety are the real royalty of the Church.

Public rank is no index of spiritual greatness. We can spend years trying to amass titles and public honors and the public will never know that we may have lost our soul in the process.

There is the opposite of all this. Spiritual depth is not guaranteed by a "race for the bottom" either. To refuse positions of authority or rank can be a subtle kind of pride. We end up being very proud of our humility, using it as an indictment against those who are forced to stand in the spotlight.

Public position is no guarantee of spiritual vitality. Saints and sinners are found on every rung of the social ladder.

Our background, our education, our achievements in the Church, our penances, our involvement in the parish, our friendships all pale in comparison with the single question that tells the truth about us. Is Jesus Christ our real Teacher and model?

Are we serving Christ or ourselves?

WEDNESDAY OF THE SECOND WEEK OF LENT
Jeremiah 18:18-20; Matthew 20:17-28

What do we expect from Jesus Christ? Why are we Christians? There are no questions more basic than these.

Our initial response probably would be that we want eternal life, forgiveness, reconciliation and inner peace, a sense of solidarity with God's purposes here on earth, strong values, inner fulfillment and, some might add, prosperity and blessing.

We could sum all this up by saying that we want to come to Easter and a sharing in Christ's risen life. But how do we get there? This is the theme of today's readings.

Can we find a bypass around the cross and suffering of Jesus? One dimension of Lent is a reflection upon the suffering and death of Jesus. But isn't our Lent tragically compromised and diminished if it is nothing more than forty days of sympathy for Jesus?

Lent calls us to take up the cross and reproduce in our life the same kind of love that filled the heart of Christ. That is one reason why a major focus of Lent is conversion of life, an effort to recover that baptismal grace that once filled our hearts.

We cannot do that by simply watching the suffering of Jesus even with tear-filled eyes. That restoration of baptismal dignity comes as we replicate Jesus' love and fidelity in our lives. That will carry with it some share in the suffering of Christ.

Zebedee's sons tried to find a short cut, an express lane to glory. The Lord warns them that no such "fast lane" exists. Fidelity to God exerts a toll, as it did on Jeremiah, but it also brings the glory of Easter.

The unavoidable truth of Lent is that we have to die to self to rise with Christ. Sympathy for Jesus is not enough. Because Jesus suffered, so must we. Because He rose, so will we.

THURSDAY OF THE SECOND WEEK OF LENT
Jeremiah 17:5-10; Luke 16:19-31

We have a familiar parable in today's Gospel reading with three powerful points for Lent.

It is a story of the reversal of roles. A wealthy man prospers here while the poor man suffers. In the next life, their roles are reversed.

A first point. The rich man is not in torment because he was rich but because he did nothing with his wealth. He didn't abuse Lazarus; he just did nothing with his wealth to help him.

Correlatively, the poor man is not in heaven because he was poor but because he was faithful to God even in his need. It is not the circumstances of our life that make us holy but what we do with them. What are we doing with our wealth or with our need?

A second point. The great abyss between the living and the dead teaches us that we pass this way but once. There is no reincarnation or "cosmic recycling" until we get it right. We have one life to live with which to know and serve the Lord and, after that, the judgment.

The time we lose is forever lost. We cannot erase life's tapes and start over. The one life we have lived is the offering we bring to the Lord.

A third point. The Lord says that the five brothers wouldn't believe even if someone were to return from the dead. If a person's heart and life are not open to God's Word, a miracle won't do it. Miracles can impress but they don't create disciples. Miracles attract our attention but we have to be willing to listen. Miracles open the door, but we have to walk in.

The three points of this parable converge on a great caution to us. We should not toy with grace or faith. They are matters of life and death, eternal life or eternal death.

FRIDAY OF THE SECOND WEEK OF LENT
Genesis 37:3-4, 12-13, 17-28; Matthew 21:33-43, 45-46

When we look back over the story of our life, what do we see? Do we see a journey of constant improvement, greater likeness to Christ and increasing spiritual maturity? Probably not.

What we will find, as we look back, are a series of spiritual zigs and zags, spiritual "broken field running." There were probably moments of betrayal of the Lord in our past or of indifference to Him.

Yet, we come to see now that the very One we rejected at some point in the past has, by the grace of God, become the spiritual foundation of the lives we are trying to build. This is the link with our readings.

Joseph, the brother who was betrayed, became the very one who would bring salvation to the family later on in Egypt. In the Gospel reading, the One rejected becomes the source of a new relationship with God.

It can be a profound meditative experience to look back at our spiritual history. We all have a spiritual biography. The reading of the Old Testament enables us to review Israel's epic of fidelity, infidelity and fidelity restored. In the New Testament we see parts of our own story in that of the disciples or others that crossed Jesus' path.

This Lent, take the time to look back at the places of betrayal in your life. As St. Augustine did in his "Confessions," focus on one time you turned from God. Analyze it to see the course of sin in your life. Regret it. Repent for it.

But then notice how you came back. Recall the places of grace, those interventions when you were touched by the love of God and given the courage to return. Analyze it. Give thanks for it. Celebrate it.

We all have a spiritual story to tell. The details may differ but there is a common denominator to them all. The One that we rejected at some time has become our salvation.

The stone we rejected is now the cornerstone of a renewed life. If sin abounds, God's grace abounds all the more. If we sometimes feel carried along in a river of temptation, God produces a "Niagara of grace."

SATURDAY OF THE SECOND WEEK OF LENT
Micah 7:14-15, 18-20; Luke 15:1-3, 11-32

This magnificent parable is known by many names. Traditionally, it has been called the parable of the Prodigal Son or the parable of the Forgiving Father. It can also be called the parable of the Two Sons.

It is a story of rebellion, realization, return and reconciliation. Each of these moments is worth a homily. Each of these moments is a critical point in any person's life.

We all know rebellion. We all have come to a point of realization about our wrongdoing either through the pressure of external circumstance or internal dislocation. We all have known forgiveness to some degree and maybe have had the wonderful, enlarging and humbling experience of reconciliation.

But we can focus, briefly, on the reaction of the older son.

His is a question we might ask when we hear of "deathbed conversions", people who come or return to the Lord late in life after their own dissolute living and seem to enter the Kingdom "under the wire."

The totality of the father's embrace seems unfair. But, what did the younger son miss in all those years of dissolute living? He spent his fortune in more ways than financial ones. The years that could have been spent sharing his father's love and life are gone. The years when he may have worked with his older brother and deepened the bond between them are gone. The years when he may have seen the result of his work on the estate are gone. The enhancement of the estate that may have occurred had he remained is gone. The years when he may have gained the respect of the other workers on the estate are gone.

Repentance late in life does not bring back the years of missed opportunities, of prayer not experienced, of graces forever lost and of life with the Church lost. All our years of wandering are years lost to the life of faith. There is no time machine to bring them back.

The forgiveness of Christ restores our relationship with Him and enables us to start over. It gives us back the gift of grace. It cannot give us back the time lost.

But Christ's forgiveness does work a miracle. It brings us back to life.

MONDAY OF THE THIRD WEEK OF LENT
2 Kings 5:1-15; Luke 4:24-30

Naaman the Syrian takes center stage in today's readings as we begin the third full week of Lent. He was a four-star general in the king's army but he had a single devastating problem. He was a leper.

The biblical term "leprosy" covers a wide range of skin diseases but it was a sickness that could attack anyone, anywhere. Naaman, for all of his position and power, was not exempt from its attack.

Naaman knew he was a leper. No one advised him to be comfortable with his leprosy, to blame society or other lepers for communicating it to him. Naaman squarely faced the fact that he had leprosy.

We can apply this story to ourselves and sin. Lent will be a success if it enables us, as a first grace, to face the fact of sin in our life realistically and directly. So often, we try to find rationalizations to excuse ourselves. We so easily blame the people or structures around us such as the media, the society or culture, the mistakes of our parents and our clergy for the fact that we are separated from the sanctifying life of God.

There is this difference between leprosy and sin. Leprosy happens to us. Sin is something we choose. Whatever the impacts the world has upon us in weakening our resolve and causing us to withdraw from our baptismal commitment to Christ, in the last analysis, when the dust of blaming subsides, we choose to sin. We need to face that fact.

The cure for Naaman was a simple one that he at first ridiculed. It was to wash seven times in the Jordan River. But that was where the power of God was at work. He bathed and was healed.

We know the cure for sin and it lies in the Sacrament of Penance. We might hesitate in going for any number of reasons. But whatever the priest is like, whatever his disposition or limitations, that is still the place where the forgiving power of Christ is at work. The second thrust of Lent is to lead us to our cleansing Jordan, the confessional.

As important as recognizing the fact of sin in our life is knowing the place where it can be healed.

TUESDAY OF THE THIRD WEEK OF LENT
Daniel 3:25, 34-43; Matthew 18:21-35

This parable loses none of its power even after two thousand years. It's about the double standard we use in expecting forgiveness from God while we are unwilling to forgive others. We even expect forgiveness from others and are shocked when it is refused even though we are unwilling to forgive.

The larger message of this parable to us is to be open to reconciliation all the time. There are moments that come when animosities can begin to diminish. We need to be open to such moments because they can pass and never come back again.

The Lord calls us to develop a heart open to bridge building, peacemaking and reconciliation. That is the meaning of our willingness to forgive seventy times seven times.

There is a difference between forgiveness and reconciliation. Forgiveness is unilateral. Reconciliation is bilateral.

Forgiveness, which we can do on our own, is a process. It takes time and, of course, the deeper the hurt the longer the process of forgiving. Just as deep bodily wounds need longer healing, the same is true of our soul.

Forgiveness starts with the willingness to forgive. Slowly, over time, as we move on with our lives and refuse to keep rehearsing the past and pulling off the scab, forgiveness comes. We can help the process by praying for the person who harmed us. Prayer changes our relationship to such an individual.

Reconciliation takes two people. It is a great healing moment when that occurs but sometimes others are unwilling to engage in reconciliation. In such a case, we must proceed to forgiveness and leave the rest in the hands of God.

Nowhere in the Gospels does Jesus ever say that forgiveness is easy. But, the Lord does say that forgiveness is necessary for an honest spiritual life.

WEDNESDAY OF THE THIRD WEEK OF LENT
Deuteronomy 4:1, 5-9; Matthew 5:17-19

Faith is a spiritual reality. How do we grasp it? How do we live it, keep it and teach it? Because faith is a condition of soul, we have rules, regulations and traditions to help us give shape and expression to our faith.

In today's first reading from the Book of Deuteronomy, Moses is speaking to the people of Israel as they are poised to enter the land of promise. The Promised Land, however, was also peopled with tribes who do not know the God of Israel.

Moses tells them to observe the laws of the Lord in the land they are about to enter. That is how they will remember their special vocation. That is how they will keep their identity. That is how they will live their faith. That is how they will teach their faith to future generations.

What was true for the Israelites is true for us. We are living in a rapidly secularizing culture. Our culture has a way of trivializing faith by making it marginal as economic and political concerns dominate our lives. Even the symbols of faith can become commercialized as crosses become jewelry, religious images become objects of art and ceremonies become props in movies.

In such an environment, we need to cherish our rules, regulations and traditions as Catholics. We need to preserve our times of prayer, our customs throughout the Church year, and the religious practices that give us a badge of identity. These rules and traditions are how we will keep our identity, how we will live our faith and teach it to future generations.

The traditions and customs of our faith are the vessels that help us preserve, protect and defend our faith. As we start to drop them we find our faith becoming diluted, weakened and eventually lost.

Lent is a good time to renew respect and care for the religious traditions and customs of our Catholic faith. They are the vessels that link us to each other and help us keep our faith strong.

THURSDAY OF THE THIRD WEEK OF LENT
Jeremiah 7:23-28; Luke 11:14-23

This moment of dispute with some of the Jewish leaders carries an important teaching of Jesus to us. It is repeated in Matthew and Mark's Gospels as well. Here, Jesus gives the Church and us a message of hope.

Jesus is accused of exercising demonic power. The Lord tells His accusers to recognize the good His ministry has done and to ask how Satan can be opposed to himself.

The exorcisms and healings Jesus performs indicate that a power stronger than Satan is here. The Lord says that a strong man can guard his possessions until someone stronger arrives. The stronger one can turn the weaker one's weapons against him.

For people in the grip of sin, Jesus is the Stronger One who comes along and through His healing and forgiveness turns the tendencies to sin into opportunities of grace. That is the drama of Jesus' ministry and of our Lenten observance.

Midpoint through Lent we can become discouraged. We may have had resolutions upon which we did not follow through. Our Lent may have become somewhat diffuse. Our grand intentions of Ash Wednesday may have themselves become ashes.

But our recognition that we are weak and that we can do better is a sign of hope. The fact that we want to follow Christ seriously means we are not totally captured by weakness. The urge to go to the Sacrament of Penance, celebrate the Eucharist more frequently and remodel our life are signs that the reign of sin is not total. The reign of God has entered our life.

It might be just a seed, a sliver of light, a crack in the back door, but the opening is there. We are all mixtures of strength and weakness, good and evil. Today's Gospel invites us to recognize our weakness and to build on our strengths. They are winter signs of a coming spring.

FRIDAY OF THE THIRD WEEK OF LENT
Hosea 14:2-10; Mark 12:28-34

Our Gospel reading today begins with a question for Jesus and ends with a question about the questioner. The scribe's question concerned the one commandment of the Law around which the rest revolved.

Jesus answers with two commandments: love of God and love of neighbor. Maybe in our own time, we might ask which of these two commandments is the more important. It is like asking what is more important for the earth to grow, sun or rain? The earth needs both. Without the sun, we will be flooded; without the rain we become a desert.

The path of Christian discipleship involves both love of God and love of neighbor. Part of the drama of Lent is for us to place the two in balance. The life of the solitary mystic has never been the standard path for Christians. On the other hand, philanthropy alone does not fulfill the Christian call since we have the call and privilege of a personal relationship with Christ that is activated and matured through prayer.

How do we know that our spiritual life is "off center"? If our prayer life leaves no time for others, we may be out of balance. If our outreach to others leaves little time for prayer, we may be out of balance. If our Catholicism is fed only by the Church's private devotions, we may be out of balance. If only the social issues facing the Church dominate our lives, we may be out of balance. If we feel that issues of public policy and social justice have no room in the Church, we may be out of balance. If we feel that prayer is our escape from engagement in the world, we may be out of balance. Lent is a time to look at how well we are calibrating our spiritual life.

The Gospel reading ends with a question about the scribe. He received Jesus' approval for recognizing the truth of what Jesus said about the two great commandments. But what is the rest of the story? Did he act on it? Was it simply an inquiry without any traction in his life? Did he begin to examine his life to see how he was fulfilling both commandments?

Jesus told him he was not far from the Kingdom of God. He was not yet there but not far from it. Can the same be said about us? Do we recognize the truth of what Jesus says, nod our head in agreement and leave unchanged? How far are we from the Kingdom of God?

Lent is a time for us to follow both of Jesus' great commandments. Our spiritual life needs both rain and sun to grow.

SATURDAY OF THE THIRD WEEK OF LENT
Hosea 6:1-6; Luke 18:9-14

We can all picture the scene in today's Gospel reading. The contrast between the two people could not be more stark and vivid. One leaves the Temple justified and the other condemned.

St. John of the Ladder once remarked that at the end of our life we will not be judged because we did not perform miracles. We will not be judged because we did not have mystical visions. We will not be judged because we didn't speak in tongues. We will be judged because we didn't repent.

In this short parable, we have the tragedy of the Pharisee and the grace of the publican. Both the tragedy and the grace repeat themselves today.

The tragedy of the Pharisee is not that he didn't repent but that he didn't even realize that he had any need to do so.

What repels us is the self-assurance of the man. It is one thing for us to know that we have done wrong and refuse to repent. The failure to even recognize that we have done wrong is a symptom of a profound moral tragedy. The inability to grasp the truth encapsulates us into a private fantasy structure that keeps us far from reality and away from the Lord.

Lent is directed toward serious fact-finding about ourselves. It is a time when we hold our lives up not against others but against the Gospel and look for the areas that need repair.

If up to this moment we have been gifted with the recognition of sin and of the spiritual deficits in our lives, a good portion of the work of Lent has been successful. The gift of sight, insight, is itself a grace. It's the grace of the publican in today's Gospel reading.

The first step to health is to recognize that we are ill.

MONDAY OF THE FOURTH WEEK IN LENT
Isaiah 65:17-21; John 4:43-54

The royal official in today's Gospel reading asks for a miracle and he receives two gifts: the healing of his son and the gift of faith in Christ. Of these, the greater was faith in Christ.

In this second half of Lent, our Gospel readings come from the Gospel of St. John, the Gospel of the great signs of Jesus. There are seven of them presented to us by St. John. They are not called "miracles" but "signs" because they enable us to go beyond what Jesus did (the miracle itself) to who Jesus is (the Source of life and spiritual healing). Each sign shows us a deep truth about the Lord and points to something that Jesus continues to do through His Church.

The first "sign" was the changing of water into wine signifying the new creation being brought to life by Jesus.

The official's son who was cured in this second "sign" will eventually die and so will the royal official. But through faith in Christ, they have become a new creation and have acquired eternal life.

The power of Lent is manifest not in what it does for us on the outside but what it does for us on the inside as we become a new creation and come to deeper faith and trust in Jesus.

The outside of us changes in many ways. As time goes on some look better, others don't; some gain weight, others don't; some age quickly, others don't. What really matters, however, is how we change on the inside, whether we are more Christ-like.

Therein lies the real beauty of a person. The transformation of a soul, a personality, a heart into a "piece of Christ" is the real miracle. This kind of miracle goes on every day.

The miraculous power of faith shows not in what it does for us on the outside, but what it does on the inside.

TUESDAY OF THE FOURTH WEEK IN LENT
Ezekiel 47:1-9, 12; John 5:1-16

In today's first reading, the prophet Ezekiel describes a stream of water flowing from the renewed Temple. He is speaking to a people in exile for whom the Temple was now a distant memory. This flowing water irrigates and nourishes everything for miles around. It brings a desert to life to show the dynamic power of God.

That dynamic presence of God giving life we call Jesus Christ. In this Gospel, Jesus does something for the man who was paralyzed for thirty-eight years. Jesus heals him in a wonderful miracle. Later, when Jesus sees him again, He said that he should give up his sins so something worse would not overtake him.

There is something worse than being unable to walk. There is a soul crippled by sin, a heart paralyzed by revenge; a mind trapped in hatred. These are indeed some things worse than not being able to walk. That is what Jesus is telling him and us.

The river of Christ's grace flows to us through the Mass and Sacraments to heal, strengthen and enliven us. It was a great miracle for that man, sick for thirty-eight years, to be able to walk again.

It is a great miracle each Lent when people who have been away from the Church return and can walk again spiritually.

Lent is a time to remember in prayer those who are disabled within, paralyzed morally, crippled spiritually that through someone, the healing waters of Christ will touch them and make them whole.

We can be that someone as we hold them up to the Lord in prayer.

WEDNESDAY OF THE FOURTH WEEK IN LENT
Isaiah 49:8-15; John 5:17-30

Jesus says to His opponents that His Father is at work and He is at work as well. The reason Jesus speaks these words is that He was accused of violating the Sabbath rest by healing a man. To that charge, Jesus makes three points.

First, the Father does not rest on the Sabbath. The work of the Father did not end with the act of creation, as though God set the universe in motion and then stepped back. The Father sustains creation. It takes as much power to keep the universe in being from one moment to the next as to create it.

This is a profound point for our meditation. God is sustaining us at every moment of our life. Our heart could not beat without His consent, whether we are aware of it or not.

The second point Jesus makes is that He and the Father are one. Statements such as these enraged the Pharisees. Jesus is identifying Himself with the great "Jehovah." He is doing the Father's "work."

This is another powerful point for meditation. In Jesus, we see the face of God.

The third point Jesus makes is that He came to raise the dead, not just the physically dead, but the spiritually dead.

This is another powerful point for reflection. However long and winding the road that we may have traveled away from God, whatever the condition of our soul and of our life, Jesus can give new life. If He can raise the physically dead, He can give new life to you and me now.

The Father's sustaining us at each moment, Jesus' unity with the Father and His continuing the Father's work by transmitting new life are potent reflections to help us see that our God is very close to us and more a part of our life than we realize.

Without His sustaining power, we would cease to be. That is a profound point for meditation, as profound as it is humbling.

THURSDAY, FOURTH WEEK OF LENT
Exodus 32:7-14; John 5:31-47

The calling of witnesses and the taking of testimony that we hear in today's Gospel reading recall discussions from Court TV more than the Gospel language with which we are familiar. In John's Gospel, Jesus seems to be on trial not only before Pontius Pilate but also throughout His life. His opponents are constantly trying to discredit Him. If we have ever had anyone "flyspeck" everything we do, we can understand how Jesus' every word and action were under the proverbial microscope.

One of the witnesses to which the Lord points is the works He has done. The Lord's reference is, of course, to His miracles that are called "works" in John's Gospel. Jesus' words in the Gospel are meant for Christians of every generation and not just for the immediate readers of John's Gospel.

The works of Jesus that draw people to belief in Him are not only the array of miracles that have taken place throughout history. The great work of Jesus is His Church. It is the Church that continues to draw people to the Lord today.

It is not the size of the Church or the beauty of its churches that draw people deeply to Christ but what the Church does. The Church embraces people all over the world. It is a truly universal institution. The Church speaks the truth of Christ whether politically correct or not. The Church presents and lives the Gospel in a constantly changing world. The Sacraments of the Church are the powers that flow today from the Risen Christ through her.

She is a Church that, like Moses in today's first reading, intercedes for sinners, produces saints and radiates Christ's light even in the midst of her own scandals like a dusty diamond.

But the Church as the "work" of Christ can become obscured when some of her members assert truth at the expense of charity, uniformity at the expense of unity, and traditionalism at the expense of Tradition. Our human excesses can cloud the Church's light like a fog blinding people to the lights of a city. The light is there but it is obscured.

Sometimes people identify the anger, the bitterness, the prejudice, and the constant criticism that they see in some members of the Church with the Church itself. They deserve better than that from us. They deserve to see Christ.

Jesus says that He has a witness greater than John the Baptist to speak on His behalf and those are His works, that is, you and me.

FRIDAY OF THE FOURTH WEEK IN LENT
Wisdom 2:1, 12-22; John 7:1-2, 10, 25-30

One thing is very clear as we read John's Gospel and especially his account of the events leading up to the Passion, Death and Resurrection of Christ. Jesus is manifestly in charge. He came on a mission from the Father. He will offer the great sacrifice of Himself to the Father as the start of a new creation. He will return to the Father in glory.

Appropriately, during Lent, we should reflect upon the sufferings of Jesus and the immense love that His endurance of those sufferings showed. That love is shown particularly in the fact that these are sufferings Jesus consciously accepted for our sake.

He was not a passive victim haplessly caught up in the vortex of evil. It takes an enormous and potent act of the will to accept suffering and pain. Jesus actively underwent the torments of the Passion for us. The Passion was not something that happened to Him, it was something He did.

Too frequently we picture Jesus only as a victim who was later vindicated by the Father on Easter Sunday. But Jesus sacrificed Himself to the Father for us. He was, as the liturgy says, "victim, altar and priest."

This can be an encouragement to all those people who accept pain in their life. Of course, one can easily say that a person confined to a hospital bed has no other choice. Indeed, they have no choice about their physical circumstance.

But they certainly have a choice about their experience of pain. It can be a time of constant anxiety and rebellion or strong, powerful, prayerful acceptance. This is what we see in Jesus.

Pain exposes our human weakness and fragility. The acceptance not only of the voluntary pains of penance but of unwanted pain and the offering of our fidelity in pain to the Father is an act not of passivity but of power.

To offer our suffering to the Father is to share in the majestic priesthood of Jesus Christ.

Saturday of the Fourth Week in Lent
Jeremiah 11:18-20; John 7:40-53

St. John records the specific detail in today's Gospel reading that each went off to his own house.

There had been a vigorous debate about the identity of Jesus and the Messiah and then each went off to his own house. What did each take with him to his own house?

For some, all this had no impact on them at all as they went back to their own house.

For others, their minds were not changed and they refused to accept Jesus as they went back to their own house.

For others, this caused them to think and examine Jesus of Nazareth as they went off to their own house.

We are in the last two weeks of Lent and what impact has Lent had on us this year?

Maybe Lent had no impact. We came to church and then each of us went back to our own house unchanged and unchallenged.

Others heard the call of Lent, faced the opportunity for renewal in Christ but, realizing the cost, left it for another time as they went back to their own house.

Others have taken the personal call of Lent to heart. Each Lent carries a special call to each of us. Maybe it's a call this year for courage or for patience or to go into deeper spiritual waters. They have taken that back to their house.

What are we taking back to our house this Lent? Are we taking back indifference, refusal or the beginning of a deeper spiritual life and commitment to the Church?

This Lent, like the people in the Gospel, we are all taking back something as we return each to our own house.

MONDAY OF THE FIFTH WEEK OF LENT
Daniel 13:1-9, 15-17, 19-30, 33-62; John 8:12-20

The story of Susanna, which has been read for centuries during Lent, dominates our Liturgy of the Word today. As we hear it read, we can picture the characters: the dishonest judges, innocent Susanna and Daniel the forthright prophet.

This is more than a story about good versus evil or someone being rescued in the nick of time. It is a story of Susanna's rescue from the clutches of people who would destroy her. It is an Old Testament preview of what our Baptism is all about.

Baptism is a rescue from darkness into the kingdom of light. Each year, Lent is a time for us to reflect upon what that means in our life. Have we come to an appreciation of the power of darkness in our world? Do we see what the darkness of sin can really do to communities, to families and to individual lives? Do we see its intrinsically corrosive nature?

Do we appreciate the darkness of ignorance about God? We can only guess what it must be like to be a spiritual vagabond searching for some meaning in life, something larger than the years we are given on this earth. We can only guess to what kind of crutches such individuals turn in their anxiety. The business of superstition is thriving these days. There is a sadness in intelligent people, endowed with reason and will and perhaps even gifted with faith in their youth, planning their future on the basis of amulets, charms and the supposed clairvoyant powers of others.

There is a sadness in seeing people move from god to god, groping for rituals to enlarge and maybe even sanctify their life.

There was a popular song years ago entitled "Imagine" that asked us to imagine no heaven, no God, nothing to die for. Such a universe would be a very lonely place.

These are the kinds of darkness from which we have been rescued in Baptism. We have been saved from the darkness of sin and confusion about God by being given the light of Christ.

The light of Christ is light for us and for the world. It is a light that can overcome any darkness. Like a single candle in a darkened hall, the light of Christ is always stronger than the night.

TUESDAY OF THE FIFTH WEEK OF LENT
Numbers 21:4-9; John 8:21-30

Our first reading from the Old Testament Book of Numbers recounts a strange incident that is also another light for us on the way to Easter.

The journey to the Promised Land was not what the Israelites had expected. They knew it wouldn't be a sleigh ride but they didn't imagine it would be as difficult as it turned out to be. They complained often and lost faith in God.

The Lord allowed these saraph or "fiery" serpents to bite them. The desert of Sinai evidently is filled with these venomous snakes whose bite leaves a bright red inflammation at the place of contact. Hence, they are called "fiery" serpents. God withheld His special care from the people of Israel to show them what life without His grace is like.

It was only when they looked at the bronze serpent, which God commanded Moses to lift up, and renewed their earlier obedience to God's Word, that they were healed. None of their doctors and no part of their natural immune system could help them. It was only by obedience to God's Word when they renewed their faith in God that healing came.

It wasn't, of course, the bronze serpent by itself but their obedience and renewed faith in God that brought about the healing.

Today, we are saved from sin and given strength for the journey by looking to Jesus' saving death on the Cross. Nothing else can save us from sin except the power of Jesus' Death and Resurrection.

During Lent, it is not our fasting and penances by themselves that save us. They do so only if they draw us to deeper faith in Christ, to embrace the Crucified One by repentance and discipleship.

On our journey of faith, we know inner healing not only by looking at but by embracing the teaching and truth of the Cross.

WEDNESDAY OF THE FIFTH WEEK OF LENT
Daniel 3:14-20, 91-92, 95; John 8:31-42

In our first reading from the Old Testament Book of Daniel, the three young men were saved from the fires of the furnace by a supernatural being that entered the flames and stood with them.

It is a metaphor of the Incarnation when God became flesh and entered our world to be beside us and give us strength.

Our natural inclination is to seek deliverance from the fires around us. But the Lord did not choose to take us out of the world and transport us into a risk-free, pain-free, antiseptic world. Instead, He chose to enter our world and by the gift of His Spirit give us a way to remain strong and secure whatever may be the destructive powers around us.

The Lord says in today's Gospel that His truth is a liberating truth that can free us from all the sham, deception, false starts and anxieties that can attack us, confuse our minds and do us real harm. Whether we like it or not, we live in a fiery furnace. It is not the physical fire of Nebuchadnezzar's huge oven. It is the furnace of flashy frenzy, media hype, deception labeled as truth, inflammatory advertising and spin galore. We live in a world that swirls in excitements that shift, twist and turn from one week to the next.

In the middle of all this is the serene, powerful Teacher of Truth, Jesus Christ. He is beside us as the quiet center in the storm. He can keep us sane and focused in a neurotic and often sociopathic world where values are for rent and truth is for sale.

He can free us not by transporting us away from this world but by His being our strength, truth and Life.

The truth that we learned from Jesus when we were young remains true. Since then, the world has changed many times. Since then we have changed. "Astronomies change; the stars remain." The truth of Jesus remains as valid and liberating today as it ever was.

THURSDAY OF THE FIFTH WEEK OF LENT
Genesis 17:3-9; John 8:51-59

Our readings today are about Abraham and Jesus. To people who revered Abraham, Jesus says something shocking.

Abraham was the great Old Testament patriarch and father of the Jewish people. God had made a covenant, a solemn alliance with Abraham and all his descendants. They would be God's own special people with a mission to save the world. The sign of this covenant would be the ritual of circumcision. All Jewish people trace themselves to Abraham.

Abraham is the father not only of the Jewish people but also of all Semitic peoples (Jews and Arabs). If the Jewish people trace themselves to Abraham through Isaac, the Arab people trace themselves to Abraham through Ishmael.

Also, St. Paul traces all people who believe in God to Abraham. In fact, he is called "our father in faith" in our liturgy.

Abraham is, therefore, a major figure to all Jewish people. To them Jesus says something startling. The Jewish people looked back with great awe to Abraham. Jesus stunned them by saying that Abraham was, in fact, looking forward to Him because Jesus fulfilled the old covenant by creating a new one.

In the Old Testament, God blessed and guided Israel from the outside in. In the New Testament, the Trinity enters the life of Christians on the inside. The more we open ourselves to His grace, the more God works through us.

Lent is not only about renewing ourselves in the Lord personally but also renewing our world through becoming bearers of His truth and grace to others. Each one of us is given the same mission that was given to old Israel.

In Jesus Christ, the individual Christian has a far greater dignity than Abraham ever had. It is the dignity of being God's agent through an inner transformation given us not in the physical surgery of circumcision but in the inner healing of Baptism.

That dignity is ours to use or lose.

FRIDAY OF THE FIFTH WEEK OF LENT
Jeremiah 20:10-13; John 10:31-42

The Gospel readings from this section of John's Gospel recount the growing tension between Jesus and the Pharisees, Scribes and Sadducees. It is a tension about His identity, His purpose and His activity, really everything about Him. That tension is escalating toward His death and Jesus knows that.

We have a detail at the end of today's Gospel reading that is seldom noticed but shows the human side of Jesus and, as with everything about the Lord, carries a message for us.

The Gospel says that Jesus went back across the Jordan River to the place where John had been baptizing before.

By now, John had been executed so Jesus went to the spot where John had baptized Him, where He had heard the Father's voice, where He had been confirmed in His mission.

Now, towards the end of His earthly ministry, Jesus goes to the place where His earthly ministry began with the voice from heaven to draw strength to complete His mission from the Father.

That is what we do at Easter. We go back to our Baptism, review our baptismal promises, renew them and revive our calling as followers of Jesus. We go back to the time when we were "bathed" in Christ, anointed by the Father, clothed in Christ, given a candle to light the way as we were commissioned to be agents of Jesus Christ.

Now, after our time in this world, like Jesus we go back to the "place" of our Baptism to renew the vision and our strength. It was in the Sacrament of Baptism that the Father made us His beloved ones.

Are we still convinced of our mission on earth? Easter is a time to restore it, to revive the truth that we are living not for ourselves alone but to testify to Jesus Christ and that we are an agent of Jesus Christ in our world today.

Easter doesn't tell us something new. It affirms something true. Like Jesus, you and I are sent by heaven for a mission on earth. Everything we do is part of that mission.

SATURDAY OF THE FIFTH WEEK OF LENT
Ezekiel 37:21-28; John 11:45-56

In this Gospel reading, we overhear the decision by the Sanhedrin to put Jesus to death. If this had been taped, it would be the moment of the "smoking gun."

The high priest Caiaphas says something of great irony and great significance, that it is better for one man to die to save the nation.

Politically, he was wrong. The Romans would destroy Jerusalem years later. On the supernatural level, however, he was right. Jesus' death would bring salvation not only to Jewish believers but also to all who believe in His name.

As this is going on in the Sanhedrin, Jesus goes to a place called "Ephraim" to pray. It was an out of the way place to which the Lord went not to escape but to determine the timing of events so that His death will coincide with and fulfill the Jewish Passover.

Jesus is about to do spiritual battle so He goes to be alone with the Father in prayer. The resources for spiritual battle come not from books, discussions or videotapes but from prayer, communion with God.

If we are preparing for spiritual battle in our life we need to enter into prayer. That's what Jesus did.

Before His public ministry began, Jesus went to the desert to pray; before He chose His apostles, Jesus went to the mountain to pray; before the events of the Passion begin, Jesus goes to Ephraim to pray and before His actual betrayal, Jesus will go to the garden to pray.

It is said that in medieval times, a knight would prepare for battle the next day not by jousting or sword practice but by a night of prayer.

We prepare for spiritual battle as Jesus did, by prayer in our personal "Ephraim" where we join our will, our life and our future to God.

MONDAY OF HOLY WEEK
Isaiah 42:1-7; John 12:1-11

The readings on these first three days of Holy Week compare the quiet majesty of Jesus in the hours before His Passion in contrast to the confused swirl of anxiety, treachery and weakness in those around Him.

Today's Gospel shows Jesus as the servant whom Isaiah describes as coming to bring God's justice not with threats but simply by being the Way, the Truth and the Life.

As Jesus dines in Lazarus' home, Mary, a woman who had experienced His forgiveness, comes to Him with a gesture of gratitude and of ominous prophecy. She expresses her thanks and also signals His coming death.

Jesus never demanded dramatic gestures of gratitude for His healing. But to those who were indeed transformed by what He had done, expressions of thanks did come. Perhaps the greatest gift He gave them was the ability to see Him as the new Lord of their life.

In contrast to this woman's generosity, Judas laments her extravagance. There is a mysterious untold story of the relationship between Jesus and Judas. Was Judas always a traitor? When did he become one? What went through the Lord's mind as He spoke with Judas in these last weeks?

In His ministry, Jesus did not change. Judas did. Again, the Lord did not demand gestures of loyalty nor did the Lord expel the hesitant from His presence. He remained as always the Way, the Truth and the Life. But slowly something inside Judas wavered then he turned away.

Mary turned to the Lord, Judas turned away. In effect, they pass each other, one on the way into the Kingdom and the other on the way out.

In these Gospel relationships as well as in His relationship with us, Jesus remains the Way, the Truth and the Life. The story of our life and of this past Lent is the story of how we have come closer to the Lord like the repentant Mary or further from the Lord like Judas.

The repentant Mary represents for us the glory of what can be. Judas represents the tragedy of losing what might have been.

TUESDAY OF HOLY WEEK
Isaiah 49:1-6; John 13:21-33, 36-38

This scene in today's Gospel reading is portrayed in Leonardo da Vinci's Last Supper that we all have seen.

Jesus tells the disciples that one of them will betray Him. We recognize in those words Jesus' reference to Judas. But it can be true of any one of us. At the end, we have Peter's bravado and his bold commitment to Christ to which Jesus responds that Peter will disown Him before daylight of the next day.

It is very easy for us to feel superior to Peter and be condescending toward his weakness. Yet, there is the weakness of Peter in each of us.

What happened to Peter can happen to us as well. We can make great affirmations of our loyalty to Christ. Launch a crusade? I'll be there! Start a campaign? I'm with you! Battle evil? Count on me! Begin a march? I'm on board!

But then, when the time comes to take the first step, something always seems to come up that keeps us from following through.

When someone says something negative about the Church, about the Faith or about others at the coffee break, at lunch, in the car, we either say nothing or we agree with them.

At that moment, deep inside us, the cock crows! We have repeated Peter's denial.

We all need the grace and strength of Christ not only to be faithful but also to remain faithful to Christ anywhere and everywhere.

WEDNESDAY OF HOLY WEEK
Isaiah 50:4-9; Matthew 26:14-25

The season of Lent comes to an end with a focus on Judas, the betrayer.

Traitors have always been held in particular contempt not simply because of their deception but because they betray the nation or the person who nurtured them. To a traitor, nothing is sacred. Everything has a price tag. Everyone, including those who purchased the traitor's services, holds a traitor in low regard.

Judas was a traitor. Whom did he betray?

He betrayed his Teacher and Master. He knew the special places and times when the Lord gathered with His disciples. Judas used that information to hand Jesus over.

Judas betrayed the other Apostles who had confidence in him, relied on him because he kept the common funds.

Finally, Judas betrayed himself. For thirty pieces of silver he sold himself. He sold out his own integrity, his ministry, his mission and his years of discipleship. He betrayed himself and all that he could have been.

Part of the tragedy of sin, any sin, is that we exchange the glory of what we are called to be in Jesus Christ for something far less and even for something that can destroy us.

Still, if we repent Christ will restore our dignity, our mission and our self-respect.

Judas remains a lesson for us. Whenever we sin, we betray the Lord, we betray the Church, and we also betray ourselves. When we return to Christ, we strengthen the Church, build up our fellow Christians and recover our baptismal dignity.

As we conclude Lent, we should keep in mind the tragedy that was Judas and the glory that could have been his and still can be ours by grace.

Easter Season

MONDAY OF THE OCTAVE OF EASTER
Acts 2:14, 22-33; Matthew 28:8-15

One of the striking things about Jesus' Resurrection appearances is that each time the Lord appears to someone, He sends them on a mission to tell others and to spread the news. He makes them missionaries of the new Easter truth that He is risen.

In this Gospel reading, when the women embraced Him, Jesus tells them to go and carry the news to His brothers that they are to go to Galilee to meet Him.

Through these appearances, Jesus is reweaving His community, broken apart and scattered by His Passion, into a new community centered on His Resurrection.

Our liturgical experience of the Paschal mystery through Holy Thursday, Good Friday and Easter will hopefully make us missionaries of Easter truth as well.

If we have experienced closeness to Christ this Easter, we should share that with others.

If we have experienced forgiveness and revival, we should share that with others.

If we have experienced a deepened faith and commitment to the Church, we should share that with others.

We should not only radiate Christ's peace to others but also let people know the source of our peace, the Risen Lord Jesus Christ!

Jesus' Resurrection appearances are never only to comfort, assure or convince single individuals alone. They are triggers for a mission and a vocation that extend beyond the appearance itself. They are given to individuals but intended for the world.

The closeness of the Risen Christ to us that we experience is not just for us but for others.

The words of Jesus in today's Gospel reading speak to us: Do not be afraid. Go and carry the news that Jesus is risen, truly risen!

TUESDAY OF THE OCTAVE OF EASTER
Acts 2:36-41; John 20:11-18

We have a magnificent and encouraging appearance of the Risen Christ in our Gospel reading today.

The fact that Mary Magdalene did not recognize the Risen Lord is a piece of evidence supporting the reality of the Lord's appearances and of His Resurrection.

If through some kind of autosuggestion His followers expected to see Jesus rise, they would have seen Him everywhere. Yet, the very opposite happened. They fail to recognize Him at first.

Jesus tells Mary not to cling to Him. Mary quite naturally wanted to put her arms around Him. That was a thoroughly understandable and natural thing to do but she couldn't stay that way. From now on, she would stay close to the Risen Christ by the embrace of faith rather than by physical contact.

It is a contact that is different but just as real. It is a kind of contact that is much more intimate and filled with grace than is physical contact. It is also portable, it can happen anywhere. That contact with the Risen Christ through faith is now open to all of us.

The Lord tells Mary Magdalene to go to His brothers with the news that He is risen. One sign of a healthy Easter faith is that we build up the Church by embracing and enhancing the Church's life.

The Jesuit, Gerard Manley Hopkins, used the word "Easter" as a verb in one of his poems as he prayed to let Christ "easter in us, be a dayspring to the dimness of us...." We do that by immersing ourselves in the Church's sacramental life, her teaching life and her community life. We build up the Church by living and sharing Gospel truth.

Easter is not a private possession. We should try to make Easter not just a noun but a powerful verb in our life as we build up the Church by making the community of faith stronger.

WEDNESDAY OF THE OCTAVE OF EASTER
Acts 3:1-10; Luke 24:13-35

Several reflections flow from this Emmaus story. Two disciples on the road to Emmaus have their eyes opened to the presence of the Risen Christ in the "breaking of the bread."

This appearance teaches us some powerful Easter truths.

These two followers of Jesus do not appear anywhere else in the Gospels. We do not hear about them before or after this incident. Here, the scene shifts from the major Gospel figures such as Peter, John and Mary Magdalene to two ordinary people like us and the Risen Lord comes to them. The Risen Christ is accessible now not just to saints and spiritual heroes but to millions of ordinary people like us.

This appearance happened on the road to Emmaus. This little known town not far from Jerusalem was neither a revered spiritual center nor a great historical center. It was just a small, unremarkable village and Christ appears there. The Risen Christ is now accessible anywhere.

Their eyes were opened in the "breaking of the bread." They were focused on their broken hopes and their disappointment that Jesus was not the kind of savior they had imagined. Now, they see that something larger and more majestic than what they had dreamed has taken place.

So in the Eucharist when we reflect on events in our life through the Liturgy of the Word and the Liturgy of the Eucharist, the Lord enables us to see that larger picture, the drama of His grace, in which we all have an important part.

Whoever we are, wherever we are, the Lord is with us now not in visions but in the "breaking of the bread."

THURSDAY OF THE OCTAVE OF EASTER
Acts 3:11-26; Luke 24:35-48

Jesus shows these Apostles His hands and His side. When they see the marks of the Passion, they realize that this indeed is the Jesus of Nazareth they knew. But now, He is in glory. Let's consider the deep truth in all this for us.

We all have read many deep reflections on the sufferings of Christ. In the face of all He suffered, the Resurrection is more than Christ's assurance that there is life after death. The Resurrection of Jesus shows us that the eternal life that awaits us is a life of glory, fulfillment and peace to which we come not despite our wounds but through them.

Through death to new life!

How we take up our crosses adds depth, seriousness and honest spirituality to our life. As one writer put it a while ago, when faced with strong winds, the skillful sailor knows how to use the wind to reach his goal. Our sufferings can bring us closer to Christ. Leonard Feeney once wrote a moving poem about a crippled girl searching the chapel walls to find the three "pictures" where Jesus falls. Her disability united her to Christ.

The meaning of Easter for us is that we come to eternal life not despite our wounds but, like Jesus, through them.

Wounds and crosses will come to each of us. They are part of our life like the bumps and scars we carry on our bodies from childhood. They can take us from the world of spiritual romance to reality. They can take us from the world of childhood to adulthood. They can take us from the surface of life to its depth. They can take us from self-absorption to empathy with others. They can take us from self to God.

Like Jesus, we come to Easter through our wounds.

This is another truth of Easter for us from this appearance. Our wounds are avenues to the glory of eternal life.

FRIDAY OF THE OCTAVE OF EASTER
Acts 4:1-12; John 21:1-14

This is another important Resurrection appearance of the Risen Christ.

The Lord had appeared to the Apostles in the upper room

on Easter Sunday. There they had been given evidence of His Resurrection. Maybe they didn't know what to do with that truth. Here, in this appearance, Jesus turns the fact of the Resurrection into a mission to spread Risen life to others. This is what we see the Apostles doing in today's first reading as they heal and give witness.

There is an important message in all this for each of us. The Lord not only called them to the meal but also provided the catch. When the Lord asks something of us, He also gives us the means to do it.

The Lord never asks us to resist temptation without providing a way to handle the pressure.

The Lord never asks us to sacrifice for others without giving us the gifts that allow sacrificial giving.

The Lord never asks us to take a public stand without giving us the strength to endure the arena.

The Lord never asks us to endure a hardship without giving us the grace to handle the challenges.

Every contribution the Lord asks of us is drawn from resources He has already provided.

In whatever the Lord calls us to do, He gives us the grace and the gifts to be faithful to that call.

As with the meal on the seashore in today's Gospel, Jesus gives us His Eucharist as strength for the particular mission in life, the quiet building of a piece of His Kingdom that He has planned for each of us.

SATURDAY OF THE OCTAVE OF EASTER
Acts 4:13-21; Mark 16:9-15

The priests and elders were amazed at the self-assurance of Peter and John and then recognized them as "companions of Jesus."

There is an old saying from the past to the effect that we are "the company we keep."

If we associate with cynics, we become cynical.

If we associate with pessimists, we become pessimistic.

If we associate with people who are bitter, that bitterness will enter us.

If we associate with people who are deeply Christian, that will change us as well.

Part of the power of the Risen Christ is the Lord's ability to change us to make us more like Himself. It's not just knowing about Jesus but knowing the Lord in prayer that can profoundly transform us. The Sacraments are our continuing contacts with the Risen Christ

Baptism is about more than the elimination of original sin. It's the start of a lifelong commitment to Christ and His mission.

Marriage is not just a bond between two people but the start of a lifelong commitment to show forth Christ's kind of fidelity to each other and to the world.

Holy Orders is not just the transmission of priestly power but a commitment to serve the Church and its people.

The Eucharist is not just receiving Holy Communion but a commitment to the sacrificial love that the Eucharist embodies.

Penance is not just the forgiveness of sin but a commitment to resetting our life around Christ.

Confirmation is not just receiving the Holy Spirit but a deeper commitment to the mission of the Christ.

The Anointing of the Sick is not just strengthening the sick but a commitment of our pain and suffering to Christ for the good of others and of the Church.

The Sacraments are our ways of becoming companions of Jesus and of being changed by Him.

MONDAY OF THE SECOND WEEK OF EASTER
Acts 4:23-31; John 3:1-8

This week, we overhear the nighttime conversation between Jesus and Nicodemus. Nicodemus was a member of the Sanhedrin, a Pharisee who came to Jesus at night. For Nicodemus it was not only night outside but on the inside as well.

Jesus speaks to him about a wonderful miracle, the wonder of a second birth available to all who believe in Christ.

Nicodemus misunderstood the nature of this second birth as though it was some kind of biological restart.

Jesus tells him that this wondrous rebirth happens through water and the Holy Spirit in Baptism. Through Baptism, the Holy Spirit can give us new spiritual vigor, move us in a new direction, give us new strength for dealing with old problems and confirm our faith when we face difficulties.

The gift of the Holy Spirit in Baptism, is a life-long gift, a source of energy, vision and wisdom that we can let work in our lives or which we can ignore.

It is like a program built into our computer. We can struggle for months to perform certain operations with our computer and only months later discover that there is a program, built into our PC, that makes it all easier but which we never bothered to open.

So it is with us on the level of our spirit. We should not neglect the gift of the Holy Spirit given us in Baptism to guide us and lead us through any problems toward Christ.

The Holy Spirit is our personal connection to the Risen Christ.

TUESDAY OF THE SECOND WEEK OF EASTER
Acts 4:32-37; John 3:7-15

Jesus continues to speak with Nicodemus about the mysterious spiritual rebirth, the second birth by water and the Holy Spirit in Baptism.

The Lord compares the Holy Spirit to the wind. Just as the wind is invisible and comes and goes through our homes, yards and lives, so the Holy Spirit is invisible and comes through our homes and lives.

We can't put the wind in a box nor can we do so with the Holy Spirit. We can't control the Holy Spirit or the direction in which the Spirit leads the Church and us. Sometimes an inspiration can come to us which is so compelling that our life will not be at rest until we follow it.

We also know the power of the wind. If we open a window of our home, a refreshing breeze can fill the house. The Holy Spirit is like that.

We have seen the power of a hurricane to overturn homes and buildings. The Holy Spirit is like that as well.

We have seen the power of compressed air to raise automobiles and houses; the Holy Spirit also has such power.

One action of the Holy Spirit is always to gather us into the Church as we see in today's first reading.

One sure sign that it is the Holy Spirit at work in our life is when the Holy Spirit joins us more deeply to the community of the Church. In the Church, we experience the Holy Spirit, verify our inspirations, nurture the graces and deepen the roots of the Lord's teaching in our life.

The Spirit blows where it will but the place where the Holy Spirit always is ready to strengthen and inspire is the Church.

One effect of our spiritual rebirth in Baptism is that we are born into the spiritual family of the Church, the family of Jesus Christ.

One sign, therefore, of deep Easter renewal is when we share more deeply in the life of the Church and the Church's life becomes our life.

WEDNESDAY OF THE SECOND WEEK OF EASTER
Acts 5:17-26; John 3:16-21

Today's Gospel reading contains the famous verse of John 3:16 that we see displayed at so many sporting events announcing that God so loved the world that He sent His only Son.

Some have said that this is the whole Gospel in capsule form or, as we would say today, a "sound bite" of Gospel truth. We can reflect on that one verse repeatedly during our life and always derive fresh inspiration from it.

Jesus is speaking to Nicodemus about spiritual rebirth in which we are taken out of darkness and born into the light. Darkness and light constitute a great theme of the Bible. We recall at Christmas that people who walked in darkness have seen a great light.

Darkness is the place of crime, deceit and danger especially years ago when villages had no street lamps. Although our streets today are well lit, we still live in a time of moral darkness.

By Baptism, we are called to live in the light. In today's Gospel, Jesus gives us one way of gauging whether we are living in the light, doing right or wrong and that is whether we do it in darkness or light.

Are we furtive, secretive, speaking in half-truths and studied ambiguities, refusing candor? Then, we are walking in darkness.

Do we hide things we are doing from people to whom we are responsible and accountable? Then, we are walking in darkness.

Do we hide things we are doing not because they are private but because we want to keep them secret? Then, we are walking in darkness.

The Lord teaches us that those who practice evil hate the light. The one who acts in truth delights in the light.

There is a great deal of darkness today. We are called to be people of the light with clear motives, clear intentions and clear purposes. "Transparency" has become the word of the hour as it should be.

In an age of so much darkness, the world needs people of light. For our own salvation as well, we need to be people of the light.

Thursday of the Second Week of Easter
Acts 5:27-33; John 3:31-36

One of the effects of the Resurrection was a transformation in the Apostles. They were not easily silenced about Jesus. They were beaten, jailed and ordered to cease preaching but they continued proclaiming that it is better to obey God than men.

That is a strong and direct statement of Christian priorities. It is better to obey God rather than men. How many times do we face that choice? How many times do we have to choose between obeying God rather than doing what people want or expect? More often than we realize.

We are not called before the Sanhedrin of Israel. But we are called before the "Sanhedrin" of our friends and neighbors.

When we want to cut corners at work because everyone does it, we face the choice.

When we want to sleep in on Sunday morning rather than go to Mass because others do it, we face the choice.

When someone at work engages in gossip or tells suggestive jokes, we face the choice.

When we are tempted to infidelity so commonly portrayed in the media, we face the choice.

When someone's good name is being maligned around us, we face the choice.

In dealing with people who "don't count" we face the choice.

When issues about Church and morality come up in conversation, we face the choice.

A dozen times a week we run into such a fateful choice. Nicodemus in today's Gospel faced such a choice after his conversation with Jesus. We don't know how he answered because the dialogue simply ends.

But we do know how the Apostles replied to the question of serving God or man.

How do we answer that question not in theory but in our life?

We are given such a choice virtually every day.

FRIDAY OF THE SECOND WEEK OF EASTER
Acts 5:34-42; John 6:1-15

If the Lord's conversation with Nicodemus was about Baptism, one of the great Easter Sacraments of the Church, the Gospels this coming week will be about the Eucharist, the second great Easter Sacrament.

Today's Gospel gives us a splendid and generous miracle of Jesus. The multiplication of loaves foreshadows and predicts the miracle of the Eucharist.

We can reflect on the Apostle Philip and on the boy. The Lord asks Philip from where food will come to feed such a giant crowd. Philip admits that even several months' wages would fail to feed such a crowd.

Financial resources are not necessarily the most important resource we bring to others. There is compassion, understanding, patience and the power of Christ that we can bring to others. Philip focuses on what they could not do. The Apostles thought that since they did not have enough, they could do nothing.

Then we have the unnamed boy who gives to Christ what little he had and the Lord made of it a spectacular miracle, the only one recounted in all four Gospels.

As we read and reflect on this miracle, we can meditate on Philip and the little boy.

Philip was intimidated by the huge crowd and the Apostles' meager resources. He was overwhelmed by what they could not do. The boy gave Jesus what he had and Jesus did the rest.

We should never underestimate what the Lord can do with the gifts we have. If we give what we have to the Lord, He will do the rest.

The gifts of simple words, simple gestures, and simple acts of compassion can be filled by Christ with grace and power, more than we can ever imagine.

Saturday of the Second Week of Easter
Acts 6:1-7; John 6:16-21

They say that the Sea of Galilee is not really a "sea" but a huge lake. It is several hundred feet below sea level and is surrounded by hills. Storms can arrive suddenly and violently.

Being alone, at night, several miles from shore in a storm there can be very terrifying. The miracle in today's Gospel reading is not that Jesus walked on the water. It is the realization of the Apostles that Jesus was with them in the storm to give them safe passage.

That is the message of this incident for the Church and for every Christian. Jesus is with us in any storm to give us safe passage.

The Church has faced many crises. Today's first reading gives us one of the initial ones, the conflict between Greeks and Hebrews as the number of disciples grew. As the Apostles prayed and decided, the Lord led them at that moment to create the office of deacon.

Our storms may not have to do with weather. They can be personal, emotional or spiritual. These storms can come in all shapes and sizes. They are not only "out there" but also "in here." That is a particularly dangerous kind of storm. Like those storms on the Sea of Galilee they can come to us suddenly and violently.

Jesus is with us in the storm. He can give us guidance and direction. When we pray and then make a decision consistent with the Gospel, we can be sure that the Lord is with us.

This moment of Jesus' walking on the water comes between the miracle of the loaves and Jesus' teaching about Himself as the Bread of life.

Through the Eucharist, the Risen Christ is with us. Let the Eucharistic Lord be your anchor, your sail, your rudder, and your peace in any storm.

Each time we receive the Eucharist, Jesus says to us, "Be not afraid. It is I." He will give us a safe passage and safe harbor.

MONDAY OF THE THIRD WEEK OF EASTER
Acts: 6:8-15; John 6:22-29

The Gospel readings this week are about the second great Sacrament of the Church's Easter life, the Eucharist.

Baptism (the subject of Jesus' conversation with Nicodemus) gives us new life in Christ. The Eucharist sustains that new life in Christ within us and among us.

Most churches had beautiful flowers surrounding the sanctuary for Easter. They were a burst of beauty at Easter. To sustain that beauty, however, they need to be watered every day or else they will wilt and die. It is the same with our spiritual life.

The Eucharist sustains our new life in Christ.

In today's Gospel reading, the people are looking for Jesus because they see in Him a miracle worker, a way to enhance their material life. But Jesus calls them to eternal life, to take care that their soul is in union with Him.

We all know how we are supposed to enhance our material life. We need to have savings, investments and a lifestyle proportionate to our income. One of the things we fear is a recession, a material decline in the quality of a nation's life and of our daily life.

There is such a thing as a spiritual recession, a decline in the spiritual life of an individual or a nation.

Receiving the Body and Blood of Christ in the Eucharist implies recommitment, the imitation of Christ's love, the embrace of dying as the way to life, the acceptance of Christ's mission as our own and the personal graces of the Eucharist. These are all ways that we can prevent a spiritual recession or even a spiritual depression from occurring in our lives.

The Eucharist is how we sustain and strengthen our new life in Christ. It is our protection against spiritual decline.

TUESDAY OF THE THIRD WEEK OF EASTER
Acts 7:51-8:1; John 6:30-35

There is a fascinating sentence in today's first reading, which carries a great truth for us. The Acts of the Apostles describes the crowd's fury against Stephen and how they dragged him outside Jerusalem to stone him and then says that they were placing their cloaks at the feet of a young man whose name was Saul (whom we know later as Paul).

It is here, in the middle of all this antagonism and hatred of Stephen, when the early Church is under siege, here, not on the road to Damascus but here where Saul's conversion to Christ begins. The seeds are being sown into Saul's mind and heart. They will later burst into life on the road to Damascus.

Stephen's fidelity, Stephen's faith and Stephen's example had a powerful impact on Saul, more potent than Saul himself realized and maybe even more powerful than Stephen, had he known of it, would have realized.

We can draw from this event evidence of the power of example, our example. For better or worse we are sowing seeds in the lives of others by how we live and how we believe.

It also shows us the power of good example. When the world is filled with shadows and darkness, the Christians life stands out all the more.

Given a choice between trusting what we say and how we live, people will look at how we live. Whether we know it or not, evangelization is a component, even an unconscious one, of every Christian life.

A powerful way of showing forth Jesus Christ to people today is the honesty of our Christian life. More significant sermons are preached outside the pulpit than in it.

The impact of Stephen on Saul is an example of that.

WEDNESDAY OF THE THIRD WEEK OF EASTER
Acts 8:1-8; John 6:35-40

In today's Gospel, Jesus teaches us that He is the Bread of Life referring to His Eucharistic presence. He satisfies our spiritual hungers and gives us a pledge of eternal life.

The ritual act of receiving Holy Communion at Mass carries many meanings.

To receive Holy Communion means that we accept the teachings of Jesus.

It means that we are opening our lives and hearts to the Lord symbolized by receiving the Lord in our hand or mouth.

It means that we are trying to live according to the example of Christ.

It means that we are in communion with the life and grace of His Church.

It means that we are trying to build communion among our fellow Christians.

Receiving Holy Communion is a very personal moment but not a private one. That is why receiving Holy Communion outside of Mass should be an exception (unless one is sick).

The reason is that receiving Holy Communion is not an independent moment but the culmination of the entire Mass.

When we have received the teaching of Jesus in the Liturgy of the Word, have presented our self and our lives to God through the gifts of bread and wine, have indicated our desire to reconcile with our brothers and sisters through the sign of peace, then the Lord gives us Himself in Holy Communion as a pledge of His grace and eternal life.

Receiving Holy Communion is not a private devotional moment in the Mass. It is part of a much larger communion of mind, heart, soul and life with Christ and His Church.

Receiving Holy Communion is the highest expression of a wider communion of ourselves with Christ and His Church that should be going on in the rest of our life.

THURSDAY OF THE THIRD WEEK OF EASTER
Acts 8:26-40; John 6:44-51

In today's first reading, we have a moment of grace as the Lord brings together two people. One of them, Philip, has a gift and the other, the court official, has a need. The official is baptized on the spot. What happened to him afterwards? How did he sustain his faith in Jesus Christ? We don't know.

This incident is recounted to show that the Gospel spread in the world not only as a result of human planning but also by divine grace. The Gospel continues to spread today not only as a result of evangelization programs but also through the unpredictable and unexpected workings of God's grace in the lives of individuals.

In today's Gospel reading, the Lord teaches us how the Gospel grows in our life through the Eucharist. Just as bread is a staple of any diet and we need it to develop and sustain strength, the same is true of the Eucharist. Jesus gives us His own self as food not to create faith which is the work of God's grace but to sustain, strengthen and deepen faith.

We all have seen pictures of people suffering from malnutrition in various parts of the world. Without the Eucharist, we can suffer from spiritual malnutrition. In fact, our material prosperity can mask the spiritual hunger with which our society is plagued. We have the Eucharist as the abiding, nourishing presence of Christ where we can always renew contact with the Risen Lord and receive Him more deeply into our life.

We can only imagine the difficulty the court official had the day after his Baptism. He had no fellow Christians with whom to pray. He could not take part in the Eucharist since there was probably no celebration to which he had regular access. His was a courageous but lonely journey. We have the Eucharist and the community built around it to counter that.

The official in today's first reading had a moment of grace in his Baptism. Through the Eucharist, we can develop a life of grace living each day in the power, truth and grace of Jesus Christ. The Eucharist and the community it creates can save us from spiritual malnutrition.

FRIDAY OF THE THIRD WEEK OF EASTER
Acts 9:1-20; John 6:52-59

Today's reading from the Acts of the Apostles gives us the account of two conversions. The first one some people may experience. The second conversion is one we all have to experience.

The first conversion that some people may undergo is a conversion like that of Saul. He was an opponent and persecutor of the Church who was transformed into her greatest missionary. He was going in one direction in his life and the Lord stopped him and turned him in another.

That is the model of the classic dramatic conversion of the sudden, life changing experience that causes us to see everything in a new way. We see the same world through new eyes.

There is another conversion in our first reading and it is one through which we all have to go. That is the conversion of Ananias.

Ananias was already a Christian but he could not believe that the Lord would choose and work through someone like Saul. This is the conversion of realizing that God's ways are not our ways. It is the insight that God is not God to fulfill our expectations. The reverse is true. We are here to fulfill the Lord's expectations.

This is a conversion we all need when we come to see that God's wisdom is at work in ways we least expect.

The conversion of Saul is an experience for some. The conversion of Ananias is a conversion for us all.

Every time we receive the Eucharist, we are submitting ourselves to God's wisdom and God's way of redemption. The drama and simplicity of the Eucharist teaches us that God can use the things of earth, things we least expect, to bring us the things of heaven, things we most desire.

SATURDAY OF THE THIRD WEEK OF EASTER
Acts 9:31-42; John 6:60-69

The word "truth" is a beautiful word. It sounds clean, liberating and honest. People say they want the truth. People say they seek the truth. People say they need the truth.

But, do we really want the truth? Can we really "stand the truth"? We love to hear the "truth" about others but are we willing to face the truth about ourselves?

Why did the people leave Jesus in today's Gospel reading? They didn't want the truth not only about the Eucharist but all its implications of Jesus as the very Bread of life, the living bread come down from heaven for us to receive as food.

In the Eucharist, Jesus presents us with the truth. We have the truth of the Real Presence, of course. But there is also the truth of our sinfulness for which He died. There is the truth of our need of grace, which He gives us at Mass. There is the truth of our call to mission with which every Mass concludes.

These are hard but liberating truths.

We would much rather discuss the sins of our culture and of others than face our own sin.

We would much rather admire the sacrificial love of Jesus made present in the Eucharist than imitate it.

We would much rather discuss the mission of the Church today than face the truth of whether we are actually taking part in that mission.

It is easier to walk away from these hard truths in a bubble of our own illusions, of our own private devotions and our own ideas of what the Lord teaches.

It is much more difficult, but ultimately liberating, to recognize the truth, or truths, to which the Lord calls us in the Eucharist.

The Eucharist calls us not only to receive Christ but also to replicate Christ in our life.

Monday of the Fourth Week of Easter
Acts 11:1-18; John 10:1-10

In today's first reading, Peter recounts the extraordinary vision he had in which he was told to embrace the Gentiles and bring them into the fold of Christ. Peter responded immediately. His problem will be one of convincing the rest of the Apostles that this is indeed the Lord's will.

This was a pivotal moment in the life of the Church. Embracing the Gentiles, the non-Jews, was to make the Gospel universal. The Church was not intended to be only for a few but like a flowing stream was to be available to all who would come to her.

Through this vision that Peter had, Jesus the Shepherd is leading the Church into new and wider pastures. In our lives, we can see change as either a threat or an opportunity. Many people do not embrace change easily. We become accustomed to our settled ways. We have adjusted to a certain state of affairs. Change disrupts that. It is much easier to go back to a world of "golden oldies" than to engage the world as it is.

Change in the neighborhood, change at work or change in our health can be destabilizing. This is precisely the area where we need to trust the Good Shepherd. The famous and lyrical twenty-third Psalm has the words, "Though I walk in the dark valley, I fear no evil. You are there with your rod and staff and with these you give me comfort."

Engaging the world as it is is the thread that runs through and unifies the Acts of the Apostles. Ultimately, the early Church will trust the will and the call of the Good Shepherd. The embrace of the Gentiles will be a magnificent, providential and energizing moment in the life of the Church. First, however, they had to trust the Good Shepherd.

Change in our planet can be gradual as in the slow subsidence of land or it can be dramatic as the earth's plates rip against each other in an earthquake. Likewise, change in the Church has been gradual and at other times dramatic. Throughout her history, the Church has been given the grace of following the Good Shepherd through massive political, cultural and economic changes.

We can pray that the Lord will give us the grace to trust Him in all the seasons of our life. We cannot halt change in our neighborhoods, in our careers or in our health. We can, however, embrace the Good Shepherd in all the turnings of our life. Whether in green pastures or in dark valleys, He is with the Church and with each of us.

TUESDAY OF THE FOURTH WEEK OF EASTER
Acts 11:19-26; John 10:22-30

We have all read about purse-snatchers or may have even experienced them. A person walks along and someone grabs a purse or wallet and runs with it unless it is secured by being firmly attached to us.

There are also sheep snatchers, people who steal members of the Church. Some do it actively such as cults who regularly proselytize to take members from one church to themselves. Others do it by sowing seeds of doubt which is much more insidious.

Jesus says in today's Gospel that there will be no taking of sheep from His hand. How do we secure ourselves in Christ's hand?

It is important to know our faith by knowing what we believe and why. It is at least important to know where we can find out about our faith. An intentional faith, rather than an "inherited" one, secures us in Christ's hand.

It is important to have a personal relationship with Christ through prayer and time before the tabernacle. This secures us in Christ's hand.

It is important to strengthen our relationship with Christ through membership in a parish. A parish is not just a convenient organization of believers. It is the very Body of Christ of which each of us is a cell.

It is important to be consistent in our practice of the faith. We need to come to church rain or shine, when at home or on vacation. This not only strengthens our faith but also gives public expression to others that we are Catholic and proud of it.

We secure ourselves in Christ's hand by knowing our faith, praying it, living it through a parish and practicing it.

Secured in Christ's hand, we never need fear being taken away by a "sheep snatcher."

WEDNESDAY OF THE FOURTH WEEK OF EASTER
Acts 12:24 – 13:5; John 12:44-50

The word of the Holy Spirit came upon the community at prayer to set apart Barnabas and Saul for the work given to them. So begins the first great missionary thrust in the Church.

There will be many more waves of missionary efforts in the Church's history: Patrick and Columba, Boniface, Cyril and Methodius and then the vast number of missionary orders in the 19th century. We should not forget our missionaries today. They are all over the world and need our prayer.

The words from the Holy Spirit to set these men apart for the work planned for them by God deserve our reflection.

There is a work that God has for each of us to do. It may be grand and glorious or silent and serious.

Sometimes that work is obvious when a great task is thrust upon us. At other times, it is not obvious. Prayers of intercession before the Blessed Sacrament, teaching in a religious education program, bringing a potential convert to Mass, listening to the problems of a friend, sending a letter of encouragement to a missionary all create a history of consequences that can have an impact far larger than we can imagine.

Many years ago, some teacher unknown to us taught a future Pope or President to read.

Months ago, someone prayed for the grace of comfort or wisdom to come to a friend and it did.

Years ago, someone brought a non-Catholic to Mass, which

led to that person's joining the Church, and later all his children and grandchildren were raised Catholic.

Years ago, a letter sent to an overworked missionary gave her the encouragement to continue to bring the Gospel to the ends of the earth.

Months ago, time given to listen to a friend's worries prevented that friend from doing damage to herself.

We should pray that the Lord would enable us to be faithful to the work He has for us to do, whether we know what it is or not.

Thursday of the Fourth Week of Easter
Acts 13:13-25; John 13:16-20

Jesus' teaching that no servant is greater than his master follows His washing of the Apostles' feet at the Last Supper.

It was a dramatic gesture which showed that the dignity of an Apostle and of any follower of Jesus comes in service to others. That does not mean being a slave but in letting our life give light, letting our struggles with illness, age and the treachery of people be an example to others of practical Christianity.

Most of us in our life knew a priest in some parish who gave no great homilies, was involved in no major parish activity but whose gifts were stability, predictability and everyday fidelity. People may never have gone to him for advice but it was comforting to know that he was there. That was his gift, his service to the parish. It was how his life served others. Comets may make the news but they don't help us navigate. The stars that abide give us direction.

Frequently at funerals, some time is given for personal recollections or remembrances of the person who died. In the overwhelming majority of those remarks, little mention is made of the amount of money that person made or awards given.

The emphasis is usually on how that person's life touched other lives.

How we will follow the Master, the form of our service may well be in giving life, help, direction and confidence to others just by being ourselves.

We are true servants of the Lord and His people when our life is light to others, a light along their way.

FRIDAY OF THE FOURTH WEEK OF EASTER
Acts 13:26-33; John 14:1-6

St. John in his Gospel records for us the magnificent words of Jesus, "I am the Way, the Truth and the Life." This is one of the great and powerful affirmations of Jesus about Himself.

He is the Way. If ever we travel into unknown territory, we know how important a map is. Without a map we can easily become lost. To come to heaven, the map we are given is Jesus. The Lord says, "Follow me. Follow my example and you will be on the right road."

Jesus didn't give us only a teaching but the example of His life. He is the Way.

He is the Truth. Today, many ideas and opinions swirl around us about the purpose of life, wealth and health. Because of the media, we might sometimes feel as though we are caught in a philosophical blender. Jesus teaches us that He is the Truth, the abiding Truth, about the things that don't change. Intellectual fashion and fads come and go, the truth Christ teaches us remains.

He is the Life. We all want the most out of life but so many things disappoint. The Lord teaches us that He will give us a level of living deeper than the biological, the emotional and the professional. It is a life in union with the Trinity, a life that will never end.

These words of Jesus, "I am the Way, the Truth and the Life" are words we can say repeatedly. When we are worried, in doubt, in trial, in the morning of life, in the noontime of our life, and in the evening of our life, these words of Jesus carry remarkably comforting power.

111

These words sum up the teaching of Jesus in St. John's Gospel. They will give us strength in every season of our life. "I am the Way, the Truth and the Life."

They are not only easy to remember but are powerful vehicles of Christ's grace.

SATURDAY OF THE FOURTH WEEK OF EASTER
Acts 13:44-52; John 14:7-14

Jesus promises that the one who has faith in Him will do greater things than Jesus did. This is a striking promise. It is not the promise that we will perform miracles but that the number of people Christ will reach through us will be gigantic.

With Christ, we too will be able to bring life from death.

There is an instance of that in today's first reading. The Jewish people rejected Paul and Barnabas. That became the catalyst for them to go in a new direction, to the Gentiles.

They could have spent the rest of their lives analyzing what went wrong, why the Jewish people didn't accept them. They could have stayed in the same place wringing their hands but they moved on to the Gentiles. One direction in their ministry died so a new one could come to life.

The same is true of us. A part of our life dies and a new direction comes to life. In each moment, there is a presence of Christ expanding His Easter life in us.

The Acts of the Apostles can be read, on the one hand, as a story of failure, the dying of the Church as a branch of Judaism. It can also be read as a magnificent success story and the coming to life of the world-wide Church of Jesus. With that comes the expansion of His Risen life to thousands and later billions of people.

The Lord will lead us, in fact is leading us now, into greater things. The frustrations in our life, scandals in the Church are the seeds of new life, deeper union with Christ and a deeper share in His dying and rising.

Every dying we experience in our life can be an avenue to deeper life in Christ.

Because of His Church, Christ is no longer limited to Palestine but is present all over the world. The period of His earthly life died, so His new Risen life can come to life and be multiplied through His followers.

Through the dyings and risings of our life, Jesus is constantly leading us to do in His name the greater things He promised.

MONDAY OF THE FIFTH WEEK OF EASTER
Acts 14:5-18; John 14:21-26

There is a popular phrase, "killing the messenger." When someone brings bad news, some people express their anger at the envoy. It is said that some tyrants in history would kill the messenger of bad news.

It happens in a parish that people who are not satisfied with diocesan or Church policy take out their anger on the local parish priest.

In today's first reading, the opposite happens. Here the people are worshipping the messengers, treating Paul and Barnabas as gods because of the Gospel they brought. Paul and Barnabas try to direct them to God but the people would not be dissuaded.

This incident reminds us of the graces, inspirations and guidance we have received through others. We should thank the Lord for the agents of His grace that He sends into our lives.

It is important to remember that they are just instruments of the Lord. When they fail, do wrong or err we need to recall that they are earthen, fragile vessels carrying the grace and truth of Christ to us. People come and go. The truth of Christ and the grace of Christ endure.

Sometimes after a wonderful homily, people are more drawn to the preacher than to what is preached. It has been said that the sign of a good spiritual director is that he or she makes himself useless. The preacher, leader and spiritual director are paths that lead us to Christ and should then disappear.

The utility company brings us water but the utility company does not give life. It's the water that gives nourishment and life. So, messengers lead us to Christ but it is Jesus who gives peace and purpose.

If we have been graced with wonderful messengers of Christ, we should thank the Lord for the messengers but remember to embrace the message.

TUESDAY OF THE FIFTH WEEK OF EASTER
Acts 14:19-28; John 14:27-31

Paul and Barnabas did not always find a warm welcome when they came to town. It has been remarked that a visit from St. Paul would spark either a revival or a riot. Even when they were welcomed, old enemies stalked them from place to place stirring up trouble. These troublemakers harassed them as they spoke and fueled opposition to Paul and Barnabas.

They were so successful in today's first reading that the people stoned Paul and dragged him outside the city leaving him half-dead.

Then we have a marvelous moment as Paul's Christian disciples formed a circle around him and before long he was better and went back into the town.

This is a wonderful picture and model for the Church. After he was mobbed and stoned, caring fellow-Christians encircled Paul. That is what our Church should be, a community of care.

Regrettably, Christians often do the wounding by tearing each other down. There is enough malicious wounding of body and spirit in our world. We need places of healing.

The Church should be the place where we can come for repair, renewal and restoration.

Do we encourage each other, take the time to listen to each other and be part of a circle of care such as Paul experienced?

That is one great mission for any parish in a world that knows so much pain and wounding. The Church can be a hospital for the soul.

WEDNESDAY OF THE FIFTH WEEK OF EASTER
Acts 15:1-6; John 15:1-8

This is the time of the year when people start taking care of their gardens by planting and pruning. Jesus uses this agricultural image in today's Gospel reading to describe our relationship with Him.

The Lord tells us that He is the vine and we are the branches. We are directly connected to Christ through Baptism. His life and grace flow to us when we become a branch of the vine.

The Lord warns that branches that become unproductive need to be cut off. This is a stark reminder that Baptism in our past alone does not save us, it does not automatically complete our life. Baptism is a beginning not an end.

The question we face is what we are doing with that Baptism today. We may be going through the motions, saying the words, singing the songs while the living connection with Christ is gone. We can be like dead branches. For a while, they look alive but the juice is gone.

If we are not spiritually productive today, we will be like those dead branches.

The Lord also teaches us that the fruitful branches will be trimmed to increase their yield. It happens that the Lord simplifies, clarifies and cleanses our life to increase our union with Him. Lots of things can distract us from Christ. When changes occur in our life, it may well be the vine grower trimming our life to increase our product.

How are we caring for our connection to Christ? It needs to be tended and nurtured. As Christ lives more fully in us, His grace flows more freely through every part of our life.

Our connection to Christ is something for which only we ourselves can care. Nobody else can do it for us. It is uniquely our own.

The majestic and intimate Last Supper teaching of Jesus continues. In today's Gospel reading, the Lord instructs His disciples to live on in His love.

There are three aspects of Christ's love, which we need to imitate to live in His love.

First, Jesus' love is obedient to the Father. The Lord tells us that we will live in His love if we are faithful to the Commandments. Our love of Jesus is verified and proven not by our words but in what we do and how we live. The touchstone of Christian living, however, is not only the Commandments. They are the baseline from which the distinctively Christian life begins. The Lord calls on us to go further than the Commandments and to imitate His love in letter and spirit.

Secondly, Jesus' love is a redeeming love. We live within His love if we accept its cleansing power into our life. Jesus' love is a dynamic power that brings us forgiveness and sets us free. If we want to be liberated from sin, we must experience the personal drama of repentance and the resolution to walk once more with Christ. This turning to Christ finds concrete expression in the Sacrament of Penance.

Lastly, Jesus' love is a sacrificial love. It entails not simply a warm feeling toward another, but giving up something of ourselves, even our rights, for the good of others.

The Acts of the Apostles recounts a controversy that could have ripped apart the early Church. But each side sought compromise on nonessential things and the Church grew.

Sometimes it happens that people want Church or parish unity but exclusively on their own terms expressed in the popular phrase, "my way or the highway." Sacrificial love entails a giving up of our prerogatives for the good of others. As a line from a popular book says, "It is not only about us."

To live in Christ's love is to imitate His love through obedience to the Commandments, to receive His redeeming love in the Sacrament of Penance, and to show His sacrificial love by being willing to give up something of ourselves for the good of the Church.

This kind of love is not easy but it gives life.

FRIDAY OF THE FIFTH WEEK OF EASTER
Acts 15:22-31; John 15:12-17

We have some extraordinary words of Jesus in today's Gospel reading. The Lord says to His Apostles, "It was not you who chose me, but I chose you." In those days, students would select a teacher or rabbi by affiliating themselves with him and follow him. Here, Jesus reverses that in that He, the teacher, chose His students.

We are used to choosing our classes in college. The situation described by the Lord is similar to a distinguished college professor would call us to join his class. We would not only be honored but surmise that we were called for a reason.

The Lord chooses us. We might think that we have made a decision for Christ, that we have chosen to be serious about our Catholicism. We are, in fact, responding to God's grace that has come to us. God's grace leads us, guides us and draws us. Each of us has been chosen for a reason.

Some have been chosen to speak in Christ's name. Others have been called to comfort others in His name. Some are called to correct or teach in His name. To be called by Christ is a great privilege but also a responsibility.

None of us is called only for our own spirituality. We are called to bear fruit abundantly. A priest is not ordained only for himself but for the good of the Church. A couple does not marry only to express their love but to manifest fidelity to the world and to give life. We are given a position at work not only to make a living but also to show forth something of the peace and care of Christ to others.

We did not choose Christ. He chose us for a reason. Knowing that we are called to be an extension of the Lord's ministry gives our life profound meaning in any circumstance and in every situation. Each place where we work or live is the place where the Lord wants us to bring His light.

A question for all of us is whether our faith is bearing any fruit. Our discipleship is not a private possession to clutch and keep isolated from contact with others. It is meant to build bridges as the Apostles do in today's first reading, to speak truth and give light to others. Christ chose each of us for a reason. That reason may be evident to us or known only to the Lord. Each of us is part of a great divine strategy for our world.

SATURDAY OF THE FIFTH WEEK OF EASTER
Acts 16:1-10; John 15:18-21

Paul had laid out a missionary strategy and itinerary for himself that included a great many closely connected towns. For some reason that Paul did not at first fully understand, he was prevented by the Holy Spirit from preaching in those towns. He then moved to another place and was again "prevented" by the Holy Spirit.

That is a strange wording from the Acts of the Apostles, to be "prevented" by the Holy Spirit from preaching. We often think of the Holy Spirit as assisting us or enabling us to make the best of reversals, but the Acts of the Apostles speaks of the Holy Spirit "preventing" Paul from preaching in certain locations.

Maybe when things don't quite work out as we plan, there is more than human error or dysfunction involved. Maybe it is the Holy Spirit "preventing" us from engaging in some activity.

Finally, they stopped at Troas and there Paul was given a dream of a man in Macedonia calling him to come to them. Finally, Paul realized why the other plans did not work. God had wanted him to take the Gospel to the North and to the West.

We can read the Acts of the Apostles as a kind of template or pattern of how the Lord guides His Church and His followers in mission.

When our endeavors don't seem to work, it may be that the Lord does not judge the time opportune or that the Lord has other plans to which He wants us to direct our energies.

The message in all this for us is that despite our planning, our programs, our strategies and our time lines, we are not the only ones involved in the spreading the Gospel. The Lord is with us guiding, directing, and sometimes even "preventing" our proceeding in a particular direction.

This incident from the life of St. Paul is a lesson to us that we should view even our failures in mission as signs that the Holy Spirit is at work among us directing us as the Risen Lord wants.

MONDAY OF THE SIXTH WEEK OF EASTER
Acts 16:11-15; John 15:26-16:4

There was a monumental movie years ago entitled, "The Agony and the Ecstasy" about the tension between Pope Julius and Michelangelo as the ceiling of the Sistine Chapel was being painted.

These words, the agony and the ecstasy, can be said of the life of the Church and of every Christian. We see both in today's readings.

In the first reading, Paul continues his missionary journeys and comes across a businesswoman named Lydia. She dealt in "purple goods." Purple did not mean "racy" but expensive. Paul spoke to her and her heart opened wide to the Gospel.

It was a great success story. It is always a splendid moment in the life of the Church when the Gospel takes hold in one more person's life as it does in so many lives every day.

Then there is the agony, which the Lord describes in today's Gospel: the persecutions, harassment and expulsions from synagogues. Opposition to the Church goes on today as well.

Such moments of trial should not be a surprise. They are predicted by the Lord as the inevitable conflict between Truth and half-truths.

Furthermore, persecutions are like storms. They clear out the dead wood and make room for new growth as the Church gets stronger. Persecutions can take many forms. It may not be an outright assault on the Church but the cultural demolition of faith by materialism and consumerism or the culture of complaint and scandal that envelops us.

The agony and the ecstasy. Great moments of grace and trial mark the rhythm of the Church's life and of every Christian life. Moments of grace and moments of trial both give life and purify. The Lord is with us in both of them.

TUESDAY OF THE SIXTH WEEK OF EASTER
Acts 16:22-34; John 16:5-11

In today's first reading from the Acts of the Apostles, we have a story of deliverance, but whose deliverance?

On one level, it is Paul and Silas. They were delivered by an earthquake from the chains of imprisonment. On a deeper level, however, it is the deliverance of the jailer from unbelief as he comes through this crisis in which not only his job but also his life is at stake and comes to believe in Jesus Christ.

He and his household are baptized and then celebrate with Paul and Silas his newly discovered faith in God.

The jailer is the one who is truly set free from the inner darkness of unbelief.

Ignorance can be a kind of bondage. When, for example, we live our lives not knowing the laws of biology and hygiene, we live at peril because the laws are true whether we know about them or not. If, however, we do learn about them and abide by them, we can lead healthy and safe lives.

The same is true about God's law. His laws govern our life whether we know about them or not. We disobey God's law at our peril. If we learn about God's law and abide by it, we can lead spiritually healthy and safe lives and receive eternal life.

If we do not, we place our souls at risk even to suffer separation from God forever.

It is the jailer who was really set free, free to know the Lord, to experience His forgiveness and the new life that is ours in Christ.

We live in a politically free society today. But sin, inner disorder, addiction, hate and infidelity are the stronger chains from which only Jesus Christ can set us free.

WEDNESDAY OF THE SIXTH WEEK OF EASTER
Acts 17:15, 22-18:1; John 16:12-15

In today's reading, we have Paul's speech in the Areopagus, the public forum of Athens. He knows that he is speaking to people who are religious and attuned to things spiritual because he sees altars dedicated to many gods, even to the "unknown god."

There is a strong religious sensitivity today as well. There are many religions and an atmosphere of religiosity, however unfocused, in our time. Television programs and books dedicated to ancient mysteries, the occult and the supernatural abound. In this sense, we too are a very religious age.

However, when Paul became specific and spoke about God's requirements of us, how we should therefore live and how this call to repentance and holiness is made concrete in Jesus Christ, people began to drift away.

They remarked that they would see him at another time. That too is a very contemporary phenomenon.

Many people prefer a religion that requires little personal change. If it condemns the world, it is seen as a needed message but not if it condemns me. If a religion requires society to change, it is welcome. If it requires me to change, it interferes.

The preoccupation we see today with miracles and angels is a manifestation of a religiosity without cost and requiring no conversion. Often, people recount stories of supernatural beings entering and leaving their lives without any prerequisite or consequent conversion of life on their part.

True religion requires a commitment and change of life,

making not only the person but also the teachings of Jesus part of our life.

We are not called to admire Jesus. Jesus doesn't want admirers but disciples who will take Him seriously and will follow Him with their life.

THURSDAY OF THE SIXTH WEEK OF EASTER
Acts 18:1-8; John 16:16-20

"A little while" is a phrase that none of us liked to hear as a child when we were told that our expectations would be met in "a little while." Yet, as adults we spend a lot of time in that "little while."

Jesus is speaking in today's Gospel reading to His disciples in the Garden of Olives. He is referring to His coming Passion and Death. They will not see Him again until His Resurrection.

The Lord is also speaking here to the whole Church about the time between His Ascension and His return in glory. That is our "little while."

We all dwell in that "little while" until the Lord comes to us. What are we doing with our "little while"? We should not simply be waiting but preparing for Christ's return.

There is a lot of work to do in this "little while." St. Paul in today's first reading moves on to the Gentiles. Rather than dwell on the lack of receptivity to his preaching among the Jewish people, he moves on to new territory so as not to waste his "little while."

Because of his work and mission, many will come to know Jesus Christ as well as their families and descendants. That is how St. Paul spent his "little while."

There is the Lord's familiar parable of the talents given to several servants. Two used them to produce more. One servant, however, buried it awaiting the master's return. That servant received only condemnation.

We have a great deal to do in our "little while." It is not just a matter of waiting with arms folded for Christ's return.

It is a time to prepare our world and ourselves for Christ's return so that the Lord will see how carefully and productively we have used our "little while."

FRIDAY OF THE SIXTH WEEK OF EASTER
Acts 18:9-18; John 16:20-23

In today's first reading, St. Paul is anxious about beginning his ministry in the city of Corinth.

Corinth was a dazzling, cosmopolitan city of the ancient world, a magnet for all kinds of ideas, fads and immoralities. It was the ancient world's "city that never sleeps." Yet, St. Paul knew that if the Gospel could make it here, it could make it anywhere. Corinth was the premier challenge of his ministry.

In his anxiety, the Lord tells him not to be afraid. Not only is Jesus with him, but the Lord says that many of His people are in this city to assist Paul.

We all have a Corinth about which we are anxious. It may not be a city to which we are moving but an illness, a new career challenge, problems in the family, local politics or a change in our life.

The Lord is with us to help us and so are His people. In the Corinth about which we are worried, there are many Christians who have undergone the same problems we are experiencing and are ready and able to support us. We can trust that God will direct us toward them and them toward us.

But a question we can ask ourselves is whether we are one of the Lord's people ready to help others when they are worried about the Corinth they have to face. Can they depend on us to bring them strength and support?

We are commissioned by our Baptism to be one of Christ's people not only for ourselves but also for others on our part of the world.

It is a great mission and a great vocation to be one of Christ's people for others. No one should have to face his or her personal Corinth alone.

Saturday of the Sixth Week of Easter
Acts 18:23-28; John 16:23-28

A teacher named Apollos appears in our first reading. He was a Jewish convert to Christianity, a very charismatic and popular teacher. But he evidently knew only part of the story. The Acts of the Apostles indicates that he knew only of John's baptism. Apollos probably taught about the importance of repentance and of conversion. That is an important and crucial message for every age.

Then, Priscilla and Aquila took him aside and explained the new way to him in greater detail. They probably spoke with him about the union with God through Jesus described in today's Gospel reading.

The Gospel is not only about turning away from sin. It is also about living the life of grace, union with God, everything that goes under the title "the spiritual life."

Just as some people know how to fight a war but not how to live in peace; just as some know how to campaign but not how to govern; just as some know how to criticize but not how to encourage, so we can so focus on sin that we forget about the life of grace.

Repentance is critical because it opens the door to the wide-open spaces of real spiritual vitality.

Like Apollos, we can stay only at the doorway and forget about the rich spiritual life to which the Lord calls us on the inside.

The Gospel is not only about what we should avoid but also, as importantly, it shows what our life can be, a life lived for the Father, with the Son and in the power of the Holy Spirit.

Priscilla and Aquila told Apollos the rest of the story. We leave sin to embrace Christ.

The Christian life has to be both a departure from sin and an embrace of Christ.

MONDAY OF THE SEVENTH WEEK OF EASTER
Acts 19:1-8; John 16:29-33

The Lord tells His disciples and us in today's Gospel reading that we will experience affliction in the world but we should have courage because He has conquered the world.

Affliction, courage and conquest are three points for reflection on Jesus' words.

The Lord's words about our experiencing affliction probably ring true in all of our lives. The world brings its afflictions to every one of its inhabitants in one way or another. For the Christian, however, this affliction is intensified since we try to live by a Gospel that is rejected sometimes in theory but always in practice by our world.

We should expect affliction because the world is still groaning for redemption. The power of Christ's redemption has not yet reached every sector of our world and so we experience affliction. It is a component of every Christian life.

Secondly, the Lord tells us to have courage. In the face of affliction and opposition, we are not alone. Hopefully we have fellow Christians to stand by us but we always have the Lord and the entire Church triumphant on our side. We are assisted by an invisible army, unseen to outsiders, who stand by us with prayer, support and guidance. In any affliction, we are never alone.

Finally, the Lord tells us that He has conquered the world. His fidelity to the Father was stronger than His pain. His sacrificial love was stronger than the hatred hurled at Him. His Risen life is stronger than death. When every army, every evil and every power of this world is gone, there will remain standing alone at the end as glorious as ever the Risen Christ.

Jesus' Resurrection teaches us that, with His grace, whatever the world might place in our path, if we keep faith, our Christian dignity, our trust in the Lord and our fidelity to Christ, we will be the conquerors and victors. Whatever people may do to our body, they cannot destroy our soul. This is how we can have victory in Christ.

Affliction, courage and victory. Affliction is part of every life on earth. Courage and victory are possible for every Christian.

TUESDAY OF THE SEVENTH WEEK OF EASTER
Acts 20:17-27; John 17:1-11

A theme that joins today's readings might be "mission accomplished." Jesus prays to the Father at the Last Supper saying that He has finished the work the Father gave Him. St. Paul says to the elders at Ephesus that he is ready to finish the race and complete the service assigned to him.

Our life is a mission. Our purpose here is, first of all, to grow in the knowledge and love of Jesus Christ as we know, love and serve God here to be with Him forever in eternity. That sense of mission should affect everything we do. When facing a decision about anything in our life we can always ask whether this will help me know, love and serve the Lord here and be with Him forever in eternity.

In addition to our personal growth in the Lord, we are also assigned a specific service in our world. Some people have a very vivid revelation of what that service is. For others, most of us, it becomes clear over time as we are faithful to each responsibility given us. It is like the gradual emergence of a photo image in developing solution used years ago before the digital age. Slowly we will see a pattern emerge as doors open, paths are taken and responsibilities assigned to us that point us in a specific direction. Events and the commitments we prayerfully make along the way can reveal to us the special task God has for each of us.

The third point for reflection is to realize the truth that our life here is not for ourselves alone. We are members of the Body of Christ and everything we do should have the intention of building up and strengthening the Body of Christ.

After a life spent deepening our personal relationship with Christ, doing the service God has given us, and building up the Body of Christ we too will be able to say, as did Jesus and St. Paul, "mission accomplished."

A word and a theme that occur in both of today's readings flow from the word "guard." Paul instructs the Ephesians to be on guard against "savage wolves" who would distort the content of the faith they have received. In His Last Supper prayer, the Lord asks the Father to guard His disciples from the Evil One.

We always need to care for the life of faith, for the truth of our faith by guarding the gift of faith that we have been given. The best way we guard that faith is not, of course, by metaphorically placing it away in a safety deposit box effectively insulating it from the world.

We guard our faith by living it, by uniting our faith with the life of the Church and by praying it. Faith is not like a precious jewel that we keep. It is something we share, live and pray.

Faith is a spiritual good, which means that the more we share it, the more it truly becomes our own. A refusal to share our faith with others indicates that our possession of it is tenuous if not fragile. To keep our faith private is to put it at risk of being reduced to personal feeling rather than guiding our public action. It loses its power to witness to Christ.

There are always distortions of faith that can occur. That is why our life within the Church is important. As we make the teaching of the Church our own in all the different ways it comes to us, we are grafting our faith onto the great tree of Christ's truth. By doing that we are allowing it to be nourished by Scripture and Tradition rather than jargon and slogans.

Lastly, we need to pray our faith. Faith is not simply an intellectual construct or a set of ideas that is nice to know. It is a relationship with Jesus Christ that is fed and enlivened through a life of prayer. Faith should connect us with the person of Jesus so that He becomes our constant companion and Master. Without prayer, faith can lose its purpose and its power.

Faith is a great gift we have been given. To call it a gift is to recognize that it is not ours by right. Faith is something we can guard or lose. We guard the gift of faith we have been given not with a lock or a gun but by sharing it with others, living it within the Church and praying it each day.

THURSDAY OF THE SEVENTH WEEK OF EASTER
Acts 22:30; 23:6-11; John 17:20-26

When Paul was arrested in Jerusalem, a dispute broke out at his arraignment between Pharisees and Sadducees. It disintegrated into a fight and Paul was sent back to headquarters. Later, when he had his hearing in front of the governor, he claimed his right as a Roman citizen to have his case tried in Rome where he was held under house arrest.

The politics of all this is fascinating. The law governing the interaction between Romans and Jews (who were treated as a unique minority in the Empire) is interesting. However, the New Testament sees this whole series of events in a different light.

It shows more than the dynamics of a political process or a legal process at work. These events provided preaching opportunities. At the end of today's first reading, the Lord tells Paul that he must give witness to Christ in Rome.

Do we look at the occurrences in our life through the glasses of faith as spiritual opportunities, apostolic opportunities or missionary opportunities to grow in the Lord and spread His Gospel?

To the person of faith, illness is not only an illness; conflict is not only conflict; change is not only change; and setbacks are not just setbacks.

Add the will of God to any of these and they are transformed into something positive and apostolic.

Faith discerns what the eyes cannot see. As with St. Paul in his appeal to Rome, there is more that is going on in our life than meets the eye. The Lord is at work in our life shaping a disciple and maybe even an apostle.

Friday of the Seventh Week of Easter
Acts 25:13-21; John 21:15-19

We have a powerful and memorable scene in today's Gospel reading. It shows Jesus forgiving Peter. For his three denials, he is given three chances to reaffirm his love for Christ.

If we fail the Lord, we too are given chances to renew our fidelity to Christ. Often, in fact, the Lord gives us more chances to renew our fidelity than we are willing to give to others.

Notice, however, that Jesus wanted more than words from Peter. Each time Peter expresses his love for Christ, the Lord tells Peter to show that love by feeding and caring for the flock.

Repentance shows itself in action by trying to change how we live. Without concrete action, repentance is only regret and regret is cheap. Add regret to a dollar and all you have is just a dollar.

Regret looks to the past. We all have things we regret. Repentance, on the other hand, looks to the future. If we are truly repentant, then we will try to change how we live.

It is not regret but repentance that ignites true maturity and real change in a Christian. Without repentance, we will find ourselves repeating the same sins over and over in Confession as though we were on an endless treadmill, filled with regret each time but lacking honest repentance. Repentance gives traction to our sorrow so that we can grow in grace.

Like Peter, we will show our love for Christ not by words or emotion, not even by beautiful words and soul-wrenching emotion, but by the action of feeding the flock in any way we can.

If we truly love Christ, we will care for His flock.

Saturday of the Seventh Week of Easter
Acts 28:16-20, 30-31; John 21:20-25

Can a burden become a blessing?

Paul would have wanted to continue his missionary work as he had planned. But, he was charged with sedition and was being taken to Rome for trial. He traveled to Rome in chains as a criminal.

From all appearances, this was a disaster in Paul's life. He would no longer be free to continue his missionary work. But, as it turned out, his arrest and transfer to Rome was a splendid chance to carry the Gospel to the very heart of the Roman Empire. He preached for two years in Rome while he was under house arrest. He had finally realized a dream that had seemed impossible earlier in his life.

A burden became a blessing.

In our life, an illness can stop us in our tracks and cause us to re-evaluate what is important in our life. A job loss can open entire new areas of work, which we had never considered before. Disillusion can make our commitments more realistic. By the grace of God, burdens can become blessings.

Burdens come to us about which we can do nothing except to carry them. But, like St. Paul, we can discover embedded within them a blessing in disguise. Most of our disguised blessings are heavily disguised but they are there.

It makes a world of difference to our personal life and our spiritual life to know that every burden carries a blessing. It is a great grace to be able to discern, receive and follow that blessing.

Everything that happens in our life carries a special grace if we have the faith to see it.

Sanctoral Cycle

January 2 – Sts. Basil the Great and Gregory Nazianzen (Memorial)

Basil and Gregory were two great teachers of the Faith. In fact, they are Doctors of the Church, great teachers not only for their time but also for all time. They lived in the 300's and were two very different types of individuals.

Basil was a great administrator bishop who was energized by Church politics. He protected the rights of the Church against government intrusion. He cared for the needs of his diocese and wrote a rule for monasteries that would be a model for all monks of the Eastern Church. In the doctrinal debates of the time he was a "warrior bishop." Cardinal Newman describes him politely as a "diligent laborer in the field of ecclesiastical politics." Gregory, on the other hand, did not have the stomach for politics and preferred a more reclusive life. Basil drew him into controversies and Gregory became a great bishop preacher and theologian. If Basil was the great defender of the Nicene Creed, Gregory was its great preacher.

Both were good theologians with excellent educations. They met at school and began a lifelong friendship. In those days, the debates about the nature of Christ and the Trinity were as intense as the rugged Cappadocian landscape in modern day Turkey. These "Cappadocian Fathers" along with Gregory of Nyssa developed the concepts which we take for granted but which enabled the Church to put its Trinitarian faith and experience into words. They gave us a language by which we can express the profound mystery of God as "three Persons in one substance." This avoided the unorthodox extremes of seeing the Trinity as three gods or the Persons of the Trinity as three dimensions or aspects of one God.

For both of them, faith was not only preached but also lived. They pointed to Christ in word and action. The Office of Readings today repeats a reflection from Gregory in which he describes his friendship with Basil as two streams that came together to form a river leading to Christ.

One of the gifts we receive in our life is the friendship of fellow-Christians to help us on our way with the Lord. Each of us has only a handful of very true lifelong friends. Here at the start of a new year, we have a chance to thank God for them, to make sure that we do not take them for granted and to let the Lord reach us through them. We can try to make our friendships a river that leads ourselves and others to Christ.

Such friendships are true gifts and wonderful anointings of strength in our life.

January 3 – Most Holy Name of Jesus (Optional Memorial)

One of the important and moving moments for parents after the birth of a child is the naming of that baby. To give the child a name is to give him or her an identity. It may be a name that honors a family member, a name that creates a bond with a special patron in heaven or the name of someone who represents a virtue the parents seek for that child. As children grow, they will give their name its own personal history and meaning to all the people they will encounter.

The Holy Name of Jesus was not a name chosen on earth but given by God through the angel Gabriel. The name of Jesus, a version of "Joshua," means "one who saves". It embodies the core truth of Jesus' mission to save and redeem the world. This is the truth to which John the Baptist referred when he identified Jesus as the "Lamb of God" who would take away the sins of the world.

The name of Jesus will acquire added meanings through His life. It will also come to mean forgiveness, peace, healing, power and sacrificial love. To His followers the name "Jesus" will evoke all the moments, miracles and teachings of His earthly life.

The name of Jesus can be a powerful source of meditation. There was a great devotion to the Holy Name during the Middle Ages. There is a magnificent litany of the Holy Name of Jesus that evokes the many facets of Christ's impact on the lives of Christians. Each title in that litany can be material for a powerful reflection. In our time, devotion to the Holy Name has centered on restoring reverence for the name of Jesus.

To come to know someone's name is to begin to develop a relationship with that person. As we use the name of Jesus with reverence, we also start to develop a personal relationship with Christ.

The Jesus of the Gospels comes to us as Teacher, Savior and Redeemer. We can also know Him as friend. There is a contemporary hymn called "Jesus the Lord" that evokes the power, majesty and beauty of Jesus' name.

Today's memorial calls us to renewed respect for the Holy Name of Jesus and to let it be the subject of our contemplation so we can appreciate all that Jesus means in our life.

The name of Jesus is not just another name. It gathers, evokes and embraces all that Jesus is and can be for each of us.

JANUARY 4 – ST. ELIZABETH ANN SETON (MEMORIAL)

We all recall how Jesus fed the people with the few loaves and fish that were given Him and that much was left over. This Gospel scene represents the life of Elizabeth Seton. She is the first native-born American to be declared a saint. She opened the first Catholic parochial school in the United States. She was the first American born founder of a religious community of women.

Nobody would have dreamed that Elizabeth Ann Bailey would achieve all this when she was born in New York City in 1774, two years before our Declaration of Independence.

Part of a prominent Episcopalian family, she married William Seton, a wealthy businessman, when she was nineteen. Together they had five children. Later, William's business went bankrupt and his health failed. They went to Italy hoping that the climate would bring improvement. Instead, William's illness worsened and he died.

Elizabeth was left alone with five children and huge medical bills. She had been drawn to Catholicism while in Italy and joined the Church when she returned to New York. Because of her conversion, her entire social support network in New York withdrew from her. To make ends meet, she opened a girls' boarding school in Baltimore.

She eventually founded the Sisters of Charity and relocated her headquarters to Emmitsburg, Maryland where she helped establish the first parochial school at St. Joseph's Church. From those headquarters, her congregation established orphanages, hospitals and schools. She died at the age of 48.

In the half-century of her life, Mother Seton was a wife, widow, teacher and founder of a religious congregation. In her debutante days back in New York, she could not have dreamed of the challenges and graces that were in store for her. The Lord took the desert her life had become after her husband's death and transformed it into a wonderful journey of grace and achievement whose impact continues to our day.

After her husband died, the great loves of Elizabeth's life became the Eucharist and the Church. Elizabeth Seton shows us how God can use the threads of our life, good and bad, to weave a great tapestry of faith and holiness. With His grace, she wove all the difficulties in her life into a life of great service to the Church.

Like the Apostles on the mountainside many centuries ago, we might feel we have little to give the Lord. He can take the few loaves and fish we give Him and make an abundance from them that will surprise us and overflow to others.

JANUARY 5 – ST. JOHN NEUMANN (MEMORIAL)

"Passio Christi, Conforta Me" – Passion of Christ, Comfort Me. This was the episcopal motto of Bishop John Neumann. Chosen from his Redemptorist background, it expresses the comfort and strength he received from the Passion of Christ in his difficult life.

He was born in 1811 in Bohemia. He studied for the priesthood but, faced with a glut of priests, bishops in Eastern Europe were delaying ordinations. With great courage and daring, he came as a seminarian to the United States where the archbishop of New York indicated he would ordain him to work among the growing number of German immigrants.

Father Neumann's work centered on Western New York. The loneliness of missionary life debilitated his health and he joined the Redemptorists to be part of a community of priests who also worked among the German Catholics. Quickly his practical administrative bent became evident. After several positions in the Redemptorist Order, he was nominated to become bishop of Philadelphia and reluctantly took the position only by order of the Pope.

During his time in Philadelphia he increased the number of parochial schools, established some 80 new parishes (almost one a month!), wrote a catechism, visited parishes, and established the practice of the Forty Hours Devotion in parishes (an early form of diocesan-wide "perpetual adoration"). He died in 1860 at the age of 49.

He was a builder, a bishop, a teacher, a writer but above all a priest who cared for his flock and met whatever needs crossed his path. Although he was ordained a bishop of a great and growing diocese, he remained at heart a parish priest never far from his flock. With a kind of poetic appropriateness, he died in the streets of Philadelphia.

The elite of Philadelphia had wanted a more sophisticated man as bishop. They were given a saint whose impact on the average Catholic was shown by the many thousands who grieved at his funeral.

St. John Neumann reminds us that the material of holiness is not principally composed of extraordinary phenomena, great miracles, a life laced with divine interventions and inner locutions. He shows us that the material of holiness is found in fidelity to our given responsibilities.

He was a model of correct belief and honest love. Before all else, he was a disciple of the Lord faithful to his duties. That is something we all can be and something we all can do.

January 6 – Bl. Andre Bessette (Optional Memorial)

No one could ever have imagined that a relatively uneducated Holy Cross brother, the doorkeeper, would become known as the "Wonder Man of Mount Royal" in Canada.

Brother Andre was born in a small town outside of Montreal in 1845. His family was very poor. His parents died when he was young and he went from job to job to support himself as best he could. He was unable to read or write until he was 25 years old. An intestinal disorder burdened him throughout his life.

He joined the Congregation of the Holy Cross in 1870 and became the doorkeeper at their residence. He once remarked that after his novitiate they showed him the door and he stayed there for 40 years!

He was a man of prayer and penance. Gradually, people began to discover that his prayer seemed to have unusual efficacy. He became known as a healer as hundreds, later thousands, came to his door seeking prayer and healing.

His dream was to build a church in honor of St. Joseph to whom he himself had a special devotion and who was also the patron saint of Canada.

Gradually, through his labors, prayer, and fund-raising, St. Joseph's Oratory rose on Mount Royale in Montreal. It stands today, taller than either St. Patrick's Cathedral in New York City or the Cathedral of Notre Dame in Paris, a monument to Brother Andre's faith and God's grace. It is the largest church in the world in honor of St. Joseph.

Brother Andre died in 1937 with his last words being, "St. Joseph." His heart was encased in a reliquary kept in the Oratory. In a bizarre incident in 1973, thieves stole his heart and demanded a ransom for its return. The Oratory refused to pay anything and the heart was recovered a year later. Still, whatever might have happened to his heart, the spirit of Brother Andre still fills every corner of this spectacular Oratory.

He was a man of paradox: a healer who was himself in pain throughout his life; an uneducated man who reached millions of people with the truth of the Gospel; a simple doorkeeper who built one of the great shrines of the world; a man small in stature who was a spiritual giant.

For this Holy Cross brother, the Holy Cross of Christ was not simply devotion for him. It shaped his life.

JANUARY 7 – ST. RAYMOND OF PEÑAFORT (OPTIONAL MEMORIAL)

There is an old saying, "When you are 40, half of you belongs to the past and when you're 70, nearly all of you does." That certainly was not true of Raymond of Peñafort. He lived to be a hundred years old and his last 35 years were arguably his most productive.

Raymond was born in 1175 in Spain. He was teaching philosophy at 20, joined the Dominican Order when he was 47, and worked in Rome to consolidate and organize a whole array of legal decrees and legislation that had grown up over the years by putting them into accessible order. For that reason, he is the patron saint of canon lawyers.

At the age of 63, he was elected Master General of the Dominicans, remained in that post for two years and retired at 65.

At an age when most men may think about retiring to the golf course, Raymond began a life of preaching, instructing converts, and establishing friaries and religious houses. The second half of his life found him imitating the Lord by feeding multitudes with the bread of instruction and the Bread of Life.

His work in Church Law was indeed a service to the Church. But in his later years, he served the Church by sharing the Word of life with thousands of people.

Raymond of Peñafort did not spend a great deal of time looking at life through the "rear-view mirror." His gaze was always forward and the work he could still do for the Gospel. Sometimes we might feel that our best years are behind us, but every stage of life has its own strength and grace. As physical sight weakens in our senior years, insight grows. We are given the gift of time to use our accumulated experience to bring spiritual and emotional nourishment to others.

Although not formally declared as such, Raymond of Peñafort might well be the patron saint of senior citizens. He lived for a hundred years and used them all productively in the service of the Gospel.

When most people would feel their productive years were over, he discovered a future to be spent in the service of the Lord. Remembrance of the past should not blind us to the potential of our future in Christ.

JANUARY 13 – ST. HILARY (OPTIONAL MEMORIAL)

St. Hilary of Poitiers is probably one of the least known and least studied doctors of the Church these days. He was born in the early 4th century and died about 70 years later in 386. Yet, despite the fact that he is virtually unknown today, his life was a dramatic and influential one.

There is the drama of his conversion. He began life in a household where many gods were invoked. He experienced a mid-life conversion to Christianity through his study of the Scriptures especially through reflection on the prologue to St. John's Gospel. The verse, "the Word became flesh and dwelt among us," struck him with stunning power and changed his life. In a sense one can say that all of Christian theology is an extended conversation and reflection on the meaning of that verse. He converted to Christianity and later became a bishop.

There is the drama of his life as a bishop. He engaged the Arian controversy defending the divinity of Jesus against the "anti-Christs" of his day who denied the full divinity of Jesus, the Christ. In some way, such challenges are present in every era. Hilary was sent into exile where he wrote a book called "On the Trinity" which developed concepts and arguments to defend the Church's traditional faith in Christ's divinity.

There is the drama of his impact. He became the bridge from which the thought of the East flowed to the West. He influenced many bishops at the time and many later Doctors of the Church. Though his work may not be studied much these days, he is still among the great ones in the Kingdom of Heaven because of those he inspired.

St. Hilary reminds us today of the importance not only of believing but also of defending the truth of Christ. We live in an age when ideas, concepts and faiths are blended, diluted, caricatured and commercialized. Feelings are often substituted for doctrinal truth. Our call today is to stand fast on the hard rock of Catholic truth that Hilary defended.

And whether we are remembered by others or not, like Hilary, we will still be great in the Kingdom of Heaven... where it counts.

JANUARY 17 – ST. ANTHONY, ABBOT (MEMORIAL)

The Anthony we celebrate today is not Anthony of Padua but the Anthony of Egypt who was born around the year 250. He came from a wealthy family and inherited a great deal of money and land. He took the Gospel words of Jesus quite literally and sold what he had to dedicate himself to a life of prayer away from the city for about twenty years.

Anthony lived at a time when Christianity was starting to become popular, almost the chic thing to do. Huge numbers of people became Christian without any strong commitment.

Some individuals, intensely serious about the Gospel, decided to leave the world of half-hearted commitment they saw around them and dedicate themselves to full Gospel living in the desert. These were the early monks and hermits. Anthony was one of these.

But he discovered a strange truth in the desert. He went to the desert to flee the temptations of the city but the temptations went with him. He suffered terrible onslaughts of the devil. He discovered that no place is immune from temptation. There is no "temptation-free environment." Our struggle is not with flesh and blood but with spiritual powers that do battle from within.

The struggle of the Christian life (the key word is "struggle") goes on in the desert, in the monastery, the convent, the rectory as well as in the city. There is no immunity against that struggle. We have to work to follow the Lord and struggle against the powers of evil that exert their force from within us.

Through our prayer, we try to clear a space within where we can gather the threads of our life, discern Christ's presence, and open ourselves to Him.

In the desert, Anthony learned a lesson for us all. The places of good and evil are not geographical. They are found in the spiritual interior of every heart. Slowly, as we clear aside the brush and weeds of sin, we discover that clearing in our soul where the Lord speaks to us and with us.

The greatest battles we fight in our life are the battles within.

JANUARY 20 – ST. FABIAN (OPTIONAL MEMORIAL)

Fabian was one of a group of heroic third century Popes who strengthened the structure and the witness of the Church.

Elections of the bishop of Rome were very divisive in those days and when the electors were deadlocked any odd circumstance might tip the balance in favor of a particular candidate. When such a deadlock occurred, it is said that a dove landed on Fabian's head and was taken as a sign from heaven that he should be elected.

Fabian was Pope during a pause in persecutions and he used that break to structure the Church of Rome into districts to better handle the growing needs of a growing flock.

The period of peace came to an end when the Roman Emperor Decius wanted to restore the good old days of Roman glory by eliminating all non-conformists and requiring public allegiance to the religion of Rome. The resulting persecution was empire-wide, systematic and especially brutal. All those who did not adhere to the official Roman religion were required to take an oath of allegiance and engage in a loyalty ritual before the statues of the Roman gods.

Pope Fabian refused and became a martyr. In the Office of Readings for today, St. Cyprian remarks on Fabian's courage. He notes that just as a defection from the Faith by a leader can have a tremendously demoralizing effect, so loyalty to the Faith by a leader encourages the faithful.

His example of fidelity may have been Fabian's final and greatest gift to the Church when, in the midst of persecution, the Lord asked him, "Do you still love me?" Fabian's answer was, "Yes!"

Sometimes we forget that our Christian faith is not simply an internal drama worked out in the privacy of our soul. The fidelity we show in church attendance, living the Gospel, speaking truthfully and charitably can have a powerful effect on others.

People need living examples of Christian discipleship. That is something we all can do.

JANUARY 20 – ST. SEBASTIAN (OPTIONAL MEMORIAL)

Holiness and martyrdom are many-splendored things.

St. Sebastian was evidently a model soldier in the Roman army and as a Christian he secretly helped Christians who had been arrested during persecution. He was discovered to be a Christian and was ordered to be executed by being shot with arrows. He was then left for dead.

A fellow-Christian carried him back to her home and nursed him to health. Once recovered, he went to the Emperor to denounce the persecution publicly and this time he was beaten to death.

He is the patron saint of archers and police personnel.

Persecution can take many forms. There are the arrows of slander, detraction, deception, and the harsh words in office and Church politics. There are arrows of betrayal, abandonment, defiance and ridicule.

St. Ambrose in today's Office of Readings calls this a "secret martyrdom." Those who are the object of these arrows experience a martyrdom others do not see. It is not as obvious as a public martyrdom but as real. We need the strength of a Sebastian to endure such secret martyrdom.

Just as there are many roads to holiness, so there are many ways of martyrdom. The subtle opposition expressed in satire, humor and ridicule can replace the public persecution of Roman times.

We honor St. Sebastian because his martyrdom gives us courage to face opposition. In each of our lives, we will have the chance to give witness to Christ and to suffer for it. Whether we endure suffering publicly or privately, it is still a way of giving witness to Christ.

Public martyrdom and "secret martyrdom" are both places of grace and ways of acknowledging Christ. "Secret discipleship" is not.

January 21 – St. Agnes (Memorial)

St. Agnes, a martyr around the year 300, was only a young girl of about 14. She refused to marry, was reported for being a Christian and was put to death in the particularly gruesome way of piercing her throat.

She showed extraordinary courage. St. Ambrose in today's Office of Readings remarks that a youngster of 13 will cry over the slightest rejection but Agnes endured chains and tortures for Christ. We all know how tense we feel when we are pulled over for a speeding violation. Here, a young girl was confronted with the machinery of State torture and didn't flinch.

Agnes reminds us that Christian discipleship is not an ephemeral enthusiasm but a way of life as we try to live a holy life not only in the world but also for the world. To paraphrase the liturgical Preface for Martyrs, God chose one of the weak creatures of our world and made her strong in giving witness to Him.

We can apply the example of God's grace at work in St. Agnes to ourselves.

For us today, the sign of Christian maturity is not the occasional burst of enthusiasm but sustained Gospel living year in and year out.

For us today, effective witness to Christ is less the dramatic act of charity or a brilliant turn of phrase to defend the Church but the constant and continuing work of following Christ.

For us today, the measure of our discipleship is found not in feelings but in fidelity.

St. Agnes shows us what we can do and what we can endure when we open ourselves to the Holy Spirit, which is the Spirit of Christ alive in us.

She showed her faith by how she died; we can show our faith by how we live.

JANUARY 22 – ST. VINCENT, DEACON (OPTIONAL MEMORIAL)

St. Vincent of Saragossa is one of the three martyred deacons honored by the Church during the liturgical year. Vincent was martyred during a persecution in the 300's. After ghastly tortures, he died courageously.

St. Augustine gave several homilies on his memorial. In today's Office of Readings, St. Augustine makes three points about Vincent's death that apply to us and to our witness to the sanctity of human life today.

First, St. Augustine says that in speaking out the truth, we should not feel that we have to rely on our own strength and ability. Our wisdom and strength come from the Lord. We do not know how the Lord will use our witness for the sacredness of life this year. Maybe many consciences will be changed, maybe a few will begin to reconsider, and maybe seeds will be planted. But in our witness, it is Christ speaking through us.

Secondly, St. Augustine says that the enemy will use two lines of attack against our faith. The first is temptation: the effort to distract us, lure us away, weaken our resolve, question our motives and doubt our success. The second is frontal assault: opposition, ridicule and even violence. Recognizing that these are attacks and knowing the ultimate power behind them can make us stronger and more committed.

Thirdly, St. Augustine says that when these attacks fail to deter us, we become the winners in Christ. Whatever the opposition may do to us materially, if they strengthen our faith and our spiritual resolve, then we are the victorious ones.

St. Vincent gave his bold witness to the truth of Christ 18 centuries ago. We are called to give witness today to the truth of Christ. The same Holy Spirit that gave him courage will give us strength as well.

JANUARY 24 – ST. FRANCIS DE SALES (MEMORIAL)

St. Francis de Sales was a bishop, a Doctor of the Church, a spiritual director, author, preacher, co-founder of the Order of the Visitation, all of this in 55 years of life.

He was born in 1567, studied initially to be a lawyer but really wanted to become a priest. Eventually, he was ordained and went to a province of France where people were poor and whose faith was weakened and confused by the Reformation.

His sermons were clear and short. He used to remark that "the more you say, the less people remember." He wrote out his teachings in leaflets or pamphlets, which centuries later caused him to be made the patron saint of journalists.

While he was bishop of Geneva, he wrote *Introduction to the Devout Life*, a spiritual classic which is still read and studied today.

St. Paul says that he was given the privilege of preaching to the Gentiles about the riches of Jesus Christ. In his preaching and writing, St. Francis de Sales was given the privilege of preaching to ordinary people the magnificent possibility of holiness.

He teaches us that we are all called to holiness, whatever

the circumstances of our life. The shape of our spiritual lives may differ, but we can all be heroically holy.

He teaches us that the "present moment," not the past or the future, is the place where we come to know and live God's will.

He teaches us the significance of the ordinary done extraordinarily well as the key to holiness.

He has also been called the "Gentleman Saint." He treated everyone, even his opponents, with respect. He preached the love of God and lived it. He never took differences personally and was never caustic, cutting or biting in his response to opponents.

He preached Christ both in the pulpit and out of it. Not all of us are called to preach Christ in the pulpit. But we are all called to preach Christ in our daily life.

January 25 – The Conversion of St. Paul (Feast)

The conversion of St. Paul was a great moment in the life of St. Paul and a great moment in the life of the Church. A persecutor of the Church became an Apostle; an opponent of Christ became His greatest missionary.

The moment of his conversion, however, didn't come out of nowhere. The light that St. Paul experienced was only the final explosion of grace that had been building inside him. He persecuted the Christians but saw their courage. He hunted them down but saw their loyalty to Christ. He saw Stephen being executed but Stephen's words entered into Saul's deep memory.

In all this, seeds were being planted; a fuse was lit that finally exploded on that road to Damascus. Our words and our example are never wasted. Through them, seeds are planted and a fuse is lit.

Furthermore, Paul's conversion on the Damascus road is not the end of the story but a beginning. He would go to the desert, learn the Faith, apprentice to the Apostles and gradually transform that moment of grace into a way of life.

So it is with us. We are touched by grace at certain times

such as Christmas and Easter or by events in our life such as illness, death of a loved one, or the birth of a child. We can waste
that grace by letting it go as quickly as it came or we can build on
it and let those moments trigger a deeper commitment to Christ.

Lastly, the conversion of St. Paul shows us that we can always begin again with the Lord. Grace can come to us at any
time. We can always begin to walk a new path. Like St. Paul, we
are not chained to the past but can always have a fresh start with
the Lord.

The conversion of St. Paul teaches us that whatever our past
may be, we can always have a different future with Christ.

JANUARY 26 – STS. TIMOTHY AND TITUS (MEMORIAL)

Timothy and Titus were both converts to the Faith who later
became companions and co-workers of St. Paul. Both of them
worked with St. Paul in Corinth and later were made bishops in
different places.

The selection of Timothy and Titus as successors to the
Apostles meant that the Apostles believed that the Church's continuing presence in that world was crucial to make the truth and
grace of Christ present for later generations. The Church's mission
goes on today gathered around the successors of the Apostles
among us.

St. Paul makes three points to the young bishop Timothy that
apply to all of us and which we can all take to heart.

He calls on Timothy to "stir into flame" the gift of grace be-
stowed on him. Are we stirring into flame the gifts given us in the
Sacraments? Are we developing our full potential as followers of
Jesus or simply doing the minimum? If we dare to go beyond what
is required, we will notice how the grace given us in the Sacraments can become radioactive with power.

St. Paul also reminds Timothy that the Spirit he received is
one that makes us "strong, loving and wise." That should be the
goal of every bishop, pastor and Christian – to become strong,

loving and wise in our decisions and actions. Such strength, love and wisdom are born in prayer.

Finally, St. Paul tells him to "bear his share of the hardship" which the Gospel entails. We all have a portion of the work of spreading the Gospel. It is not only the missionaries who work hard. When we try to bring the Gospel into the workplace, our business, our school and even our family there is a resistance which shows how deeply the world still needs a Redeemer.

St. Paul's advice to Timothy is powerful advice to all of us: to activate the graces we are given, to become strong, loving and wise through prayer, and to bear our share of the hard work the Gospel entails.

JANUARY 27 – ST. ANGELA MERICI (OPTIONAL MEMORIAL)

Angela Merici was a woman of her time who was also way ahead of her time. She was the founder of the Ursulines, the first great teaching order of women in the Church.

Angela was born in Italy in 1470. The experience of being orphaned at an early age may have given her a special concern for the little ones about whom the Lord cared so much in the Gospels. She was intelligent, attractive and a natural leader.

She was shocked at the lack of education among young girls of her time. She envisioned a group of unmarried women who would dedicate themselves to teaching these young girls in their homes. These women would not wear a common habit, not be bound by vows, not live in a convent but in their own homes, and would gather regularly for prayer and study. What Angela conceived is what we would call today a "secular institute" or one of the new "movements" that have grown within the Church. She pioneered a way of living a life of consecration to God while living in the world.

She placed this company of women under the patronage of St. Ursula (hence the "Ursulines") whose story Angela had heard when she was a child. St. Ursula was a patroness of education and had herself led a company of maidens on pilgrimage. Angela envisioned her women as going on a kind of pilgrimage through the world bringing learning to young girls in a campaign of what would be called today "empowerment" and "evangelization."

In her Spiritual Testament from today's Office of Readings, Angela encourages her followers to engrave their children on their hearts, not only their names but their individual personalities as well.

After Angela's death, the Ursulines were given a more conventional rule required by those times. But for those who are neither married nor in the religious life, Angela's powerful vision of living a consecrated life in the middle of a busy world is especially compelling today as a magnificent way of glorifying Jesus Christ.

JANUARY 28 – ST. THOMAS AQUINAS (MEMORIAL)

Thomas Aquinas was a great thinker, a theologian of the Church, a Doctor of the Church and a saint!

The outline of his life is not very dramatic. He was born in a wealthy family in Italy in 1225. An average student, he decided to become a Dominican friar. His parents tried very creative ways of dissuading him but he held firm. He joined the Dominican friars and there he blossomed as the awesome range and power of his mind displayed themselves for all to see.

He was a great theologian who wrote two majestic summaries of the Catholic faith, many commentaries on the Scriptures, devotional hymns and sermons. He was on the "cutting edge" of theology in those days as he used the conceptual tools of the newly retrieved philosophy of Aristotle to help explain the Faith.

Then, toward the end of his life, during Mass, he had a vision of Christ and realized that compared to what he had experienced in that vision, all he had written was like straw. The experience of God is richer and greater than reflection about God (the unifying theme of today's readings). He died at the age of 49.

What does Thomas Aquinas say to us today? Apart from the fact that his theology has been the pillar of Catholic thought for centuries, he shows us that there is no necessary conflict between faith and intelligence. We need never be afraid of the Truth. God is Truth and Truth is one. What we do need to fear are half-truths, partial truths, half-baked truths and apparent truths.

Pope John Paul II wrote that faith and reason are two wings we are given to come to the truth of God. Faith takes us where reason cannot go. Reason is like the booster rocket that gives us lift, but faith takes us into the heavens.

St. Thomas gladly embraced the light of faith and the light of reason he was given. Reason is not an enemy but an ally of faith. As an old saying from years ago put it, "Christ came to take away our sins, not our intelligence."

January 31 – St. John Bosco (Memorial)

It is appropriate that within Catholic Schools Week occurs the memorial of St. John Bosco, a patron of youth. He dedicated his life to helping young people grow and mature in every dimension of their lives.

He was born in 1815 from a poor family in Italy. That poverty did not make him bitter but motivated him as a priest to care for young people themselves living in poor circumstances.

It is said that he would take young people from the city into the countryside where they would enjoy positive recreation with his magic shows and hear about Christ and His Church.

Later, John Bosco founded a group of priests under the patronage of St. Francis de Sales ("Salesians") to continue his work of caring for young people. Today the Salesians, numbering about 18,000, operate vocational schools in many parts of Africa and South America. Through them, John Bosco's mission of helping young people grow morally and spiritually continues as it does in our Catholic schools.

Another intriguing feature of Don Bosco's life was his dreams. From his youngest years, he seems to have had dreams of the future, of what he would become and how. And they came true. Later, he had dreams about the Church's future, her various crises and recoveries. These dreams did not leave him paralyzed in speculation but caused him to work all the more in the present to make the Church strong to face any future.

Unlike Don Bosco, most of us are not gifted with such dreams. But, like Don Bosco, we can strengthen the Church to face any future by our being faithful in the present, doing what we can to help young people grow in fidelity to Christ and His Church.

Our Catholic schools are where the Church of tomorrow is being built today.

FEBRUARY 3 – ST. BLAISE (OPTIONAL MEMORIAL)

The memorial of St. Blaise is marked each year by a simple and popular sacramental, the blessing of throats. The connection of this particular blessing with St. Blaise takes us back into Christian memory.

Blaise was a bishop in what we call modern day Turkey in the 300's. He was sentenced to death for being a Christian and a bishop. While he was in prison awaiting execution, it is said that a woman brought her son to him because the boy had a bone lodged in his throat. St. Blaise blessed the boy and his throat was cleared.

When we have the traditional blessing of throats on this day, the priest makes the "St. Andrew's cross" with two candles and asks the intercession of St. Blaise for protection from all ailments of the throat.

We can use that moment to ask St. Blaise's intercession so that we will use the gift of speech to speak truth and not lies, to give encouragement and not criticism, to build people up and not tear them down.

The tongue is a very powerful weapon. Words can make war or bring peace. The physical hurts we inflict on people will heal, but the spiritual and emotional wounds we inflict by what we say can last a lifetime. If we look back on our own lives, each of us was probably hurt most deeply by others not from any physical attack but from words harshly or cruelly spoken. The gift of speech is a very powerful gift.

Let us ask the intercession of St. Blaise that we will always use this gift in the service of Christ's Kingdom. Let our words be agents of Christ's truth and peace.

FEBRUARY 3 – ST. ANSGAR (OPTIONAL MEMORIAL)

St. Ansgar, a missionary from the 9th century, is doubly burdened. One burden that he carries is that his memorial is "bumped" in most parishes by that of St. Blaise. There are no popular sacramentals associated with St. Ansgar.

The second burden is the fact that his life as a missionary seemed a failure. He was born in France during the time of the barbarian invasions. It was a time when terror from these marauding armies of thieves could sweep down suddenly like a tsunami on towns and villages

The Church sought to convert these barbarians and Ansgar wanted to be part of that effort. He was sent as a missionary to Denmark and then Sweden. It is said that he built the first Christian church in Sweden. Afterwards, he spread the Gospel to Norway and northern Germany.

He witnessed the tragedy, however, of his accomplishments being obliterated by the Vikings. Many of the institutions he established in Denmark and Sweden were later destroyed in his own lifetime. It seemed that his work had been in vain. Christ asked him to follow yet it all seemed to turn to dust.

But was his life a failure? We cannot completely comprehend the providence of God. During his missionary work, souls were saved as people came to know Jesus Christ. During his lifetime seeds were sown in people's lives that may have deeply influenced entire families in ways we cannot imagine. His life shows us that missionary success should never be taken for granted. Finally, he was faithful to his call and that made him a saint. Today, he can intercede for all the work of evangelization being done in the Scandinavian countries.

Ansgar, the seemingly failed missionary, continues a ministry of intercession today to the areas where he worked centuries ago.

The message of his life to us is to answer the call and leave the rest to God.

February 5 – St. Agatha (Memorial)

The facts we know about Agatha's life are few but her popularity among Christians has been enormous.

She was a young girl in Sicily around the year 250 and had made a promise to remain unmarried and completely dedicated to the Lord. A Roman official made advances toward her, which she refused. He sent her to a brothel operated by a woman named, appropriately, Aphrodisia to lower her resistance. Agatha, however, refused to compromise her virginity.

She was tortured and eventually put to death. Part of the pain inflicted on her was the severing of her breasts. She is a patron today of those who suffer breast cancer.

Agatha's popularity was certainly enhanced by the regard Pope Gregory the Great had for her story. But there is more.

One virtue she displays for us today is her respect for her own virginity and her sexual integrity. Many studies today show that sexuality and personality are connected on very deep levels. One truth of the "theology of the body" is that our sexuality is a very critical part of who we are. Yet, this is also an age when people tend to sever their sexuality from their deepest selves and treat it simply as a function to be variously used.

It is no surprise when human sexuality is so trivialized that self-respect should plummet as well. It is paradoxical that an era like our own that places such high regard on emotional integrity, financial integrity and physical integrity should place such little value on sexual integrity, which reaches so deeply into our personal identity.

Agatha stands for sexual self-respect. Whatever she may

have meant to previous generations in terms of her heroic loyalty to the Faith, to our generation she shows us a person who refused to compromise her personal dignity.

The respect we have for our sexuality shows the respect we have for ourselves.

FEBRUARY 6 – ST. PAUL MIKI AND COMPANIONS (MEMORIAL)

The story of Paul Miki and his companions, twenty-six in all, is a story of tragedy and triumph. They are sometimes called "the martyrs of Nagasaki" or "the martyrs of Japan."

St. Francis Xavier had done a remarkable job of bringing the Gospel to Japan. Through his efforts, there was a substantial Catholic community in Japan. Still, Japanese leaders were somewhat suspicious of Europeans.

Almost a half century after Xavier's death in 1552, a powerful Japanese official listened to and believed some gossip from a Spanish businessman to the effect that the Christian missionaries were agents of Spanish domination.

This set in motion a chain reaction leading to the arrest of twenty-six Christian leaders. Six were Franciscans, three were Japanese Jesuits of which Paul Miki was the leader, and seventeen were lay leaders. They were tortured and then fastened to individual crosses outside Nagasaki and put to death simultaneously. They were, quite literally and dramatically, "crucified with Christ."

Among other things, this is an example of the tragic consequences of gossip.

Many thought that was the end of Christianity in Japan. When missionaries were allowed to return centuries later, they did not initially see any signs of Christianity. Then, slowly, they discovered some Christians, then others and then thousands around Nagasaki. The Faith was kept alive in families, thanks to the magnificent work and heroism of Paul Miki and his companions.

We see in these events the triumph of the Gospel. Opponents could slay missionaries but they could not kill the Word of God. We are all responsible for the Church, keeping it alive, credible and strong.

Enemies may kill Christians, but they cannot kill the Truth of Jesus Christ, the Gospel that lives in the hearts of all who believe.

FEBRUARY 8 – ST. JEROME EMILIANI (OPTIONAL MEMORIAL)

One of the modern phrases we have to describe the honesty and genuineness of a person's commitment to something is to "put your money where your mouth is." A person's financial support of a cause is a proof or guarantee that his enthusiasm for it is not simply rhetorical. Unfortunately, we have people today who are enthusiasts for a cause who wish to put our money where their mouth is.

St. Jerome Emiliani was born in Venice in 1486. He had come from a family of means, ran away from home and joined the army. His mysterious, almost miraculous, deliverance from prison sparked a conversion in his life. He gave up politics for the priesthood.

He devoted his life to caring for children who were abandoned and orphans. Despite her wealth, 16th century Venice was not a great place to be if you were poor. Beneath the beautiful façade of bobbing gondolas on the Grand Canal and masked balls in the palaces was a dark and brutal world largely indifferent to the needs of the poor.

Jerome Emiliani spent all he had to provide shelter and food for the children who were "left behind" in Venice. Gradually, others joined him in his work. He begged for money from the wealthy to continue caring for these poor children. Jerome established six orphanages in his life. He tended not only the physical needs of the children but their spiritual needs as well, as he taught them the Faith. It is said that he introduced the "question and answer" method of instruction which is with us today.

In his own way, Jerome Emiliani was prophetic of a new

kind of world that would provide for and care for its children. Today, he is the patron saint of orphaned children.

His feast reminds us today of people among us who "put their money where their mouth is." These are couples who adopt children with disabilities of various kinds and welcome them into their families. In a world that exalts physical beauty and perfection, these individuals are profoundly pro-life as they care for children who would otherwise be kept at the margins of our society.

It is said that some people today have a "checklist" of physical attributes they prefer in children they will adopt, like buying a car. Jerome Emiliani had no such "checklist." His only criterion was need, which is the same criterion God uses in regard to each of us.

February 8 – St. Josephine Bakhita (Optional Memorial)

Josephine Bakhita is a new saint recently added to the Church's universal calendar. Her life is a witness to the tragedies of our time and also to the power of God's grace in our time as well.

She was born in 1869 in Sudan in the Darfur region, the "land of tears," that has seen enormous strife. The result has been hundreds of thousands dead, two and a half million people displaced and left to starve to death. The U.S. government has labeled the atrocities in Darfur today as genocide.

Josephine (her original name is unknown) was kidnapped at age seven. She was whipped and permanently branded on her body in some sixty places by one of the many "owners" to whom she was sold and resold over the years. This trafficking in human beings, buying and selling them as items, is not a thing of the past. It goes on today even in cultures we thought were Christian or at least humane. It is a multi-billion dollar business today.

She was finally "sold" to an Italian diplomat who brought her to Italy where she lived in a convent. Later she was baptized taking the name Josephine, was legally emancipated, and became a nun. In the convent, she then served as cook, seamstress and doorkeeper. After a long illness, she died in 1947, beloved by the community.

Through her difficult life, Josephine came to hear the Gospel and come to know Jesus Christ, whom she called her real Master. For all that had been done to her, Josephine did not become bitter. In fact, the tragedies inflicted on her made her compassionate and open to God. However much her body was scarred, her heart was intact and filled with forgiveness.

There is much in the world and in our personal life that can make us bitter. Josephine Bakhita shows us that it can also make us holy as we try to be different from the world around us. Josephine Bakhita shows us that we can follow another path, the path of Christ.

The conflict in Darfur has today exploded from the government's persecution of civilians into a violent, genocidal free for all. Josephine Bakhita has been called the "patron saint of Sudan," a land whose people are yearning for peace and peacemakers. May their prayers be answered.

February 10 – St. Scholastica (Memorial)

Special moments do not come often in a person's life. When they do come, however, they give our life lift and new enthusiasm.

The life of St. Scholastica captures such a special moment. She was the twin sister of St. Benedict. Just as he had established a monastic order of men, so she founded a convent of women a few miles away from his monastery. Brother and sister would meet annually to have spiritual conversation and prayer together.

On one occasion, they had met for a long while and nightfall was approaching. Benedict rose to leave but Scholastica asked that he remain a while longer. When he refused in obedience to his own monastic rule to stay overnight only in the monastery, she prayed for a storm to prevent his departure. Her prayer was answered and the two of them were able to continue their meeting long into the night.

As it turns out, that was the last time they would see each other because she died soon after. It was a special moment not only between brother and sister but also between fellow Christians.

Maybe in the busy schedule of our life, we might think of times of joined prayer and Christian conversation as optional extras. But they invite us into the substance of life. The ancient words of Genesis are true for all of us, "It is not good for any man to be alone."

We need times of shared prayer, laughter, conversation and even sorrow. Whatever form they may take, they are gifts from God. That is surely one point the Lord is making to Martha in today's Gospel reading. It is important to pause and let the Holy Spirit work in our life through others, especially through their friendship.

In the routine of life, such shared moments are islands of refreshment, faith and light.

Such moments as these may be brief but they have the power and grace to fill a lifetime.

FEBRUARY 11 – OUR LADY OF LOURDES (OPTIONAL MEMORIAL)

The liturgy frequently tends to apply the praises sung of the city of Jerusalem in the Old Testament to Mary. Part of the reason is that Jerusalem was, in the early Church, a center of devotion to Mary. The other reason is that Mary was herself, in effect, a "city of God." Just as Jerusalem and the Temple were the places were God dwelled, so Mary was the place where for nine months God dwelled among us.

All the strength, comfort, welcome and embrace that the city of Jerusalem offered to pilgrims back then is true of Mary herself.

This is very much the case with the devotion to Our Lady of Lourdes. The story of her appearances to Bernadette Soubirous in France on eight occasions from February to July in 1858 is well known. Over the years since then, Lourdes has become a place of wonderful, warm and universal pilgrimage.

It shows the worldwide embrace of Mary to all people. The pilgrimage to the healing waters of Lourdes can be a powerful experience. But we can all know the healing waters of Mary's intercession wherever we are.

The appearances at Lourdes are a reminder to us of the presence of Mary who is close to us all the time.

Some people try to diminish the significance of the words given by Mary in various apparitions because they are not part of the binding revelation given us in the New Testament. Yet, the words of Mary to those who have the privilege of experiencing her presence have always had the same theme as her words at Cana, "Do whatever he tells you."

Devotion to Mary is not a rival to our love for the Lord Jesus. Authentic devotion to Mary always leads us to her Son.

One of the features of Marian shrines around the world is that they are places where all people can feel at peace. This is seen and heard most dramatically in the hymn sung during the evening procession at Lourdes in many languages each time ending with the universal refrain, "Ave, Ave, Ave, Maria."

In a world of so much fragmentation and in a time when the Church has experienced so much division, Mary today can show us the way to unity and peace as a family.

Every mother wants to see her children get along together. Mary is no different.

February 14 – Sts. Cyril and Methodius (Memorial)

Saints Cyril and Methodius were splendid laborers for the harvest. Cyril was a monk and Methodius a bishop who brought the Gospel to the Slavic peoples. Their mission was to bring the teaching and liturgy of the Church into the very heart and soul of a people by translating it into the popular language.

They were always careful to remain united with the See of Peter and to ensure that their preaching was consistent with the apostolic tradition. But they were equally zealous to clothe the Gospel of Jesus in the garments of the Eastern peoples.

They lived around the mid 800's before the split between the Eastern and Western Church. Cyril and Methodius remind us of a unity that can be regained.

They were early advocates of what is today called "inculturation." This means that the truth of Jesus and the life of the Church are not generic abstractions. They always live in a particular time and place and wrap themselves in the language, hopes and dreams of various cultures.

Cyril and Methodius gave the Slavic peoples Christian roots and a common Christian heritage. They are a bridge between East and West and remind us that our divisions are not from Christ but from elsewhere and they can be overcome.

Diversity is not at war with unity. Today, as people all over the world are discovering the richness and beauty of our differing ethnic roots, perhaps we will be able to rediscover as well the real places of our unity. For a world that knows so much division and subdivision, the worldwide Church can be a splendid model for the entire family of mankind to see that unity is not only plausible but also possible.

The same Church that is so magnificently universal is also deeply local. That is a gift of the Holy Spirit to us.

FEBRUARY 17 – SEVEN FOUNDERS OF THE ORDER OF SERVITES (OPTIONAL MEMORIAL)

Jesus speaks about surrender for the sake of the Kingdom. St. Paul speaks about the profound depths of prayer. Renunciation and prayer frame the story of the seven founders of the Order of Servites.

They were all prosperous businessmen in Florence of the 13th century. They had belonged to a religious confraternity but wanted to dedicate their lives to the Lord in a more complete and permanent way. They founded a religious congregation dedicated to prayer and contemplation.

The focus of their meditation was on the Sorrows of Mary and the Passion of Jesus. Even though they had somewhat secluded themselves, people still sought to join their community.

Eventually, contemplation became one aspect of their vocation. Any deep reflection upon the suffering of Jesus will lead us to consider His Mother's part in that suffering. The meditation on one leads to the other. And any contemplation on their suffering must lead to a care for those around us who are suffering in any way.

This is exactly what happened to the Servants of Mary, the Servites as they came to be called. Their Marian prayer life led them gradually to care for the Church as Mary cares for the Church. Care for the people of the Church should be the normal outcome of all Marian devotion. Under her patronage they entered a variety of ministries which continue today.

The service they and their followers showed is one sign to us today of the Gospel's continuing power to heal as it mends us within and prompts us to look at the wounds of others.

The Gospel brings a double cure, healing to those for whom we care and healing from a self-absorbed life to those who do the caring.

FEBRUARY 21 – ST. PETER DAMIAN (OPTIONAL MEMORIAL)

St. Peter Damian lived at the turn of the first millennium. He became a Benedictine monk whose great learning was coupled with a personal asceticism, which he encouraged other monks to follow when he became an abbot.

He was a man widely recognized for his fidelity to Christ in the Church. He was asked to mediate various controversies and eventually became a bishop and a cardinal of the Church.

It was Damian's call to live during a time of a huge "knowledge explosion" and a time of scandal. It was a time when many new ideas were pouring into Europe. Schools and the teaching professions were coming to new life in a very vigorous way.

The dark side of all this light was that the foundations of the apostolic faith were being questioned as well. It took a while for this new learning to be integrated with the ancient Faith.

Peter Damian stood for the proposition that philosophy was the "handmaid" or assistant of faith, not its master. That is why he insisted that all learning be used to illuminate faith and not replace it. If we cannot understand how some secular truth can be integrated with our faith, we should still trust the Faith. Peter Damian's offensive was against an intellectual elite who popularized their opinions without regard for the faith of people who did not have the background for discernment as these teachers had. Peter Damian encouraged, therefore, a prudent reserve.

He also faced a time of scandal. He called churchmen back to simplicity of life and to live by the Gospel they preached. Churchmen are called to a higher standard of life and, if they fail, to a higher standard of repentance.

In a time of secularism and scandal, St. Peter Damian issued a summons to faith and repentance, to stay close to the vine that is Jesus Christ. Deeper faith and deeper repentance were the antidotes then as they are now.

FEBRUARY 22 – THE CHAIR OF PETER, APOSTLE (FEAST)

In the apse of St. Peter's Basilica in Rome is a brilliant creation by Bernini called "the Chair of Peter." It captures the power and drama of the office of Pope. Behind the chair is a representation of the Holy Spirit. The great chair itself is supported by four doctors of the Church, Saints Ambrose and Augustine of the Western Church as well as Saints John Chrysostom and Athanasius of the Eastern Church.

Significantly, the chair is empty because it is not meant to exalt any particular Pope but the office itself that Jesus gave to the Church as a point of unity and continuity.

We have been blessed with many great Popes in the past century. We must, however, be cautious in assessing their years in any negative way. We can only look back at their time from the outside. We cannot fully recapture the inner dynamics and subtleties of their years. We were not there.

In our national life as well, we cannot fully understand the subtleties of the politics and mood of the twenties, the thirties, forties or fifties. Complete historical empathy is virtually impossible for us to attain. We have the words but not the music.

The crises facing Leo XIII, Pius X, Benedict XV, Pius XI, Pius XII, John XXIII, Paul VI, and John Paul II are now a world away from us.

Each of these Popes in his own way worked for unity within the Church by "tending the flock" in the words of St. Peter in today's first reading in times that were troubled in ways different from each other. Each of them tried to maintain continuity with the apostolic faith expressed by Peter in today's Gospel reading. In these Popes, the promise of Christ was kept.

We pray that the Lord will give the Holy Father today the strength and the grace to do the work he has been given to do. Each Pope brings his own grace and accent to the office created by Christ. In the election of each Pope, Christ's promise is renewed.

Just as Bernini's majestic chair is the focal point of St. Peter's Basilica, the office of Pope is the point of unity and continuity of a diverse and worldwide Church. Through the Holy Spirit, the Pope keeps the Church one and linked to Christ.

FEBRUARY 23 – ST. POLYCARP (MEMORIAL)

St. Polycarp was a bishop and martyr of the early Church. It is said that he was a disciple of John the Apostle. He lived in a time of seething hostility toward Christians. Almost anything could spark a local or regional persecution.

Evidently, a young man was killed at a pagan festival; the crowd was worked into a frenzy and called for death to the "atheists" which meant the Christians because they didn't worship pagan gods.

They seized Polycarp and sentenced him to death. What is striking about Polycarp was his reported calm in the middle of this feeding frenzy and his profound Christian dignity in the face of his impending death. At his interrogation, he was ordered to deny Christ and responded by refusing to reverse his 86 years of service to Christ by betraying Him at this most important hour of his life, his death.

He was then burned at the stake. Polycarp reminds us of the dignity and witness in Christian dying.

St. Francis de Sales once remarked as a comfort to those facing death that if our life has not been very Christian, our dying still can be. That can be our witness to Christ.

Polycarp's life was truly faithful. But it is his fidelity to Christ in facing death that has been preserved in Christian memory and remains an inspiration to us today.

In the middle of the madness of those brutal days, Polycarp kept his "eyes on the prize" and knew that his ultimate future, his everlasting future, was not here but with Jesus Christ.

We can give witness to Christ not only by how we live but also by how we will die.

MARCH 3 – ST. KATHERINE DREXEL (OPTIONAL MEMORIAL)

In the Old Testament story of Jonah, Jonah did not want to preach repentance to the Ninevites. He saw these ancient enemies of Israel as outside the reach of God's mercy.

The saint we honor today, Mother Katherine Drexel, was a Jonah in reverse. She showed special care for African Americans and Native American Indians who had been marginalized by society. She was born to a wealthy family in the middle of the 19th century. She wanted to become a religious sister from her early years. After her father died, she and her siblings were heirs to a good part of his substantial fortune.

She was moved by the poverty and suffering of the American Indians and African Americans in our country that she had

165

witnessed on family trips. She used the considerable funds available to her to build schools, provide food, clothing and shelter for them.

In a private audience with Pope Leo XIII, she requested missionary priests to assist these minorities in the United States. The pope responded by suggesting that she become a missionary herself. That set her course for the rest of her life.

She founded the Sisters of the Blessed Sacrament. They established boarding schools and churches around the country for minorities. She was instrumental in founding Xavier University for black Americans. This apostolate was especially difficult in a time when discrimination was widespread. People saw them as negligible minorities. She saw them as brothers and sisters in Christ.

What St. Paul said of Christ, Pope John Paul said of Katherine Drexel that "she made herself poor so others could be rich." She spent the money bequeathed to her (some $14 million) in the service of Native and African Americans so they could acquire a sense of dignity through education and faith in Jesus Christ. She died in 1955 after almost a century of service to the Lord.

Pope Leo's remark to her that she herself become a missionary can apply to us. We can lament the absence of attention or care in our community or parish to people with a particular need. That may be the Lord's call to us to become involved.

On a personal level this Lent, we can imitate Katherine Drexel by choosing someone in our life that we may have neglected or avoided. We can raise them to the Lord in prayer by name, give them some of our time and assistance, and try to see beneath the stereotype to the person within.

When we choose a neglected stranger, we may discover a brother or sister in the Lord.

March 4 – St. Casimir (Optional Memorial)

Where we are born is not necessarily that to which we are called. This is profoundly true in the life of St. Casimir.

Casimir was born in 1458. He was a prince of the royal line in Poland. Although he was born of a royal family, was third in line for the throne, was called to wage a campaign to become King of Hungary and then withdrew, the world of domination and command was not for him.

From his earliest years he was attracted to prayer and penitential practices. He showed early signs of mysticism in the length of his prayers. He lived in the midst of the royal court but chose not to live its lifestyle. His clothing, his approach to others and his demeanor were different from the rest of his family members. He followed the command of the Lord in today's Gospel to treat others as we would have them treat us.

He realized that his great work in life would be the life of prayer. After his failed military campaign in Hungary, he retreated to a life of meditation and reflection to which he had always felt called. He was drawn to meditation on the Passion of Jesus, the power of the Mass and the intercession of Mary. His favorite hymn, in fact, was a Marian one, *Omni die dic Mariae*, which we know as "Daily, daily sing to Mary." A copy of that hymn, in fact, was buried with him.

Casimir might seem a world apart from some of our great warrior saints. Yet, it takes a different kind of courage to stand out from the crowd, follow where the Holy Spirit is leading us despite family pressure and come to know what the Lord wants us to be.

That was Casimir's gift. He was not a great general, not a great king, not a great leader, not a great administrator, but he was a great saint. In the larger view of things, his life was a great success.

St. Casimir reminds us that our environment doesn't have to define who we are. Where we are born does not determine what we shall be. What we can be comes from God and His grace.

March 7 – Sts. Perpetua and Felicity (Memorial)

Perpetua and Felicity were joined together in life, in death and in Catholic memory for centuries. Their names have long been linked in the Roman canon and in the liturgical calendar. It is difficult for us to recapture the terror of the Roman persecutions in the early Church. Perhaps the closest we can come is found in the Nazi persecution of the Jews.

Persecutions it seems came in waves and the one under Septimius Severus was empire-wide and particularly vicious. The net of government sponsored violence swept young and old, rich and poor, male and female, slave and free together who shared the single characteristic of being Christian.

Perpetua and Felicity lived in North Africa in the early 200's. Perpetua was from the upper class while Felicity was her slave. Both were young mothers. Perpetua gave birth to a child who was entrusted to her father when she was imprisoned. Felicity was pregnant and gave birth to her child in prison. The story of their united heroism is contained in accounts attributed to Perpetua's diary. Some say that later writers amplified the events that are recounted.

There is no need to embellish the fact that these two young women gave their lives for their faith in Christ in a very vicious death. There is no need to embellish the fact that they allowed nothing to separate them from Christ's love. There is no need to embellish the fact that their common witness inspired their generation. There is no need to embellish the fact that they gave up their families, their children and their spouses for Christ.

As we look back on the heroism of the martyrs like Perpetua and Felicity, we find the sources of their strength to be their trust in the Gospel, the grace of God and the community of fellow-believers. In their prison cell they strengthened each other in faith. Today, many centuries later, we draw our strength from the same sources of trust in God's Word, the grace of God that comes to us in the Sacraments and in the fellowship of believers.

The joining of Perpetua and Felicity in our liturgy and memory is not simply an historical acknowledgment of their friendship. It is also a statement that we cannot fight the battle of fidelity alone. We need to identify the spiritual resources available to us that help us remain faithful to Christ. Those resources are found in the powerful and strategic triad of Word, Sacrament and Church. What protected and sustained Christians from the very beginning will protect and sustain us today.

MARCH 8 – ST. JOHN OF GOD (OPTIONAL MEMORIAL)

The Lord counsels us to be as merciful to others as God is merciful to us. The receiving and giving of mercy mark the life of St. John of God. John lived in Spain in the 16th century. His life can be divided into two parts.

In the first part, he was a wanderer, an adventurer, a laborer, a "jack of many trades" but master of none. His amorality reflected his errant and undisciplined life. One day, he heard a powerful preacher speak on the evil of sin and the necessity of conversion.

This threw John into a tailspin. His repentance became extreme, erratic and excessive. His behavior was so frightening that the townspeople committed him to an asylum. Fortunately, the very preacher whose sermon had such a profoundly disorienting effect on John visited him at the hospital and helped him center his life on the Gospel of Jesus Christ. This made all the difference for John as his life found new direction. This began the second half of his life.

The negligent and often brutal treatment he had received at the hospital was the spark that caused him to care for the sick, the mentally infirm and the dying. The Brothers Hospitallers continue his work today in a vast and diverse ministry to people with all sorts of illness and affliction.

There are those in our society who look to attack the root causes of poverty and illness. They are the great crusaders that address the conscience of a generation. That was not the core charism of John of God.

His mission was to help the hurting who crossed his path.

Social reform was not his calling but extending the compassion of Christ to people around him was. Sometimes, people engaged in societal reform can become so engrossed in the programmatic transformation of society's structures that they can forget the hurting individual.

John of God reminds us that whatever reform movements might engage us, we still have an obligation to care for the hurting person who crosses our path.

Working for societal change may or may not be an option for us. Mercy never is.

March 9 – St. Frances of Rome (Optional Memorial)

There is a familiar saying to the effect that service of others is fine but "charity begins at home." There is validity to the truth that charity begins at home as long as it doesn't stay there.

Frances of Rome is a case study of this truth. She lived in Rome in the 15th century. Born in 1384 of an aristocratic family, she married a member of the nobility. They had six children. By all accounts, she was a loving wife and caring mother. At the death of her mother-in-law, she took over management of the family castle.

With all this responsibility, she also had an extraordinary care for the poor of the city of Rome. Not only did she fulfill this Gospel reading by stepping from her social circle to care for those trapped in another, she did this while caring for her own family.

Through all kinds of natural disasters and political calamities that escalated the number of people in need, Frances was there. In fact, she often opened her spacious house as a hospital. For thousands of people, she was the only "social safety net" they knew.

She founded a group of women, the Oblates of St. Francis, who lived at home but cared for the needy as a personal apostolate. Gradually, they continued their work from a convent and when Frances' husband died and her children were grown, she joined them.

Her charity began at home but it didn't stay there. It reached out to all the corners of her world. So often it is the case that people who are dedicated to their families manage also to find the time to reach out to others. Generosity and compassion are naturally expansive.

Often enough, as well, people who don't have time for others frequently don't have much time for family either.

Indeed, charity begins at home but it shouldn't stay there.

March 17 – St. Patrick (Optional Memorial)

Patrick, the patron saint of Ireland, was himself born in Britain. As a young man he was kidnapped and put into slavery in Ireland. He escaped but felt drawn back to that land. He was ordained a priest and then went as a missionary to bring the Gospel to Ireland, a land at that time filled with Druids and tribal conflicts. Patrick's work was not easy. He met with resistance and some success but he stayed the course.

He used simple things to explain the Faith as represented by the story of his using a shamrock to image the Trinity. His greatest clash was with the Druids. On a March night when all the Druid fires of the kingdom were extinguished, the chieftains assembled to start the new fire. As they looked into the darkness, they saw on the next mountain a new fire lit by Patrick. It was Holy Saturday and there Patrick for the first time lit the Paschal fire, a symbol of the Church's Easter faith that was to light up the land for generations. After that incident, Patrick's fame spread throughout Ireland.

Patrick was not Irish but he became the spiritual father of Ireland. He began a fusion of Irish culture and Catholicism that continues to our own day. He gave the Church a strong institutional base to enable it to survive and thrive. He used education to enable women to be perceived not as possessions but as persons.

A problem we face today is a different one, the drama of the growing split between culture and faith. That is why our traditions are vital to keep our faith and Catholic identity alive. We need to give our Church a strong institutional base as a base for re-evangelizing people in the next millennium. We can use education to help people realize their dignity as sons and daughters of God and not see themselves only as consumers or voting units.

Patrick was a great missionary of faith and in doing so he transformed Irish culture. His example can inspire us to begin to permeate our culture with faith once again today.

MARCH 18 – ST. CYRIL OF JERUSALEM (OPTIONAL MEMORIAL)

Faithfulness to the Gospel was quickly disappearing during the 4th century in which Cyril of Jerusalem lived. If there was not complete faithlessness, there was certainly plenty of confusion.

Cyril became bishop of Jerusalem in 348. Christianity had been made legal and so deep-seated differences previously relegated to the proverbial "backburner" began to surface. Those were quarrelsome days. The great cancer that infected the Church was Arianism, a distorted and diminished view of Christ that blended politics and personal animosities and convulsed Church and Empire for over a century.

After the Second Vatican Council, some people complained about confusion in the Church. The confusion and disorder at the time of Cyril was mammoth. Bishops were openly opposed to each other. They excommunicated and exiled each other. Episcopal sees teeter-tottered back and forth from Arian to orthodox bishop. None of this did very much to edify a very confused group of lay people.

Cyril was drawn into this seething political vortex. He suffered enormously for the faith of the Church. He was accused of heresy, misfeasance and malfeasance in office and was sent into exile several times. Eventually he came back to his diocese and died there at the age of seventy.

Cyril is credited with something that has endured the controversy with Arianism. It is the development of the catechumenate as we know it. In those days, many people were becoming Christian without proper preparation. In Cyril's effort to bring them to a commitment to Christ, the catechumenate, which has been restored today as the RCIA, was established. Many of his homilies from that process survive.

A structure for strong faith formation remains Cyril's enduring gift to the Church. We should know what we believe and why. Our faith should not be simply an emotion, an impression, and an opinion. It should be a solid rock in which to erect our lives. The importance of parish membership in this process is vital.

In an age of confusion, Cyril showed a way to help people remain firm in Christ. Our age today needs strong structures and programs to help people know what we believe and why.

MARCH 23 – ST. TORIBIO DE MOGROVEJO (OPTIONAL MEMORIAL)

The graces of revival and healing were gifts that St. Toribio brought to the people he served as bishop.

Toribio was a lawyer in Spain in the 1500's and was renowned for his brilliance. One day, he was informed that he had been appointed archbishop of Lima, Peru. This shocked Toribio since he wasn't even a priest. But Pope and King insisted that he accept the appointment.

He was ordained priest and then bishop. When he arrived in his diocese of Lima, he found a serious illness in the Body of Christ. It was a kind of spiritual atrophy or paralysis in that many in the Spanish upper class were viciously exploiting the native Indians.

Toribio began a truly heroic effort of renewal. He visited the parishes of his diocese to revive faith and the pastoral care of the clergy for the people. This was especially courageous since the clergy were largely corrupt and catered only to the wealthy.

Toribio traveled thousands of miles through unusually rough terrain to visit his sprawling diocese. It took seven years to visit the entire area. Eventually he called a local council to set new rules for the clergy and try to restore right order.

Enacting laws is one thing, implementing is another. That was the second phase of his ministry. We can only imagine the loneliness of a bishop like Toribio. He was treated as a stranger in his own diocese, branded a reformer when nobody wanted to reform and called a teacher to the poor in a diocese where money talked and had a lot to say.

But Toribio not only legislated; he lived the life he wanted his clergy to follow. He died in 1606 at the age of 68. As a result of his labor, the Church in Latin America was stronger, the clergy were more attentive to all the people, the poor had the Gospel preached to them and Toribio became a saint!

The renewal and the healing of Jesus finally came to a whole diocese through one man.

APRIL 2 – ST. FRANCIS OF PAOLA (OPTIONAL MEMORIAL)

The life of Francis of Paola is fascinating because he began his adult life as a hermit and ended up as a statesman. Usually, it is the other way around, politics being what they are.

Francis was born in 1416. He lived in an age that experienced a rise of secular culture in the Renaissance and a diminishment of Christian fervor. When he was young, he made a pilgrimage with his parents to Assisi and was very much drawn to the life and spirit of St. Francis of Assisi.

Afterwards, he went to live as a hermit and very soon other men came to join his simple, austere way of life. Not only did others join this hermit group but also people from the surrounding area began to come to him for advice, prayer and healing.

His order had the usual three vows with an added fourth vow of a perpetual Lenten fast.

Gradually, he became known for his miracles and cures. Very soon, the nobility of Europe were seeking him out for spiritual counsel and for prayer. There came a point in Francis' life when he began to speak out publicly on behalf of the poor and used his popularity to preach the Gospel of Jesus as a Gospel not only of compassion but also of justice.

As his fame spread, he became a counselor to many leaders of Europe. He was called to use his healing power on an ailing French king and was gently compelled to remain at court for many years.

What made this hermit popular was his transparent holiness that came from his faith in Christ. Jesus says in today's Gospel that if people do not believe Him because of His words, they should believe because of His works. The same was true of Francis of Paola. The miracles he was said to have performed drew people to the message of Christ that he preached rather than the other way around. He died while the Passion according to St. John was being read to him on Good Friday.

Francis of Paola lived what we would call today a "countercultural" life. But he was more than a social contrarian. He exhibited a life of communion with God, simplicity of life and service of neighbor without compromise. These are dimensions of life that every human heart seeks because they are "echoes of Paradise" planted deep inside us. People saw in him some reflection of the Kingdom of God for which we are all designed. That was the greatest miracle in the life of this miracle-worker.

When we strengthen our communion with God, the simplicity of our life and the service of our neighbor, we will notice the Kingdom of God coming to life for us as well.

April 4 – St. Isidore of Seville (Optional Memorial)

It may be easy to confuse Isidore of Seville with the title of an opera called "The Barber of Seville." Although he is less known today than Rossini's fictional barber, he is a very significant figure in the life of the Church. Dante includes him in the circle of holy ones around Thomas Aquinas in heaven.

Isidore was a bishop in Spain who lived in the late 500's. Some have called those days the "dark ages" but Isidore kept the light burning in those years. He lived in a time of huge transition. The institutions, learning and culture of the Roman Empire were disintegrating. Spain was becoming dominated by the anti-intellectual, brutal influence of the Visigoths. Isidore sought to create a new world view from the cultural fragments of Roman and Gothic culture that surrounded him.

As an influential bishop, he persuaded local councils of bishops to mandate seminaries in every diocese, to commit themselves to education and to make their churches and monasteries centers of learning. He himself wrote abundantly. His goal was to rescue the remains of learning that had not been destroyed by the barbarians. His works are many but perhaps his greatest work was an encyclopedia of all truth known at his time in any field. He preserved in writing whatever was known of the sciences at that time. He sought to preserve not only the lamp of learning but to engage a rapidly changing culture and give it direction. For him, the Church was not a hideout from change but an agent to preserve and advance learning.

Although he was not a creative theologian, his claim to fame was in gathering and condensing the learning of his time. His work became a major source of information about the wisdom of the ancients throughout the Middle Ages.

Isidore was not simply a polymath but a bishop. Everything he did was to bring people closer to Christ and show the path to God. In his later years, recognizing the coming end of his life, he began to distribute his possessions to the poor. Because of his life, the light of learning continued to burn after his death in 636.

There has been a kind of revival of interest in Isidore of Seville as a patron saint for the Internet and computer users. Although his writing could be called an early version of a database, he shows us more importantly that the Church never has to be afraid of the truth. Today, we are living in a time of enormous change. It is not necessarily competing philosophical systems that present a challenge but the pace of technology. Every day an increasing number of people receive their information and shape their opinions not from sermons, conventional newspapers or network broadcasts but from web logs on the Internet. The velocity of the flow of information and opinion has increased exponentially. The impact of this change on the Church's life will be far more decisive than that of the automobile.

It took a while for the Church to embrace newspapers and television in its work. The Church cannot come into the arena of the Internet "breathless and little late." Perhaps we can pray that St. Isidore will help us use the powerful tool of the Internet to spread the Gospel of Jesus Christ. If the Internet can be an agent of temptation it can also be an instrument of grace.

April 5 – St. Vincent Ferrer (Optional Memorial)

He liked to call himself the "angel of judgment." Vincent Ferrer was a powerful preacher who spoke forcefully about the end of the world, the coming judgment and the need for repentance. He gave extraordinarily effective and popular "fire and brimstone" sermons yet he is largely forgotten today.

He was a Dominican friar in the 14th century, the time of the great Papal schism when two rival popes claimed the throne. Vincent Ferrer sided with the anti-pope Benedict XIII and was profoundly disappointed when he realized that Benedict had no interest in bringing about Church unity. Disenchanted with the possibility of institutional reform, Vincent left behind Church politics and began a grand preaching tour of Europe calling for personal reform.

His sermons were eloquent, hugely successful and accompanied by a multitude of miracles and many changed lives. He himself was very ascetic and lived thoroughly what he preached. St. Paul's charge to Timothy to preach persistently whether convenient or not certainly describes the life of Vincent Ferrer.

We have distanced ourselves from the "fire and brimstone" sermons that were so common for centuries. Perhaps some excessively graphic and imaginative portrayals of the punishment of sinners may have been overly vivid. Yet, the truth of the unpredictability of death, the certainty of judgment and the eternal consequences of sin are as true today as they ever were. The Lord teaches us in today's Gospel that the judgment can come to any of us at any age and at any hour.

Vincent Ferrer was vivid in his sermons because people had

become apathetic in an age of bewildering Church politics, divided leadership and popular superstition. He sounded a wake-up call for the Church.

We do not hear much about the Judgment today, yet do we really want a non-judgmental God? Are people who have raped, murdered, ravaged the poor and destroyed families to be exonerated in the end? It is comforting to know that the perfect justice that eludes us on earth will be found with God. It is comforting to know that the new creation will be peopled with souls that deserve to be there. It is comforting to know that repentance on earth brings fulfillment in heaven.

These teachings, central to the preaching of Vincent Ferrer, are as much of a fire bell to us today as they were 600 years ago... and as true!

APRIL 7 – ST. JOHN BAPTIST DE LA SALLE (MEMORIAL)

"No child left behind" is the name given to various initiatives to improve education. It could also be the theme of St. John Baptist de la Salle's life.

He was born in 1651 and became a pioneer in educational method, a leader in making education available to children of all sectors of society and a superb catechist as well.

John de la Salle popularized many things that we take for granted in our schools. Dividing children into grades of similar age aptitude, using the vernacular rather than Latin in classroom instruction, emphasizing the importance of visual aids such as the blackboard, and introducing all students to a range of subjects were enduring achievements in which he was a leader. His purpose, however, was not simply a secular one. He sought to enable young people to become strong in the grace of Jesus Christ, of which St. Paul speaks in today's first reading, as well as in fidelity to Christ's Church. He wanted no child to be hindered from coming to Jesus because of the circumstances of birth.

He founded "free schools" for the children of the poor, technical schools to help young people develop marketable skills and colleges to train future teachers. He truly wanted no child to be left behind. To achieve this goal, he founded the Brothers of the Christian Schools who today teach close to a million students in 80 countries.

John de la Salle's mission did not come to him in a single great burst of revelation. It gradually became clear to him through events. When he was relatively young, he had to take care of his siblings. Later as a priest, he assisted in managing a small "informal" school and gathered with men interested in committing themselves to teaching. When he began his congregation, a promising young teacher he had chosen for future leadership died before ordination. John de la Salle came to see this as God's will that the Christian Brothers would be composed exclusively of brothers.

The challenges of his time and the events of his life led John de la Salle to a strong vision of how to make Jesus Christ known. He did not retreat to the past but cleared the way to a new future. His message for us is that the past should not be a hideout but a springboard. The future does not lie in the past.

April 11 – St. Stanislaus (Memorial)

One of the striking phenomena surrounding the televising of the dying and death of Pope John Paul II was the number of people who expressed an interest in returning to or joining the Catholic Church. Perhaps more than his trips around the world, the fidelity and heroism of his last days moved millions.

This provides a connection to St. Stanislaus the bishop and martyr that we remember today. John Paul had been bishop of Cracow and so was Stanislaus, a thousand years earlier. Stanislaus had been born in Cracow, was ordained a priest in Cracow and became the bishop of Cracow. He opposed the public excesses and sins of rich and poor. He was a courageous bishop in that while condemning the sins of ordinary churchgoers is seen as part of his mission, criticizing the wealthy can have significantly negative material consequences for the life of the Church.

179

He also opposed the King Boleslaus who was violent, abusive and driven by lust. Finally, Boleslaus became so enraged at Stanislaus that he sent men to kill him. When he suspected that they were hesitant to carry out his order, he himself went to the church where Stanislaus was celebrating Mass and hacked him to pieces with his own hand.

This terrible act so enraged the people that Boleslaus was driven to leave public life. He went eventually to a Benedictine monastery to do penance where he spent the rest of his life. Boleslaus disappears from public records after that point. There is, however, more to the story. It is said that an eleventh century list of saints venerated by a Benedictine monastery in Poland includes the name, "Blessed Boleslaus, king and penitent."

The king could have gone into exile and remained there. Instead, he did penance because of the courage he saw in Stanislaus and Boleslaus became a "blessed" venerated locally at least. Sometimes when the intensity of emotion that accompanies our youth, our anger or volatile issues passes, we start to see ourselves in a clearer light. It is that moment that brings to mind the witness of people we have known who were loyal to Christ and His truth.

One point for all of us is that how we endure suffering, pain and tragedy is also a way of giving witness. Its impact may not be immediate, but our example enters people's deep memory and comes forward to them later in a moment of grace almost as a spiritual time release capsule.

Saint Stanislaus and Pope John Paul II show us that the moment of our weakness can also be the moment of our most powerful witness to Christ. Whatever else we may do in our life, fidelity and loyalty to Christ in the middle of difficulties are never forgettable. They can be the life preserver held in memory that can strengthen and save others.

April 13 – Pope St. Martin I (Optional Memorial)

Hidden deep within the history of the Church are stories of enormous heroism on behalf of the faith that are forgotten by most. Occasionally, a saint is recalled in the liturgy who reminds us of the enormous sacrifices that have been endured for the Gospel. Pope St. Martin I is one of those saints.

He was elected Pope in 649. He was faced with a threat to the Catholic faith that came from the East called monothelitism. It taught that although Jesus had two natures, He had only one will, a divine will. The result of this doctrine was to distance Jesus from us and empty His human nature of any real significance. If Jesus had only a divine will, then His human nature was an empty shell, only a kind of costume that He wore on earth. The teaching affirmed by Pope Martin and the Church today is that Jesus had two wills, human and divine.

Pope Martin gathered a council of bishops to condemn the Patriarch of Constantinople who taught this doctrine as well as the Emperor who promoted it as public policy. Martin's action enraged the Patriarch and, more importantly, the Emperor.

The Emperor sent an agent to assassinate Pope Martin. The plan was to have the Pope stabbed in the back as he gave the agent Communion. At the very last minute, he was unable to carry out the plan. He later recounted that he seemed to go blind and was unable to do the deed. The agent then told the Pope the entire story.

This did not deter the Emperor who sent another operative to kidnap the Pope. Pope Martin was very ill at this point. Knowing what was in store for him, he had himself carried into the Lateran Basilica on his bed and placed before the altar expecting respect for the church. The official and his men entered the church and took the Pope by force. He was transported from one prison to another, kept lying on a mat for an entire day exposed to the sun, ridiculed, given inedible food to eat and subjected to psychological and emotional abuse. Part of Martin's suffering was the indifference to his plight by his own people back in Rome who didn't seem to care whether he was alive or dead.

Finally, the Emperor had him condemned to death. Fearing the reaction of the populace, he sent him into exile where he died of starvation. Even though he died of natural causes, accelerated by vicious human cruelty, the Church regards him as a martyr. He was pope for only six years.

In every age and every generation, there are hidden stories of great heroism. These are people who, like Pope Martin, followed the path of the Lord not only in their hearts but in their bodies and lives as well. They have endured great suffering for the sake of the truth. They have given the passion of Christ a contemporary form.

Suffering is not a sacrament which automatically sanctifies. Suffering with and for the Lord opens the door to eternal life and the great embrace of Christ. The world may forget our suffering. Christ never will.

APRIL 21 – St. Anselm (Optional Memorial)

Anselm of Canterbury has been called the most important theologian in the Church between the time of St. Augustine and that of St. Thomas Aquinas.

His life began in Italy in 1033 and after some youthful wandering he became a Benedictine monk in France, then went to a monastery in England and was later made archbishop of Canterbury without a great deal of willingness on his part. Evidently the staff was put in his hand and he was taken to the church to be consecrated while the king ordered a hymn of praise.

While he was archbishop he was part of the usual taffy pull of politics between Church and State that dominated the 11th century. It was a continuing argument over rights, privileges, property ownership and, of course, revenues. Anselm stood firmly for the rights of the Church.

He was light in a dark time, however, in another way. During this time, theology was largely Biblical commentary. Anselm introduced rational analysis. To him belongs the famous saying to the effect that he does not analyze in order to believe, but believes in order to analyze. In other words, God has given us truth through His revelation. The work of theologian is to try to understand it and in so doing deepen our faith and marvel at God's wisdom.

Anselm was the place where reason and faith intersected magnificently and beautifully. He has quite appropriately been called the "father of medieval scholasticism."

To him belongs the famously maligned and praised ontological argument for God's existence about which one philosopher remarked that, to maintain sanity, no one should try to figure it out alone. Its thrust is to the effect that the idea of God planted in all of us is itself evidence of God.

St. Anselm also presented an analysis of our Redemption called the "Satisfaction theory of Atonement" to explain why Christ had to die on the cross. To satisfy God's justice, sin could not find full atonement through an ordinary man but only in a perfect man who was also God. The cross, therefore, shows us the evil of sin and the power of God's love.

Darkness can take many forms. So can light. In a time of darkness, Anselm was a magnificent light.

APRIL 23 – ST. GEORGE (OPTIONAL MEMORIAL)

To think of St. George is to picture the dragon. We all know the story of St. George and the dragon. A particular dragon terrorized townspeople. They assuaged its hunger by giving it various animals. Its hunger only grew more intense. At the end, it would only be satisfied by human sacrifice. St. George came, did battle with and slew the dragon dragging its carcass into the town to the rejoicing of all the people.

This story is the stuff of legend. In fact, St. George existed and was a martyr of the early Church. But the legends around him grew. Maybe the historical George did, in fact, slay some large animal to protect others and this became the basis of later stories.

The image of St. George and the dragon remains a potent one today. In parishes that have a children's parade of saints on All Saints' Day, several boys will inevitably choose to dress as St. George carrying a sword.

The picture of St. George is actually a kind of symbol of our redemption. George represents Christ who comes and slays the dragon of sin, dragging its remains into the town to the joy of all the people that Easter victory is ours. It is a strong Easter image.

The picture of St. George also represents a drama we hope to enact in our life as we try to slay the dragons of sin, abortion, and immorality in our day. We cannot do it on our own so we need the resources of Christ – the sword of His truth, the armor of His grace, the steed of His Eucharist. These are the spiritual arms on which we can rely in the battle we have to enter.

St. George and the dragon remain vivid and picturesque symbols of the drama of our redemption and of our life.

APRIL 23 – ST. ADALBERT (OPTIONAL MEMORIAL)

The rabbi, Gamaliel, once remarked that an endeavor that is from God cannot be destroyed. This can be applied to the work of St. Adalbert, who was put to death in 997, three years before the close of the first millennium.

Adalbert was born in Bohemia and took the name of the archbishop who had converted him. At the very early age of 30, he was made bishop of Prague. He sought to bring about moral reform in laity and clergy but his efforts were not appreciated and he was sent into exile in Rome.

While in Rome he lived as a Benedictine monk. The Pope then sent him back to Prague. There he met further opposition and, when he excommunicated a gang of politically connected cutthroats, he was sent into exile again.

The Pope sent him back as a missionary to Russia. He spread the Gospel but was accused of being a Polish spy. He was stabbed to death, by seven spears it is said, and died a martyr.

The spiritual and moral unity he sought, however, did not die with him. Man cannot kill the truth of the Word of God. The seeds his ministry sowed continued to grow.

Eventually a vigorous Christian community flourished in Poland and Russia. St. Adalbert's life and death teaches us not to assess the success of our life by what occurs in the years we have here on earth.

We may see the effect of our labor only in eternity. The people in Adalbert's time may have sent him into repeated exile but they could not exile the truth of Christ and the judgment of Christ.

If something is of man, it can be persecuted, hunted and even destroyed. But an enterprise that is from God will survive in our life or after it. But God's purpose will be done.

April 24 – St. Fidelis of Sigmaringen (Optional Memorial)

Probably every group and organization has its own special heroes. St. Fidelis is the protomartyr, the first martyr, of the Congregation for the Propagation of the Faith.

He was born in Germany in 1578. He became a lawyer and quickly became disenchanted with both lawyers and the legal profession. This led him to seek a deeper way of helping people by caring for their souls.

He joined the Capuchin Friars. He was sent by the Congregation for the Propagation of the Faith to preach the Catholic Faith in an area dominated by the Calvinists. During the time of the Reformation, this was like sending a tank into enemy territory. It was an "act of war."

Fidelis was a persuasive speaker and won many people back to the Faith. The politics of the Reformation were very volatile. Every action was given a sinister meaning and success was seen as a defeat for the other side. As Fidelis was preaching one day, a group of men attacked him in the church. He managed to escape but when he reaffirmed his Catholic Faith outside the church, he was clubbed and stabbed to death by a violent mob.

Still, through his strong faith in Christ he was given the grace of remaining faithful until the end. In the middle of that mob outside the church, Jesus gave Fidelis supernatural courage.

The storms we must weather today come in a variety of forms. In the time of St. Fidelis, they were the storms of religious controversy over doctrinal differences. Today, we face a different kind of storm. It is the storm of indifference and the homogenization of doctrines.

We can so easily lose what is distinctive to our Catholicism in an effort to be tolerant. Tolerance is a necessary virtue for harmony in society. Indifference can be deadly to our faith.

We need to respect the faith commitments of others. To be able to do so honestly, however, we need to know and respect our own Catholic faith even more.

APRIL 25 – ST. MARK (FEAST)

We hear the words, "A reading from the holy Gospel according to Mark" a great deal in church. Most of us do not know a great deal about this great and holy man. He was a companion to the Apostles, an evangelist and a martyr.

He came from a Christian family in Jerusalem. He was a nephew of Barnabas and had accompanied him and Paul on their first missionary journey. At one point, however, he left them perhaps intimidated by the difficulties of missionary life. When time came for the second missionary tour of Paul and Barnabas, Paul refused to take him along. Paul and Barnabas later separated from each other. Later reconciliation between Paul and Mark occurred because in his Letter to the Colossians, Paul mentions how valuable Mark was as his fellow-worker. These few facts show us that the first Christians were not plaster saints. The personal dynamics within the early Church were similar to those of today.

It is said that Mark recorded the memories of St. Peter whose companion he was as well. He witnessed the persecution and terror to which the Christians at Rome were exposed. He wanted them to know that however great the suffering they experience might be, the world is not wildly out of control. Jesus had foretold all of it. In his Gospel, he emphasizes the words of Jesus that we must pick up our cross and follow Him. This saying of Jesus is found at the heart, the very center of St. Mark's Gospel. The path to the glory of Jesus is by the way of the cross.

In today's Gospel reading, Jesus says that His disciples will be able to handle serpents and drink poisons without danger. Some Christian "snake handlers" have taken these words literally. Here, Jesus is speaking about the power of faith in Him. Nothing from the outside can destroy God's grace in our life except our own sin. Nothing from the outside can cancel the promise of Christ's victory in our life except our own sin. Nothing from the outside can defeat God's plan for our life except our own sin.

Mark experienced the cross about which he wrote. He became bishop of Alexandria and was martyred there. Mark wrote a Gospel whose simple, direct truth is a reality check for all of us. It is not the miracles but the cross that makes Jesus our Savior. It is not achieving miracles but carrying our cross that makes us disciples. In St. Mark's Gospel, the cross is a powerful lens that shows us the truth about the world, about Christ and about ourselves.

APRIL 28 – ST. PETER CHANEL (OPTIONAL MEMORIAL)

When a persecution broke out against the Church in Jerusalem scattering its members to the surrounding area, it had the effect of bringing about the first movement of evangelization.

We find the same phenomenon in the life of St. Peter Chanel. Peter Chanel was born in France in 1803. He was ordained to the priesthood and was sent to a parish for three years where he heard the call to be a missionary.

He joined the Society of Mary (the Marists) to be part of their evangelization of the South Pacific islands. Instead, he was sent to teach in the seminary for five years. Eventually, he was sent as the head of a mission band to go to the South Seas.

The Gospel was well received but as people began to take their new faith seriously, certain entrenched interests among the rulers of the islands were threatened. When the chief's own son decided to become Christian, the decision was made to kill Peter Chanel and his missionaries.

Peter was clubbed to death and became the first martyr of the South Seas. That was the bad news. The good news was that as a result of his martyrdom, within five months the entire island was converted to Christianity.

As one Church Father remarked, the blood of martyrs is the seed of Christians.

Peter Chanel's witness for Christ brought results almost immediately. It teaches us that planted within every event, even within a tragedy, is a seed of grace and new life.

Even our suffering can give glory to God in ways we least expect.

April 28 – St. Louis Mary de Montfort (Optional Memorial)

"Look for the silver lining" was the title of a song from many years ago. That is certainly the case of St. Louis Mary de Montfort, the "priest from Montfort," who lived a fascinating life filled with silver linings.

He was born in 1673 in Montfort, France. He studied under the Jesuits where he developed a strong devotion to Mary. He then went to the Sulpician seminary in Paris. He was ordained to the priesthood in 1700 and served in the hospital ministry. Deep within his heart, however, he wanted to be a missionary.

He spoke with the Pope who gave him the roving commission as an apostolic missionary to France. Louis de Montfort then began a ministry as a vagabond missionary, preaching missions in parishes, opposing various heresies and strengthening the Faith. For a variety of puzzling reasons, his work and preaching engendered opposition from clergy, various interest groups and bishops. Asked to leave one diocese, he went to another.

This harassment required him to move about and enabled him over a seventeen-year period to spread his mission work over a wide area and to spread devotion to Mary as well.

St. Louis de Montfort wrote several treatises on devotion to Mary: *True Devotion to Mary, The Secret of Mary,* and *The Secret of the Rosary.*

One of the features of his Marian devotion is a 33-day period of preparation for a total consecration to Mary. In this consecration to Mary, we commend all our talents, gifts and circumstances of life to Mary who in turn is to give them to Christ. One of the mottoes from St. Louis de Montfort expressing this dedication is *Totus Tuus* (Completely Yours).

Mary was the most completely dedicated disciple of Jesus. To consecrate oneself to Mary is to consecrate oneself to Christ. St. Louis did not see devotion to Mary as an alternative to devotion to the Lord. He teaches that the heart of true devotion to Mary is that it leads us to Christ.

St. Louis de Montfort provides us today with a muscular, virile expression of devotion to Mary, which powerfully connects us to Christ. This gift to the Church was the silver lining from the life of St. Louis de Montfort, the "vagabond missionary."

April 29 – St. Catherine of Siena (Memorial)

Catherine of Siena lived in the difficult 14th century which one writer called a "distant mirror" of our own. It was a time of wars, violence, scandal within the Church, chaos and disease. Yet, despite all that, it was a century of great mysticism in people who were very deeply into prayer. Catherine of Siena was one of them.

She came from a large family, had mystical experiences early in life and became a lay member of the Dominican Order. She engaged in various works of charity but people slowly began to discern in her an unusual wisdom. They came to her with problems, conflicts and eventually she became involved in politics, diplomacy and the tensions between the Pope and various city-states.

She learned this wisdom from prayer, the wisdom revealed to the little ones of which the Lord speaks in today's Gospel. The wisdom she learned in prayer plunged her into the affairs of society, Church and the souls of many people. There are some 400 letters of hers that still exist to people at all levels of society.

In the midst of deception, she spoke truth.

In the midst of scandal, she called for reform.

In the midst of indifference, she called for fidelity to the Church.

Faced with scandals in the Church, she repeatedly called the clergy back to the dignity to which they were ordained.

Pope Paul VI designated her a Doctor of the Church. She not only brought wisdom to her age but also served as a kind of spiritual physician to bring healing to a wounded time. Her prayer led her not to retreat from the problems of her time but to bring her faith to them. She died at the age of 33 in 1380.

We might not operate on such a large stage as Catherine did. But, like her, we can bring teaching and healing to people around us.

Our Baptism, like hers, can bring light to the darkness of any era.

April 30 – St. Pius V (Optional Memorial)

Pope St. Pius V lived in the mid-1500's. He was a reforming Pope in an age that needed reformation. It was the time of the Protestant revolt. Everyone agreed that reform was needed, but someplace else. As today, people loved to hear sermons about reform as long as nothing serious was done. The Council of Trent had been called but its sessions went on for some 18 years due to apathy and reluctance to engage serious reform.

When Pius V became Pope in 1566, he was neither apathetic nor reluctant to reform.

He began to enforce the spirit and the letter of the decrees of the Council of Trent, starting in Rome. Funds that were to be spent for his coronation as Pope were given to hospitals and to the poor. He eliminated bull fighting and gambling. He reformed the Roman Curia.

He reformed the Breviary by eliminating many legends about saints that had accumulated in its pages. He published the *Roman Catechism*, the predecessor of the *Catechism* we have today. He promulgated the Roman missal to standardize the way Mass was celebrated in a time of division and fracture.

The Papacy was very much a political office in those days and so he organized a coalition against the Turks that resulted in European victory at the Battle of Lepanto that saved Europe for Christianity. To attain victory, he asked the Christian world to pray the Rosary and has been called the Pope of the Rosary. As one poet remarked, he uplifted the Rosary like the rod of Moses to bring victory. He was a great reformer who was Pope for only six years but in those few years he achieved a great deal to keep the Church true to her mission.

It is very easy for us to drift away from the Lord in our life and in our prayer. Seldom is there any dramatic departure from Christ, just a slow ebbing away of faith. People like Pius V come to arouse us to look how far we have wandered and to call us back to the truth of Christ.

Critics are a dime a dozen. Genuine reformers are true gifts to the Church from Christ.

MAY 1 – ST. JOSEPH THE WORKER (OPTIONAL MEMORIAL)

This memorial of St. Joseph the Worker is a legacy to us of the period of the Cold War. It comes to us in 1955 from Pope Pius XII. Its purpose was to give a Christian alternative to the Communist May Day observances, which celebrated the Communist movement. Those observances were often anti-Christian and anti-Church as well as anti-democratic.

Today, Communism is largely gone and this feast remains to take on a different dimension. It calls on us to look carefully at our performance as Christians in the work we do. People should be able to depend on the quality, honesty, integrity and professionalism of our work whether it be with our minds or with our hands.

Today there is a tendency for some people to cut corners in the work they do and not take pride in what they have done. A good model for us, which is widely acknowledged, is the work done in any area by the Amish, who are known for their quality work.

People should be able to say that about all Christians. In whatever we commit ourselves to do as volunteers or as employees we should respect our work, respect our employer, and respect the work environment. We can make it a place where we can be light to people around us.

Frequently, the workplace can become a place of gossip, detraction, slander and even hostility. It may well be a place that needs something of Christ.

St. Paul once wrote to the Colossians that we should do our work for the Lord rather than only for others.

That is a splendid keynote for this feast of St. Joseph the Worker. Wherever we work, that is our place to be light to others and a place to serve the Lord.

MAY 2 – ST. ATHANASIUS (MEMORIAL)

A phrase about which we hear a great deal these days is the "culture war" in which many are engaged. It is a battle for which values will shape our society now as well as in the future. St. Athanasius was involved in a great theological war in his day. In that gigantic battle, he was both a strategist and a general.

Athanasius was a great teacher and Doctor of the Church. He lived in the 300's. He was part of a truly momentous crisis in the life of the Church. In fact, it was the first great internal crisis after the persecutions were over. It is as though the end of the great persecutions became a signal for Christians to persecute each other.

The conflict arose from the teaching of a man named Arius

who taught that Jesus was not fully God but a lesser god, a human being who became divine. Athanasius' position was that to become divine is not to be truly God in the same way as the Father. The fact was that Arius' teaching diminishes Christ. Athanasius taught that Jesus was truly God and truly man. In Jesus God became man, man did not become God. There is a world of difference between the two.

This debate ripped the Church apart. Eventually, all the bishops met in the Council of Nicaea in 325 and affirmed the traditional faith. Their teaching has come to us in an expanded version in the Nicene Creed. In its words, we can almost hear the Council fathers nailing down the truth about Jesus once and for all, "God from God, Light from Light, true God from true God, begotten not made, one in Being with the Father." Every Sunday, this Creed is an echo of that first major controversy in the Church.

Athanasius was a champion of the teaching of the Council of Nicaea. He did this not only by his own teaching but by gathering alliances, establishing support networks, influencing leaders and endorsing bishops who taught the truth. The words of Jesus predicting persecution describe exactly what happened to Athanasius. He became a bishop three years after the historic Council of Nicaea and spent the next half-century being hounded, slandered, persecuted, exiled and hunted by Arians of every kind. In fact, he spent more time out of his diocese than in it. But he stayed firm.

Athanasius is a saint not only because he affirmed the true faith but also because he was "faithful under fire." He is a good model for us. When all goes well, it is easy to be Christian. When our faith is challenged, especially by our culture, the real depth of our faith is exposed.

When we are engaged today in a "culture war" for the soul of our civilization, we can look to the example of the indomitable bishop Athanasius and ask his intercession that we would remain "faithful under fire" as he was.

May 3 – Sts. Philip and James (Feast)

Today we honor two great Apostles. Philip was the third one to be called by Jesus after Andrew and Peter. It is to Philip that Jesus speaks those great words that the one who sees Jesus sees the Father.

James was a relative of Jesus and author of the Letter of James in the New Testament. He was the first leader of the Jerusalem church and received a special appearance of the Risen Lord.

In the last analysis, we don't know much about Philip and James. We know little about their thoughts, feelings and dreams, which is the psychological aspect that so intrigues people today. Yet, in the larger plan of things it is not important how they felt. It is what they did that counts. They handed on the Faith and were a bridge from Christ to the rest of history.

That is also an important truth about our earthly life. Are we handing on the Faith? Are we a bridge from Jesus Christ to others?

To walk through a cemetery is to see many names inscribed on the stones. In some cases, the elements have over time obscured the names so that only God knows their identity. Their final and lasting reward is from God. We know few details of their accomplishments, thoughts, feelings and dreams.

What is important about their earthly life is whether they knew the Lord and whether they were a bridge from Christ to others or a barrier.

A question we can ask ourselves on this feast of Philip and James is whether we are a bridge to Christ or a barrier.

A bridge or a barrier? Baptism calls us to be a bridge. Sin makes us a barrier.

Long after our accomplishments are forgotten, the answer to that question – bridge or barrier – will be the most important truth about our life as it was for Philip and James.

MAY 10 – ST. DAMIEN OF MOLOKAI (OPTIONAL MEMORIAL)

"Father Damien" was born in Belgium in 1840. He joined the Fathers of the Sacred Hearts of Jesus and Mary and went to work among the lepers in Molokai.

Leprosy is known today as "Hansen's disease" to which the great majority of people in the world are naturally immune. That was not known in earlier days and so lepers were isolated from the rest of society. Here, they were restricted to the Hawaiian island of Molokai.

Father Damien worked among them and eventually contracted leprosy himself. It was a dramatic moment when he began his sermon one day with the words, "Fellow lepers."

He may not have been able to bring them healing in body but he did bring them healing in soul and spirit. Through his ministry, he taught them that whatever society may do, Jesus Christ loves them. Through the Church and the Eucharist the Lord came to them to dwell among them as Jesus promises in today's Gospel reading.

Society has had and always will have its prejudices and its assumptions as to who counts and who doesn't. But society's assumptions are not those of the Lord. However society sees an individual, Jesus sees a soul of eternal value that He brought into being and wants to be with Him forever.

We need to bring that message of Jesus to our society. Father Damien's work with the lepers was a message to his time that they counted and that whatever the disease with which they were burdened, they remained human beings with dignity and purpose.

One way we can serve our world today is to remind people of the inherent dignity of every individual even though that person may be stigmatized because of an illness, handicap or disease they have. The young and the beautiful fascinate our society. The message of the Church to our time is that every person counts.

Father Damien died at the age of 49.

May 12 – Sts. Nereus and Achilleus (Optional Memorial)

Saints Nereus and Achilleus were praetorian guards in the Emperor Diocletian's army. The tradition about them is that they persecuted Christians as they were ordered to do but at some point they were converted to the Gospel of Jesus Christ.

At that point, they threw down their armor and weapons and served the Gospel with the same fervor and drive they had given the Emperor. Eventually, they were sent into exile and martyred. All this occurred around the year 300.

We all have competing loyalties in our life. We have obligations to family, friends, work, parish and various organizations to which we may belong. Sometimes, we have to engage in a kind of triage to establish priorities since we cannot do everything for everyone.

What will be the ultimate loyalty in our life? If the Gospel of Jesus Christ takes first place, then we will respond to all of our other responsibilities as disciples of Christ. If consumer goods have first place, then our faith becomes a vehicle for accumulation of more goods.

With most of us, it is a matter of arranging priorities. Sometimes, however, there is a conflict between loyalties that are diametrically opposed. We cannot be a member of an anti-Christian organization and a faithful Catholic as well. In such a case, we are called to decide whom we will serve as were Nereus and Achilleus.

The choice they faced was common in the ancient world and common in our own. One difference, however, is that the early Christians made a choice. Today, people prefer to amble along with several half-hearted commitments never really embracing any one completely. When our life is crowded with opposing commitments we have no center, no rudder by which to direct our life. We are pulled in many directions. Our life is not a journey but an aimless wandering back and forth.

Nereus and Achilleus teach us that the union with the strong and Risen Christ, like branch to vine, is not for the half-hearted but for those who give themselves completely to Christ.

Blessed indeed are the single-hearted, for they shall see God.

May 12 – St. Pancras (Optional Memorial)

A government decides to exterminate a whole class of people in an effort to bring about a "final solution" to their existence. One of these targeted people, a young boy, is arrested and brought before the leader. He is cajoled and then threatened if he will not surrender his belief. He refuses and is put to death.

The facts of this story could be from our modern world but come from the 3rd century in the Roman Empire.

Pancras was a young orphan whose parents had died when he was nine years old. Raised by a relative in Rome, he converted to the Christian faith. It was at this time that the Emperor Diocletian had organized an empire wide persecution to stamp out Christianity once and for all. Young Pancras, now fourteen years old, was arrested and brought before the Emperor. He refused to betray Christ or other Christians. He was then put to death and fellow Christians later secretly buried his body.

When Constantine became Emperor, Christianity was legalized a few years later and a church was built over the place of Pancras' grave. The Emperor Diocletian is known today only for his failed persecution. Pancras is known for his heroism that inspired others and strengthened the Church.

The words of Jesus that He is the Vine and we are the branches who draw life and vigor from Him proved true in the case of Pancras. This young man showed extraordinary courage in the face of a terrible persecution.

The story of Pancras reminds us that in all the conflicts we face, there stands at our side the silent, invisible presence of the Risen Christ. We are not facing any enemy or opposition alone.

After the death of his parents and guardian, Pancras seemed to be all alone in the world. Yet, at his side, was the Risen Christ who led him into eternal life.

However it might look to the world, the Christian is never alone.

May 13 – Our Lady of Fatima (Optional Memorial)

Today's memorial remembers the apparitions of Mary to three peasant children in Fatima, Portugal in the year 1917. In the course of these apparitions, Mary spoke to the children and through them to the world about the importance of prayer and penance to reverse the disastrous moral slide of the world toward war.

In the course of these apparitions, Mary entrusted messages to the children about the sufferings which the Church and the world would endure through war and communism. Through the power of prayer and penance, however, Mary's Immaculate Heart and our continuing fidelity to Christ would triumph.

The messages of Fatima are often portrayed as messages of apocalypse and future disaster. They really are messages of hope that the power of prayer is greater than the powers of evil.

Communism is in large part gone from the world stage. Other forces that oppose the Gospel of life and of justice remain. As damaging as communism was to people years ago, human dignity today is being destroyed by the abortion industry, the pornography industry, the drug industry, the weapons industry, and corporations that place the size of their profit above the value of people. All of these are formidable forces larger than any one person, which can destroy the bodies and souls of millions.

The message of Fatima and its call to live in Christ's love as Jesus commands in today's Gospel reading is as relevant today as it was in 1917. The players on the world stage have changed. The shape of evil has taken on forms different and more ominous than atheistic communism because they are not external to but within our own society. But the power of prayer, described with such drama to Lucia dos Santos and Francisco and Jacinta Marto by Mary remains a formidable counterforce to evil.

When we feel impotent in the face of such gigantic and well-financed forces of sin, the message of Mary reminds us of the power of prayer especially the Rosary and the power of conversion of life to do battle with evil.

The appearances at Fatima remind us that the Church militant will become the Church at rest only at the end of history. Until then, we fight the good fight through prayer and penance.

May 14 – St. Matthias (Feast)

Matthias' life speaks to all of us. When he became a follower of Jesus, he probably never dreamed that one day he would become one of the Twelve. But that is what happened.

They cast lots in the Holy Spirit and he won the lottery. That could make him the patron saint of lotteries or of delayed vocations.

So often, things don't turn out as we plan them. In any profession or vocation, the circumstances of our life in our later years are far different from what we had projected when we were young. People have images of the ideal marriage, the ideal family, the ideal job and things don't turn out as we plan.

Spouses have problems, children have difficulties, and a job has a downside to it that we never anticipated.

We would love to decide what following God's call to us should be like. But God's will is not necessarily our will. Things happen that we don't expect but slowly God's will starts to become apparent to us as it did for Matthias.

One message of Matthias' life is to follow the call as it comes. Jesus says that He chose us to go forth and bear fruit. Plants don't simply grow. They need to be planted somewhere, in some location and if they take root, they will thrive. They can't simply stay on a shelf or they will die.

So it is with us. We cannot be forever planning to do God's will on our terms. Through events in our life, the Lord plants us in a particular location: this family, this job, this parish, this spouse, and this ministry.

Here is where we are to take root and when God gives the growth, we will thrive.

Matthias shows us that God calls us in ways we least expect. If we don't follow, we will stay forever on the shelf waiting for what we prefer and all the while dying inside.

If we follow the Lord's call, we will grow and thrive.

May 15 – St. Isidore the Farmer (Optional Memorial)

There is something enchanting about the life of Isidore the Farmer. He is called Isidore the Farmer to distinguish him from Isidore of Seville, a great bishop after whom he had been named.

The words of Jesus about the world hating His followers do not seem to apply to Isidore. He was born in 1070 in Madrid. He worked as a farmer for the same employer throughout his entire life. He and his wife had a child who died early. Isidore and his wife then dedicated themselves to Christ.

The world of faith was very real to Isidore. He spoke with the saints as he plowed the fields. He went to Mass before going to work each day. It is said that he was seen to have angel helpers for his plowing.

Miracles of healings and natural springs bubbling to life are attributed to him. Long after Isidore's death, the King of Spain credited a particular military victory to his intervention.

His life seems to have been a profoundly simple one, filled with faith, prayer and work for the Lord. Yet, rural life is never as simple as it appears. Human nature does not change because people live in the country. The area where he lived probably had its share of crime, detraction and complaint. Isidore chose not to take part in those aspects of life.

The apparent simplicity of his life must have taken a great deal of work to achieve and maintain. Therein probably lies the key to his holiness. He withstood the siren call of life around him and kept his focus on working for the Lord. That made him a saint.

The lesson we can learn from Isidore the Farmer is that it takes a great deal of work to remain simple and uncomplicated at heart.

May 18 – St. John I (Optional Memorial)

Things are often not what they appear to be. If a stranger were to pass by the hill of Calvary at the time of Christ's death, he would conclude that Jesus was an unrighteous sinner and therefore had been correctly condemned. Jesus taught that His Resurrection would reverse all that.

His Resurrection would demonstrate that the ones who crucified Him were the sinners. He was the righteous one suffering for their sins and His crucifixion brought judgment and condemnation on the way of the world because Jesus' Resurrection shows that dying is the way to eternal life.

This reversal of values is also manifest in the life of Pope John I. He was Pope in the 6th century for a brief period of three years. At that time the Church was split by the Arian heresy. The King of Italy was an Arian while the Eastern Roman Emperor in Constantinople was Catholic.

The Emperor had issued a decree imposing penalties on the Arians and confiscating their property. The King of Italy wanted that decree mitigated. He sent a high level delegation headed by John I to persuade the Emperor to take the pressure off the Arians.

John and his delegation were greeted in Constantinople with extraordinary honor. The crowds, the clergy and the Emperor were exceedingly deferential to him. It was evidently a glorious arrival. The result of John's delegation was some mitigation of the law against the Arians, a unifying of the Church of the West with the patriarchs of the Eastern Church and the papal crowning of the Emperor. The delegation was a great success.

Meanwhile, the paranoid King of Italy saw these events differently. He saw it as an alliance to usurp his power. When John returned home, he was thrown into prison where he was starved to death. The Church has always honored him as a martyr.

One would have thought that John's magnificent entry into Constantinople was his moment of glory. Yet, his real moment of glory was alone in the prison awaiting death. In this true reversal of values, John showed his real fidelity to Christ.

The real glory of our life is not in the moments of acclaim but in how we are willing to suffer for Christ. It is in suffering, not acclaim that the truth of our fidelity is made clear.

MAY 20 – ST. BERNARDINE OF SIENA (OPTIONAL MEMORIAL)

St. Bernardine of Siena was a Franciscan saint of the 15th century. We all know of Catherine of Siena who deeply affected her century. Bernardine's impact is still with us very vividly. He was born in beautiful Tuscany in 1380 and his family lived outside Siena.

He became a Franciscan and the most famous preacher of his day. Bernardine would draw great crowds into the city square, preach for several hours and then set up the "bonfire of the vanities" into which people would throw all their extravagances such as paintings, cosmetics and today we would add cell phones and CDs.

The other feature of his preaching is that he popularized the most familiar symbol or "logo" of Catholicism, the "IHS" with rays radiating from it. Some say the "IHS" stands for the first three letters of Jesus' name in Greek. Others say it is an acronym for *Iesus Hominum Salvator* (Jesus Savior of all men). Today, anachronistically, some say it represents the words "I Have Suffered."

He would hold up this symbol at the end of his sermon and people would venerate it. Today, we see it represented all over especially in religious houses that he founded. Eventually, it seems to have been taken over by the Jesuits.

This memorial of St. Bernardine calls us to reflect on the name of Jesus. It is a name of great peace and great power. The Eastern Church for centuries has made use of the "Jesus prayer" which is a slow repetition of the name to allow its grace and power to enter our heart. Just to say the holy name of Jesus over and over is a magnificent prayer.

Bernardine called the name of Jesus the refuge of sinners, banner of the warrior, medicine of the ailing, comfort of the suffering, splendor of the believer, help of the weak, joy of the contemplative and glory of the saints. It is a name that can release into us the deep joy of the soul of which the Lord speaks.

St. Bernardine died on Ascension Thursday many years ago but his logo, the "IHS," and the name it represents, remains very much a part of Catholic life like a time release capsule, releasing its power, joy and peace into our lives even today.

MAY 21 – ST. CHRISTOPHER MAGALLANES AND COMPANIONS (OPTIONAL MEMORIAL)

Today, we celebrate the memorial of Father Christopher Magallanes and his 24 companions, 25 Mexican martyrs of the 20th century and literally in our own backyard.

The separation of Church and State has been a part of Mexico's Constitution since the mid-19th century. In the early 20th century, however, the Mexican government began to enforce that separation with a series of laws that not only separated Church from State but also burdened and persecuted the Church.

Parochial schools were outlawed, seminaries and convents were closed, worship outside church buildings was prohibited, public wearing of religious garb by clergy was forbidden, non-Mexican clergy were expelled, and Church property was nationalized. This led the archbishop of Mexico to place the country under interdict forbidding liturgical services.

In 1926, a small group of Catholics began to fight to restore their religious freedom. They took the name "Cristeros" or followers of Christ. Soon, their ranks swelled to 50,000. The government's response was further repression.

Priests were jailed and then executed. Among these was Father Christopher Magallanes who was shot to death on May 25, 1927. He and the other priests had been available to provide the Mass and the Word of God to the Cristeros. They were implicated as aiding and abetting the Cristeros and were put to death. The battle cry of the martyrs was to shout, "Viva Cristo Rey!" as they died ("Long live Christ the King"). At that moment, as Jesus foretold in the Gospel, their earthly grief was turned into eternal joy.

The persecution was massive and nationwide. Yet, it showed the deep attachment of the Mexican people to their Faith, the loyalty of priests to their vocation, and the ultimate impotence of the government to kill the Faith.

The story of the Cristeros war should cause us to thank God for the freedom of religion we enjoy in this country and to recall that the persecution of the Church, the death of its martyrs, and the heroic efforts of priests to bring the Gospel to the people did not occur in some distant century in a far away land.

It happened in our own back yard, a few miles from El Paso!

MAY 22 – ST. RITA OF CASCIA (OPTIONAL MEMORIAL)

St. Rita of Cascia is a medieval saint from the 14th century who is also very contemporary.

She was born in 1371, the only child of older parents. Her parents seem to have been peacemakers in the neighborhood where they lived and in later life Rita would be one as well. She wanted to become a nun but her parents informed her that they had already chosen the man she was to marry.

Seeing this as God's will, Rita married the man her parents had chosen and together they had two sons. Her husband turned out to be very abusive toward her as well as her sons. After a difficult twenty-year marriage, he was stabbed to death as part of a local vendetta.

She told her sons to forgive his murderers and not seek revenge but they didn't listen and were themselves murdered shortly thereafter.

Rita wanted to then become a nun but the convent refused her because they thought she might bring the town vendetta with her into the convent. Rita managed to reconcile the families of her husband and his killers and was then allowed to enter the convent. She was a nun for forty years spending her life in prayer. For the last fifteen years of her life, her forehead was pierced with a kind of stigmata by a thorn wound indicating her closeness to the Passion and sacrificial love of Christ.

There is a touching story told from the last year of her life. A friend visited her and asked if she had any requests. Rita asked that a rose be brought to her from her parents' garden. Since it was January, the visitor imagined the request would be impossible to fulfill. She went to the garden and a rose bloomed there just as Rita had indicated. The rose became a symbol of St. Rita as the saint of impossible requests. She could as well be the patron of abused spouses.

A wife, a mother, a widow and a nun, Rita was a woman of peace in every situation. She lived a difficult life in a difficult time. Still, through her union with Christ, as the Lord says, her joy was complete.

St. Rita was a medieval saint but very much our contemporary.

MAY 25 – ST. BEDE THE VENERABLE (OPTIONAL MEMORIAL)

St. Bede the Venerable entered a Benedictine monastery when he was seven years of age and left only at his death at 65.

Bede represents the splendid Anglo-Saxon Catholic culture of Northumbrian England in the 7th century. Although he never left the monastery, he wrote some 45 volumes about theology, Scripture and history. His *Ecclesiastical History of the English People* recounts the story of Christianity from its beginnings to his day. He carefully researched sources to produce an elegant and reliable account of the growth of the Faith and of early Britain.

He was ordained a priest at the age of thirty. His formal ministry took place within the confines of two joint monasteries. His entire life, in fact, was circumscribed within a fifty-mile radius. Yet his mind traveled to the past, commented on the present and provided a history to inspire the future. It is said that he popularized the use of B.C. and A.D. to designate years before and after Christ.

Some people are called to show their faith by enduring torture in their bodies. Others show their faith with their minds. The blood of martyrs is called the seed of the Church. St. Bede also seeded the Church of the future by his history, his homilies (still found in the Liturgy of the Hours), his commentaries and his theological writings.

His life was not as dramatic as that of some martyrs but it was as important. Heroism can come in many forms. There is the heroism of courageous witness in the face of persecution. There is also the heroism of quiet, faithful study and reflection. They are different faces of faithfulness.

St. Bede's writings are his gift to the Church's memory. They give us hope for the future as they display the work of God's grace in the past.

May 25 – St. Gregory VII (Optional Memorial)

Jesus prayed at the Last Supper for His Apostles as He was leaving the world that they would have the grace of fidelity and courage. Implied in the Lord's words are the persecutions that will come.

It is important that our spirituality and reflection keep unified the Death and Resurrection of the Lord. Isolating either component of the Paschal Mystery can create a lop-sided spirituality that can result in either a mystique of pain or a religion of cheap grace.

Persecution can take many forms. Gregory VII was a powerful, reforming Pope around the year 1000. He is the Pope best known to history as the one to whom the Holy Roman Emperor, Henry IV, came to Canossa to seek forgiveness and seek the reversal of Gregory's excommunication of him.

Yet, Gregory died in exile. What appeared to be a moment of triumph on that wintry afternoon at Canossa was really the beginning of Gregory's end as the Emperor began to plot revenge.

The issue was the liberty and independence of the Church. It centered on the custom of "lay investiture" which Gregory considered the root of all evil in the Church at that time. This meant that lay people (usually government officials or royalty) had the right to nominate people to the office of bishop. That right had been acquired in all kinds of ways over the years.

Gregory sought to recover that right for the Church. He asserted that Church officials should not be the creatures or pawns of secular rulers but the agents of Jesus Christ and truly bishops of the Church and not of the regime. It was a difficult and protracted controversy.

Gregory won the first round but Henry came back a few years later to send Gregory into exile. That right would never be fully recovered for the Church in Gregory's time. But he drew a line and made a beginning, which broke his health.

There are many ways of experiencing the Paschal Mystery of dying and rising with Christ. Standing for the rights of the Church is one of them.

May 25 – St. Mary Magdalene de Pazzi (Optional Memorial)

May 25th of each year gathers as optional memorials three very different kinds of saints. The first is St. Bede living in a monastery in the lush Northumbrian hills of Britain using his formidable powers of intellect to teach and write about the Faith. The second is Pope Gregory VII, a fiery reformer, ready to do battle against heretic and emperor at the drop of a hat to defend the rights of the Church. The third is St. Mary Magdalene de Pazzi, a Carmelite mystic who went down into depths to experience the heights of union with Christ.

She was born in Florence in 1566. In her early life she displayed openness to prayer and mystical experiences. She entered the Carmelite convent. At the time of her entry, she became ill and went through forty days of ecstasies and visions.

Afterwards, she subjected herself to great mortifications by her attraction to the crucified Christ. This was followed by a very long period of depression. She experienced a dark night of the soul that lasted for years. Through all that, she came to trust in

Christ's grace without relying on any accompanying "feelings" of grace.

Out of her journey into the darkest night a human being can know, the night of depression, she emerged with a profoundly personal relationship with Christ.

Through her struggles, she manifested gifts of healing and prophecy as well as the ability to read minds. Once remarking on the subject of her visions and ecstasies, she indicated that she received them because the Lord judged that she needed them. Others whose faith is stronger do not. That is a splendidly comforting piece of wisdom for us.

She died in 1607 after a long illness at the age of 41. One lesson for us from St. Mary Magdalene de Pazzi's life is that even the darkness can serve the light. If she had known only the conventional spirituality, perhaps she would not have become the saint she was. She required something more.

We don't know the causes of depression and the dark night. The psalmist says that whatever the heights or depths to which we go, God is there. What Mary Magdalene de Pazzi's life does teach us is that however dark the night we experience, Jesus is there to lead us back to the light.

Maybe some people experience the night to be able to later lead others to the light.

May 26 – St. Philip Neri (Memorial)

Philip Neri, the saint of a joyful heart, was born in 1515 in Florence. He was ready to go into business but underwent a mysterious period of conversion that began his total dedication to Christ.

He went on a pilgrimage to Rome. There, working as a part-time tutor to earn his living, he lived in an attic almost like a hermit deep in prayer. He emerged out of this seclusion and, after some study, became a "street preacher" among the younger people of the city of Rome. People were attracted to his message at a time when the Faith had been weakened in Rome.

He encouraged those drawn to him to show their faith by caring for the sick and infirm. Eventually he was ordained and was able to continue his work of counseling and leading people to conversion through the confessional. He had wanted to go abroad as a missionary but was told that his mission was at home, in Rome.

He preached the gospel with geniality and good humor. His attractive personality drew people to him and through him to Christ. His work became so extensive that he had five of his companions ordained to the priesthood and they became the beginning of the Congregation of the Oratory.

They established a community where people could come and hear teaching, reflection, Mass and receive spiritual direction.

Jesus prayed at the Last Supper not that the Apostles be taken out of the world but that they be kept safe from the Evil One while in the world. St. Philip Neri teaches us that to be in the world does not necessarily mean to be away from Christ. Philip Neri knew the pains and sufferings of people as any spiritual director does. But he had the gift of enabling people to see in their life a sharing in the life of Christ. He brought a sense of mission and purpose to everyone he met.

He showed them that our life is a journey not to death but to glory. Pressure can crush a stone or turn coal into a diamond. Philip Neri helped people see the diamond they can become.

He died at the age of 80, himself a diamond for Christ.

MAY 27 – ST. AUGUSTINE OF CANTERBURY (OPTIONAL MEMORIAL)

Augustine of Canterbury was a great missionary. He was the very first archbishop of Canterbury and also the "Apostle of England." He can also be called the patron saint of what is called today "inculturation."

Augustine lived in the late 500's. He was a Benedictine monk in Rome when he was selected by Pope Gregory I (the "Great") along with 40 others to bring the Gospel to the Anglo-Saxon peoples of England.

After some hesitation on Augustine's part and a great deal of encouragement from Pope Gregory, he proceeded to Britain and converted the king and his court. The growth of the Catholic Faith was not uniform throughout the British Isles but where it did grow it became strong. Designated an archbishop, he began to establish dioceses and a Catholic culture began to grow.

One of the famous pieces of correspondence between Augustine and Pope Gregory concerned the pagan customs he found in abundance. Gregory's wise advice to Augustine was not to oppose but to Christianize the customs, sacred days and symbols he found. That is what Augustine did and the faith thrived.

There is discussion today about the reach and limits of "inculturation." There are those Christians who are not only counter-cultural but who hate the culture. For them, the world is corrupt and Catholicism can only survive by separating itself completely from the ambient culture.

Another approach, sanctioned by centuries of missionary activity by the Jesuit Fathers, is to be counter-cultural but to "baptize" the culture in whatever way we can. One ancient Church Father spoke of "seeds of the Word" that are present in every culture. It takes a discerning eye and a discerning Catholic faith to determine what can be used to express the Faith and what is intrinsically hostile to the Faith. It takes a careful eye to separate what is of Christ and what is of Europe.

Augustine of Canterbury reminds us that Christ is no longer limited to any one culture or place. Now, He belongs to the whole human race.

Every culture, even our own, can be a home for Christ.

May 31 – Visitation of the Blessed Virgin Mary (Feast)

Today, we celebrate the feast of the Visitation, known to us as the second joyful mystery of the Rosary. The visit to Elizabeth by Mary is not just a link between relatives but of two people graced by God in different ways and both bringing Scripture to fulfillment. Elizabeth is bringing forth John the Baptist, the herald of

Christ to Judaism, and Mary will give birth to Jesus, the Savior of the world.

On a personal level, this is more than a visit of a very short duration. Mary stayed with Elizabeth for three months to help her during her pregnancy.

Let's reflect briefly on that little detail of the three months over which the Gospel seems to slide.

There are many paintings and sketches of the Visitation scene, that initial encounter of Mary and Elizabeth. There are no portrayals of Mary during those three months. She was evidently doing the work, making the meals, keeping things in order, working behind the scenes. Nothing about those three months has surfaced in traditional devotional material.

Yet, those three months showed Mary to be a true handmaid of the Lord.

One test of our spirituality is what we do when nobody is watching, when the cameras are turned off and when we don't feel inspired and "charged-up." Are we as faithful in private as we are in public? Mary was.

Mary is still helping people behind the scenes in so many ways today. Mary assists people not only in such well-publicized shrines as Fatima and Lourdes but also in ways that will probably never be known to most of us here on earth. Every parish has people who can recount interventions by Mary, some spectacular and others less so, where Mary's prayer and intercession became a decisive part of their lives.

In this mystery of the Visitation, that holy visit of three months, we see Mary as a model of true spiritual service, quiet and silent service. She is a model of the kind of life St. Paul describes in that extraordinary litany in today's first reading in which he gives us a program to last a lifetime.

This feast of the Visitation invites us to seek the grace (and it is a grace) and the virtue (and it is a virtue) of quiet service of the Lord. It is the real measure of our fidelity to Christ.

Friday after Corpus Christi – The Most Sacred Heart of Jesus (Solemnity)

Although the feast of the Sacred Heart is a few centuries old, the devotion and reflection on the heart of Christ go back to the early centuries of the Church's life. It initially took the form of meditation on the blood and water flowing from Jesus' side.

The heart represents the center of a person. It registers our emotions. We speak about the "Valentine heart," "I heart New York," "You broke my heart," "Cross my heart," "Your cheatin' heart," "Be still my heart," "My heart sank," Without the heart, nothing else works. The brain cannot function without blood from the heart. The heart is a powerful muscle. It pumps 2000 gallons of blood a day. It beats 100,000 times a day. Over a lifetime of seventy years, it will beat 2.5 billion times. It is a powerful symbol of Christ's love for us.

In the mid 1600's, there was a heresy called Jansenism that taught that whole sectors of the human race are doomed to hell. It was at that time that the Lord appeared to St. Margaret Mary Alacoque to speak of His love for all people and His desire for all people to be saved. To show that, the Lord pointed to His heart.

This Sacred Heart devotion was later spread by the Jesuit Fathers through the "Apostleship of Prayer," the Sacred Heart television program, Enthronements of the image of the Sacred Heart, the Sacred Heart badge and Morning Offering, the promotion of the First Friday devotion of which the Lord spoke to St. Margaret Mary together with the Great Promises. All of this was to enable us to experience and embrace the transforming love of Christ. We can picture the love of Christ through contemporary images that derive from the readings for each of the lectionary years.

Year A suggests the picture of a father embracing a small child not because of the child's accomplishments or personality but simply out of love. In fact, the more the child is hurting, the greater is the father's love. God's love is like that.

Year B implies the image of a father's sacrificial love for his child. He is willing to donate a bodily organ, risk his life or spend all he has for the child. God's love is like that.

Year C points to the image of a father in search of a lost child, driving, seeking and looking for a child to bring him or her home. God's love is like that.

The feast of the Sacred Heart reminds us that however much we may have sinned, Christ's love is greater than our sin.

The Immaculate Heart of the Blessed Virgin Mary (Memorial)
Saturday after the Second Sunday after Pentecost

The memorial of the Immaculate Heart of Mary follows the Solemnity of the Sacred Heart not only in the calendar but also in Catholic logic and devotion. The Sacred Heart speaks to us of Christ's love for us and so does the heart of Mary.

There is an old saying, "There's no place like home." Home is a refuge, a port in a storm, a safety net, and a place to regain strength, to recover perspective, to nourish our roots and to be safe. Mary's heart is all that for us.

Different generations have seen different strengths in Mary: obedience, courage, fidelity, compassion and faith during grief. Now Mary shows the way to the Risen Lord, now Mary calls us to penance, now she gives us assurance of victory in Christ.

All of these aspects of Mary's heart are gathered in the Litany of Loreto. Each title in that litany has its own story to tell, its own truth about Mary. But the greatest title of Mary is, of course, "Mother." Her heart pondered the great events that took place in her Son's Life (as in today's Gospel), her heart was pierced with a sword and her heart knew the agony of Good Friday and the joy of Easter like no other. That heart is home to all of us.

Mary's heart is called "immaculate" because it was an uncorrupted heart. We all know how vices and angers can corrupt and entangle our heart. Mary's heart was uncorrupted by those forces and she can help us rehabilitate our heart to make it healthy, strong and at peace.

Mary's heart was immaculate because it was clear and open to the Father, Son and Holy Spirit. One writer called Mary's heart the "clean page" on which the Father wrote the Word. Mary can help us be open to God's Word and will.

Mary's heart was immaculate because it was never touched by sin. Ours has been cleansed from sin and Mary can enable us to now remain firm in Christ's grace.

The memorial of the Immaculate Heart of Mary reminds us that we all have a place we can call home, where our hearts can be made strong, open and firm in grace. That place, home to us all, is the Immaculate Heart of Mary.

JUNE 1 – ST. JUSTIN (MEMORIAL)

Public television and cable channels have become well known for all sorts of quest programs: the search for the source of the Nile, for the secret of the pyramids, for the ancient city of Troy, for UFOs etc.

There is something about the quest and the search that resonates within the human heart perhaps because we are all on a journey.

Justin was on a search. He was a scholar who was born early in the 2nd century. He spent his early life traveling from teacher to teacher in search of wisdom, seeking deep answers to deep questions. One day, he came upon an old man by the sea who spoke to him about the Hebrew prophets and how their prophecies were fulfilled in Jesus Christ.

That led to Justin's conversion to Christ and a life of confessing the Christian faith. He became a strong defender of Christianity in days when Christians were suspect. Justin gives us the earliest account of a Christian liturgy we have which he wrote to dispel rumors about what happens at the Christian Mass. Finally, in 165 he was put to death for the Faith. To this day he is called "Justin Martyr." For his time, he was the salt and light Jesus describes.

The message of Justin's life for us is that neither theory nor theology can redeem us and set us free. What we have in Jesus

Christ is not a theory but a saving action. Jesus is not a philosopher but a Redeemer. Jesus died for our sins and rose from the dead. If we open our lives to Him, the Lord gives us not just new understanding or a deeper view of God but the very power of God called the Holy Spirit.

There is a fallacy called "Greek intellectualism" that if we know the truth, we will follow it. Our experience shows us that is not the case. We know the truth about lots of things and the damage they can do to us, yet addicts of every sort abound. We do not need more information but redemption. We need rescue not only from bad ideas but also from the grip of sin.

Surrender to Jesus brings that redemption and rescue. Jesus is our Savior not only because of what He said but also because of what He did. That saving act was made present at the Mass Justin described with such detail and at every Mass today to cleanse us and set us free.

JUNE 2 – STS. MARCELLINUS AND PETER (OPTIONAL MEMORIAL)

The known facts of the lives of Saints Marcellinus and Peter are few. Most of what we know about them is about their death. Those details come from Pope Damasus who said he had spoken to their executioner.

They died in the year 304 during the persecution by Diocletian. Marcellinus was a priest and Peter was in minor orders. Arrested and tried secretly, they were led to a forest area, told to dig their graves and then were beheaded with their bodies thrown into the very graves they had dug.

They must have had a special standing among the Christians at Rome since their arrest and trial were done secretly. Their death was not meant to be a deterrent but to remove their influence. Of course, the opposite occurred. They were honored by the Roman Christians as great heroes and their names are included in the Roman Canon of the Mass.

Every generation and part of the Church has its martyrs. They remain examples to us of a heroism that we think to be impossible. We live in an age of lowered expectations spiritually. The example of the martyrs shows us the depth and height of commitment that can be ours.

In a time when people judge Christians by the worst among us, the example of the martyrs shows us the best in fidelity. We should judge the Church not by its worst but by its best.

There are, of course, many kinds of saints in the Church. But martyrs are given a special place because they stand for the clear, pure and undiluted fidelity to which we all can aspire. We live in an age of compromise when everything seems negotiable. The martyrs remind us that some things are non-negotiable for which they were ready to die.

Against the physical cruelties of persecution they responded with the spiritual weapons of righteousness, patience and truth. The martyrs waged the battle of faith and chose to die for Christ. Theirs was the victory.

We know the things for which we live. Is there anything for which we are willing to die?

June 3 – St. Charles Lwanga and Companions (Memorial)

The story of the martyrs of Uganda reads like an account from the early persecutions of the Church by Rome but it is about events from our own time, events both ancient and very modern.

Christianity had come to Uganda in the late 1800's. The king of a particular tribe was young, unstable and a pedophile. He regularly used the young men of his court for sexual pleasure. The Christians resisted the king's advances and some had openly criticized his immorality.

He turned on them and put them to death. Charles Lwanga was their leader. All together, there were twenty-two Catholic men. But the king's anger raged against Protestant Christians as well who refused his advances. All these martyrs were burned, beaten or axed to death.

At the moment before their sentence, they were given the

chance to renounce their faith in Christ. They all responded that they would remain Christian "until death." Their wish was fulfilled. They chose to die for God rather than live a corrupted life. How many people would do the same today?

In his homily for the canonization of the first martyrs of Uganda, Pope Paul VI remarked on the striking fact that the list of the early martyrs of Africa with names such as Cyprian, Felicity and Perpetua would now include names from our time like Charles Lwanga and Matthew Kalemba.

The evil of sexual abuse, which they resisted, is a feature of our time as well and so is the violence they suffered. But they are heroes because they resisted and God gave them the strength to remain faithful.

Every era has its own violence but it also has the grace of Christ. In the Beatitudes, the Lord shows us the unexpected places that would be places of grace for all time. He teaches us that those persecuted for the Kingdom of Heaven will experience that Kingdom without delay.

We all ask the Lord that we might live in peaceful times, in undisturbed possession of the Faith, in an environment that allows us to follow Christ. Often that is not to be.

But the Lord always gives the grace to be faithful in unfaithful times just as He gave the grace to Cyprian, Felicity, Perpetua, Charles Lwanga and the martyrs of Uganda.

June 5 – St. Boniface (Memorial)

Boniface wanted only to be a missionary. Instead, he became a religious statesman. He lived around the year 700. He was a Benedictine monk in England and was sent as a missionary to what we know today as Germany and Austria to bring the Gospel and establish the Church.

Perhaps the most famous scene from his life was his cutting down of a sacred tree dedicated to the pagan god Wotan. He then used the wood to build an altar to Christ. That heroic act sparked widespread conversion to Christianity.

Boniface spent the next 35 years organizing and establishing the Church. He seems to have been designated a kind of roaming archbishop with no diocese of his own but authorized to establish dioceses and install bishops. He proceeded to create dioceses, establish monasteries and organize the institutional Church.

One historian has remarked that Boniface had a deeper influence on Europe than any other Englishman did. He brought about the Christian conversion of entire peoples, he extended the care of the Church of Rome to Germany and Austria, he secured education and literary growth through the monasteries he built and gave the Church a strong institutional base that would survive him. He deserves to be better known than he is.

The true greatness of Boniface is reflected in his last missionary journey. He was by now an old man, tired and weak. He had given all his authority to others. He was now free to be the missionary he had dreamed of being as a young monk.

One day, he and his companions were killed by unbelievers. He had already given his intelligence, his talents, and all his youth to Christ. The one thing that remained was his blood. At the age of 75, he was put to death. He had indeed been that good shepherd of which the Lord speaks in today's Gospel.

He gave his life to help create Christians. Because of the institutions he founded, after his death there would be millions more. He was a great man in this world and a great one in the Kingdom of Heaven.

His example teaches us to support the institutions of the Church because they have a staying power longer than individual lives. They prolong and extend our faith into future generations.

June 6 – St. Norbert (Optional Memorial)

We all know the story of St. Paul's conversion on the road to Damascus when he was knocked to the ground by a light from heaven. St. Norbert's conversion took a similar form as he was thrown to the ground when his horse was frightened by a bolt of lightning. It is said that Norbert laid stunned on the ground for about an hour and when he awoke, his life was changed.

Until that moment, his life was one of carefree careerism in the Church. Through his ecclesiastical positions, he had accrued a ton of benefits with little responsibility. Such a life was not uncommon for upper class clerics. That lightning strike was his moment of spiritual awakening. He then began to take the spiritual life and ministry very seriously. He was ordained to the priesthood in 1115 and began to live a life of apostolic, even monastic, strictness.

His rigor and habits were seen as excessive to some people. Eventually, the Pope gave him permission to preach wherever he wished. He gave away all his possessions and used this roving license to convert many people and to establish an order of priests who would live an austere and apostolic life. Following a modified form of St. Augustine's rule of life for priests, they became part of what is called the "Gregorian reform," a movement to establish order and discipline in the Church that spanned the period of several popes. This "in-house" movement for reform predated the Reformation by four centuries.

He established the headquarters of his congregation in the valley of Premontre. They were known as the Premonstratensians which is quite a mouthful. Years later, they were known simply as the Norbertines. Norbert was eventually made archbishop of Magdeburg in Germany. This drew him into the politics of the time when competing popes were claiming the chair of Peter. When Norbert died at the age of fifty-three, there were over a thousand monasteries of "Norbertines."

The life of St. Norbert teaches us that reform is not an idea born in the Reformation. The story of the Church is laced with reform movements. In a very real sense, every religious congregation began as some kind of reform movement. The Church knows it is in constant need of renewal because charisms become routine, commitment becomes compromised, and faith can lose its fire and become frozen. The call to reform is a constant part of the Church's life. Secondly, St. Norbert's life shows us that we can change. Our conversion to a deeper embrace of the Gospel may not be as dramatic as his was but it can be as real. We can always take the Gospel more seriously.

Finally, St. Norbert's life shows us that the call to reform needs expression not only in books, periodicals and web logs but in concrete communities of faith where the new life in Christ is given tangible and visible expression. A life lived according to the Gospel is worth a million words.

JUNE 9 – St. Ephrem (Optional Memorial)

St. Ephrem the deacon is known more as a deacon than a Doctor of the Church. He lived in the 4th century in modern day Syria. Baptized at 18 years of age, he was educated and mentored by the local bishop.

Ephrem discerned early the power of poetry and song to "give wings to thought." He saw the potential of the hymns of heretics to spread their erroneous ideas and decided to use his own formidable gift with words to spread the Gospel of Jesus Christ.

Hundreds of his hymns and poems remain and are used in the Eastern Church today. Yet, we know few facts about his life.

When his hometown was besieged and Christians ordered to leave, he became a refugee and went to live as a hermit in Edessa. Occasionally coming to the town to preach, he lived his life as a recluse composing sermons and hymns that would inspire the Eastern Church for centuries.

He has been called the "harp of the Holy Spirit" and teaches us the power of song to convey our faith. Many people point to the dignity and power of Gregorian Chant to inspire. But the music of every era has power to express faith. St. Paul writes to the Colossians that we teach and admonish each other in psalms, hymns and spiritual songs.

Church music is not an optional extra, a melodious decoration added to her liturgy. Music is a powerful way to join not only voices but also hearts, to gather individuals into a congregation, to express the deep yearnings and prayers of the heart, and to communicate the Faith from one generation to the next. In fact, some of the great hymns of the Church can bind generations together. Church music does not have to be divisive but can be profoundly unifying.

People who may not recall much theology or the recent sermon at Mass can remember the songs and hymns of the Mass. Of course, styles in music come and go. Every generation has its own "top ten" of favorite hymns. Hymns from the past may or may not speak to us, but they spoke to that generation. If they have inspired, then they have served "to teach and admonish."

Ephrem teaches us not to neglect or overlook the huge teaching power of songs and poetry to communicate the Faith. Poetry and music are the lines of communication between people and between generations.

The Holy Spirit can speak to us very personally not only through the words but also through the music of the Mass.

June 11 – St. Barnabas (Memorial)

Barnabas' name means "Son of Encouragement." He was certainly that for the Apostles. He sold his farm to help the early Church financially. We don't often think of that dimension of the early life of the Church. Someone had to pay for the place where the Apostles met, for supplies, for the missionary journeys that were so much a part of their life.

Barnabas introduced Paul to the other Apostles when they were very wary of Paul. He accompanied Paul on his first missionary journey. He was a genuine source of encouragement on many levels.

There are people who continue his ministry of encouragement today.

Missionaries today arrive in an unfamiliar area and meet local people who assist them. Often one or several people help them with contacts, friends and material resources. A new priest in a parish meets parishioners who are ready and willing to enable him to begin his ministry with a strong start.

These are the worthy citizens in every town to which the Lord refers in today's Gospel reading.

There have been many people like Barnabas in the Church's life who have helped the Church materially and politically. There are people in every town who are willing to help new arrivals in the neighborhood and in the parish.

People like Barnabas among us help others not only materially but also with words of encouragement and support when people are going through a difficult time.

It is a very important ministry in the Church to be a son or daughter of encouragement. Hopefully most of us have had a Barnabas in our life. It is as important that we try to be a Barnabas in someone else's life as well.

June 13 – St. Anthony of Padua (Memorial)

St. Anthony is probably the most loved Franciscan saint after Francis himself. The many parishes that have statues of St. Anthony show the huge devotion to him that is found all over the world. That devotion usually centers on the tradition of his helping to find lost articles but there is much more to St. Anthony than that.

He was born in Portugal in 1295. He had been an Augustinian monk and one day witnessed a procession with the remains of some Franciscan missionaries. This inspired him to become a Franciscan and a missionary. After he had become a Franciscan friar, he sailed for Africa to preach the gospel. He became seriously ill and had to return home. His missionary career abroad was over. But a new turn was taking shape. The ship he was on went off course and he ended up in Italy instead of Portugal.

One day, a scheduled preacher did not arrive for a religious service. Anthony was asked to pinch hit and was an unexpected but spectacular success. His intellectual and oratorical gifts were admired by all. After a brief stint teaching theology, he began to preach throughout Italy. He became, in effect, a "home missionary," preaching relentlessly about conversion and God's love. His sermons attracted so many thousands that the services had to be held in the town squares. He was later made a Provincial for a few years but retired early to Padua where he spent his remaining years. He died at the very early age of thirty-six.

Devotion to him grew as reports of miracles through his intercession spread about. He was canonized a year after his death. No one is sure how he became the "finder of lost articles." One account tells a story that occurred years after Anthony's death. A young novice had stolen another's hymnal. Anthony appeared to him in a dream and told him to return the book or he would be sorry. The hymnal was returned.

Anthony is often portrayed holding a lily in one hand to represent his chastity and a Bible in the other to represent his learning. In continuity with the Franciscan tradition of emphasis on the power and magnificence of the Incarnation, Anthony had a devotion to and vision of the Christ child. His statues often picture the Christ child seated on the Scriptures Anthony holds.

The life of Anthony shows us how God can work in our life. A preacher's illness launched his ministry as a preacher. His own illness kept him from foreign missions only to make him a magnificent missionary at home. Maybe much in our life that we call coincidence is really Providence at work.

Anthony sought to reclaim lost souls. Perhaps in addition to seeking his help in finding lost car keys, wallets, rings and papers, we might seek his intercession for lost souls and people who are drifting. As he did so many centuries ago, Anthony can help them find the Lord.

JUNE 19 – ST. ROMUALD (OPTIONAL MEMORIAL)

Years ago, there was a popular song called "The Rose." Its concluding image was that of a seed beneath the winter snows that with the sun's love will become a rose. We can apply that picture to the life of St. Romuald. His is not a household name that people give to their children, but the dynamics of his life should give hope to all of us.

He was born in the 10th century and lived a carefree life

typical of the wealthy youth of his time. One day, his father required him to be present at a duel in which his father shot a man to death. That single, stark incident changed Romuald's life for good. It is as though the shot that killed one person brought new life to another.

Horrified by this unnecessary taking of a life, Romuald wanted to do penance for his father's sin. He entered a Benedictine Abbey. As is the case with new converts, he felt the monks there were insufficiently devout. He departed to place himself under the spiritual direction of a hermit and lived a life of austerity and prayer. He then wandered about Italy establishing monasteries and hermitages. He was given land known as the Campus Maldoli to establish a monastery. The monks there became known as the Camaldolese hermits. They lived separately but gathered for liturgy.

Romuald's life shows us how certain events can release a desire for union with God that until then had hibernated within us. It is not uncommon for the first-hand experience of war, violence and abuse to trigger a person's search for healing and for God. The monastic experience in its many forms only institutionalizes the quest and need of every person to find a place apart where we can experience God's presence. That need is the "monk" inside all of us.

Romuald died at the age of seventy-seven. In his life, he had seen many men begin the quest for deeper union with God through the monasteries he established. In fact, he had the grace to see his own father, whose heinous act began Romuald's own journey, enter the monastic life.

Within each of us is a need for God that is as real as our need for food and water. The energies of our life can become erratic and dysfunctional until something happens that enables us to see that God is our heart's true destination. Without God, our life is an endless quest. With God, we find our true home as Romuald did. Beneath the winter snow lies the seed that can become the rose.

June 21 – St. Aloysius Gonzaga (Memorial)

Aloysius Gonzaga was born in 1568 into the world of the Italian Renaissance, a world of wealth, intrigue, materialism, brutality and consumption, a world not unlike our own.

Aloysius decided to follow a path different from the rest of his family. He decided not to go into politics but to give his life to the service of God in the Church. He wanted to become a Jesuit.

He was very intense in his vocation seeing, at first, every human relationship and every friendship as a distraction from God. This may have been an expression of youthful enthusiasm or his way of separating himself from the addictive influence of the social circle in which his entire family moved.

His Jesuit spiritual director enabled him to come to more of a balance in his life perhaps reminding him that the Lord gave not just one but two great commandments, love of God and love of neighbor. It seems that he made that insight his own because he spent months caring for victims of a plague until he died of a fever at the age of 23. He didn't live long enough to be ordained a priest but is, of course, a member of the Jesuit family and a patron of youth.

In his soul he conquered the environment of political intrigue, materialism and Renaissance "consumerism" by following a different path of serving God.

None of us lives in a plastic bubble. We live in an environment not unlike that of Aloysius Gonzaga with its centrifugal pull away from Gospel values. We can either submit to the pull of our culture or stake out another path, the path of the Gospel.

The Gospel gives us the strength of purity in every part of our life, the vitality of a vigorous relationship with the Risen Christ, and the wisdom of Christian prudence in all our choices.

Aloysius Gonzaga shows us that whatever the condition of the world in which we live, we are not trapped in it and can make choices. Our soul can either sink its roots into the prevailing culture or be rooted in different soil, in Jesus Christ. As with Aloysius Gonzaga, that choice is always open to us.

JUNE 22 – ST. PAULINUS OF NOLA (MEMORIAL)

Paulinus of Nola was a great bishop of the 5th century. He was born in 354 in Gaul from a very wealthy family. He received a good education and became a lawyer. He married a wealthy woman and together they lived a life of upper-class luxury.

When their only child of a few weeks died, they began to undergo a transformative conversion experience. They retreated from the social circuit and Paulinus was baptized a Christian. With that began a remarkable multi-year distribution of his extraordinary wealth and properties to the poor and to the Church.

He was ordained a priest despite his personal opposition. He built a church, a hospital and an aqueduct for the townspeople. He and his wife dedicated themselves completely to the Lord. Eventually, again against his will, he was elected bishop of Nola. He led the diocese for over twenty years still living in his own home virtually as a hermit. Still, Paulinus carried on a massive correspondence with the great figures of his time: Augustine, Jerome, Ambrose and Martin of Tours.

It is said that he introduced the use of bells in churches because Nola was a center for bronze casting.

Paulinus' life highlights his virtue of generosity to the poor and to the Church. It is a great gift to be able to give of our prosperity and even of our substance to the Church. Many people today remember the Church and charitable organizations in their wills.

The life of St. Paulinus also shows us the benefit of giving during our lifetime. We can then see our gifts being put to use, take care that our donations are used as promised, and experience the satisfaction of knowing that we have enhanced and benefited the life of the Church and of those in need.

All of God's blessings toward us are gifts to be shared, whether spiritual or material. Gifts we are given should be used to build up the Church.

JUNE 22 – STS. JOHN FISHER AND THOMAS MORE (OPTIONAL MEMORIAL)

Thomas More and Bishop John Fisher were both martyrs for the Faith in England in 1535 under Henry VIII.

Thomas More was a barrister and Chancellor of England. His story was recounted in the play and movie "A Man for All Seasons." He was prayerful, scholarly and wise. He was brilliant and simple in that he could spot the moral issue at the heart of any complicated controversy.

He was loyal to the king, to his wife and family and to the Church. The crisis came when Henry's annulment of his marriage to his first wife was refused and the king then required allegiance to himself, through the Oath of Supremacy, as head of the Church in England. Thomas More refused to take the oath and was put to death. His last words were, "I die the king's good servant but God's first."

John Fisher was bishop of Rochester, England and was a scholar as well. He was also an adviser to the king. But on the issue of the Oath, he also said "no." He was nominated by the Pope to be a cardinal. Henry replied that if they sent a red hat, John Fisher wouldn't have a head to put it on. He was beheaded in 1535.

Both were men of power. Power could be as intoxicating and addictive then as it is now. Yet, their allegiance to God, the Church and moral truth came first even at the expense of their mortal lives.

Still, they stood for something. In a time when everything seems negotiable, they stood for Truth.

The lives and deaths of John Fisher and Thomas More should cause us to revisit the image of "merry old England" to realize that it was not just country folk dancing around a maypole. It was a dark and brutal place.

Today, persecution continues in various versions of anti-Catholicism. It can take the form of ridicule, a patronizing tolerance or a highlighting of unfaithful Catholics. This is our time to stand for what we believe.

The Church at the time of Thomas More and John Fisher had lots of scandal. They knew that. They also knew that the Church was also entrusted with Christ's Truth, Christ's grace and Christ's Sacraments. She was the link to Christ in our world. They lost their mortal lives for the Church but they found eternal life.

JUNE 27 – ST. CYRIL OF ALEXANDRIA (OPTIONAL MEMORIAL)

Cyril, the Patriarch of Alexandria, is forever linked with the assault of Nestorianism, the third great heresy that faced the Church in the first half-millennium of its life. The teaching of Apollinaris had diminished the humanity of Christ. Arius had lessened the divinity of Christ. Nestorius split Christ in two.

The Church at Alexandria had long emphasized the unity of Christ's divine and human natures. The Church at Antioch, of which Nestorius was a part as Patriarch of Constantinople, emphasized the difference between the two. Nestorius went further to so separate the natures of Christ as to divide Christ into two persons. The divine person led the human person like two cars in precise procession, each with its own driver.

The trigger issue was the title given to Mary as "Mother of God." Nestorius taught that Mary could properly be called the "Mother of Christ," that is, of His human nature, but not of God. He stated that he could not imagine divinity being a two month old infant. One consequence of his teaching, of course, is that only the human Christ would have died on the cross thus removing the heart from what redemption is all about.

His chief opponent was Cyril of Alexandria. Cyril, who became Patriarch in 412, was pugnacious, in no mood for compromise, highly political and fierce in his defense of the unity of Christ's two natures in one divine Person. Supported by the pope at the Council of Ephesus, Cyril led the way in the excommunication of Nestorius and preserved forever the title of Mary as "Mother of God." The core issue, however, was not about Mary but about the truth concerning Jesus Christ.

This theological battle was fought on many fronts and was

fueled from many sources. There was a personal tension between Cyril and Nestorius. There was rivalry between the Sees of Alexandria and Constantinople. There were regional differences as well, as each man came from a different theological culture. But at its heart was the issue of Catholic truth. Cyril as theologian and as bishop was in no mood for discussion, debate or euphemisms. He wanted to secure the hard, solid truth that Christ is a single divine Person with both a divine and human nature.

This teaching would find clear expression in the Council of Calcedon. At Ephesus, however, it took the form of celebrating the title of Mary as "Mother of God." This title for which Cyril fought so hard reminds us that our devotion to Mary flows from our faith in her Son. Honor to Mary leads to love of Christ. Honor to Christ leads us to love of Mary, His mother. Like the sun and its light, they go together.

June 28 – St. Irenaeus (Memorial)

Every computer user fears a "computer virus." A computer virus is a program that can spread itself through certain files or the computer system itself and then replicate itself. It can interfere with or even damage the work of one's computer program.

There was a kind of "computer virus" at large in the early Church called "Gnosticism." Gnosticism presented itself as secret knowledge filled with a melange of speculation, blends from different religions and bizarre claims that were mimicking and infecting the Christian faith.

Irenaeus, the bishop we remember today, was very instrumental in combating Gnosticism in two ways.

First, he lifted the veil of secrecy from the teachings and books of the Gnostics. In a five-volume work written in the late 2nd century, he pulled away the curtain of secrecy to reveal the "Oz" of Gnosticism as a bundle of senseless and contradictory speculations.

Secondly, he completed an anti-Gnostic defense system to guide the faithful and protect against the infection of Gnosticism.

One leg of the triad was emphasis on the local bishop as the source of legitimacy and the standard of orthodoxy in a diocese. To this Irenaeus added two other elements.

He established the canon or list of inspired books of the Bible, excluding the Gnostic works. The canon was composed of books of the Bible the Church treated as inspired and as the written norm of the apostolic faith.

He then referred to the apostolic faith as publicly taught by the successors of the Apostles in the apostolic sees, principally Rome, as the living norm of the Christian faith.

The bishop, the Word of God, and the apostolic teaching were the safeguards against the virus of Gnosticism in the early Church and remain so against our contemporary new age versions of Gnosticism.

Irenaeus was a great bishop who sought to preserve the unity for which the Lord prays in today's Gospel reading while treating his opponents in a Christian way as St. Paul recommends in today's first reading.

He helped keep the Christian faith one and apostolic. In our own time, thanks to Irenaeus, we can turn to the same sources of bishop, Scripture and the apostolic Tradition to keep our faith authentic and clear.

JUNE 30 – THE FIRST HOLY MARTYRS OF THE HOLY ROMAN CHURCH (OPTIONAL MEMORIAL)

On the evening of July 18th, in the year 64 AD there was a fire in the city of Rome. Rome was not the city of marbled buildings we imagine. Stone was used for public buildings and palaces but the houses of average people were constructed of wood.

The fires spread and panic ensued. The fire burned for six days until it eventually subsided. The result was a city virtually destroyed and people were searching for someone to blame. The first suspect was the Emperor Nero. He wanted to raze some wooden structures to begin his version of urban renewal and the fire probably got out of hand. To deflect suspicion from himself, he blamed the Christians.

With that began the first major persecution of the Christians by the Romans. They were arrested in the middle of the night and subjected to horrible tortures in an area called "Nero's Circus" which is the present site of the Vatican.

To read ancient descriptions of their tortures is to read of cruelty comparable to the Nazis, Pol Pot and Saddam Hussein. The many nameless martyrs from this first persecution are the ones we remember today. Their persecution was the opening shot in a centuries-long struggle between cross and crown that continues to our day. That struggle will take many forms from outright brutality to legal restriction or cultural marginalization. But the persecution continues.

When we read about Catholics who are unfaithful to their vocation, these martyrs and all who have been faithful to Christ over the centuries show us a different face of Christianity. It is the face of ordinary people made strong by the Holy Spirit. They are the ones who, in St. Paul's words, let nothing separate them from their love for Christ. Unlike many people today who will let virtually anything separate them from the love of Christ, these remained strong.

Jesus predicted all this. In fact, the words of Jesus in today's Gospel reading are a kind of overture to the history of the Church perhaps cautioning us to be suspicious when all goes well. When the Church is in complete favor with secular powers, it may be that the Church has compromised its mission. In fact, persecution in its many forms is the more common pattern in the Church's life.

Today, we don't have to look for persecution. It will find us in one of its many forms. Our fidelity under fire will strengthen the weaker ones among us.

July 1 – Bl. Junipero Serra (Optional Memorial)

There have been many missionaries and saints who have followed Jesus' command to bring the Gospel to the entire world. Today, we remember Blessed Junipero Serra, the "Apostle of California."

He was born on the Spanish island of Mallorca in 1713. He became a member of the Franciscan Order in Spain where he taught theology. Wanting a missionary life, he joined the Franciscan missionaries in Mexico City. Later, he was placed in charge of the Franciscans sent to Christianize the Indians in California. He established a string of missions after which many major cities in California today are named.

His missions were tiny Spanish colonies where the baptized Indians learned new agricultural methods, followed a Catholic way of life and learned the Gospel of Jesus Christ. There is controversy today about some of Junipero Serra's methods of evangelization. We should be careful about assessing his work by the standards of the 20th century. Further, the Spanish government assisted his missionary work to the extent that it could also be a vehicle for colonization. The alternative was no evangelization at all.

Finally, Junipero Serra was a very ascetic person and his natural rigor affected his dealings with others. He expected nothing less of them than he expected of himself. He was not perfect but an earthen vessel, which still carried the grace and truth of Jesus Christ to others.

He was plagued by asthma and still rode on horseback or walked close to 10,000 miles. It is said that he personally baptized over 5,000 people. He died at 70 years of age at his headquarters in Carmel, a mission that reflected his asceticism and was clearly not the Carmel of today.

In reading the life of Junipero Serra, we are watching the building of the Church in California. Today, we have inherited a Church with a strong institutional base. That is the legacy of previous generations to us. What are we doing to enhance the life of that Church? Are we simply consumers of the work done by others or are we trying to build up the life of the Church for the next generation?

Junipero Serra was not just a "consumer" of grace, he was a builder. Which are we?

JULY 3 – ST. THOMAS (FEAST)

St. Thomas, called "doubting Thomas," is known to history for his doubts. Yet, in this moment in today's Gospel reading, his faith was renewed as he said those words that have come to us as "My Lord and my God." It is said that he became a missionary to the people of India and gave his life for Christ.

St. Gregory the Great remarked that Thomas' doubts help to build up our faith because Jesus spoke to him that famous beatitude about the blessedness of those who have not seen but have believed.

Faith is not just a state of mind or an opinion. It is a contact, spiritual but real, with the Risen Christ.

Through faith, we can have the same relationship with Christ as those who saw Him.

Through faith, we can open ourselves to Christ's saving grace.

Through faith, we can know the healing power of Christ and His presence in all the events of our life.

Faith is a magnificent gift that connects us with Christ. Many who saw Him with their eyes in His earthly life never had a saving contact with Him because salvation comes not through the eyes but through faith.

It is important that we respect the gift of faith we have received. Many people take it for granted and do not nurture it or guard it. Then, one day, they realize it is gone.

We keep our faith strong, in good times and bad, by staying close to the Church, reflecting on our faith, studying it through the *Catechism*, by living it, sharing it and praying it. Faith is one of those "spiritual goods" which grows within us as we share it with others.

Those who have not seen but have believed are indeed

blessed because their faith does not depend on eyesight but on grace-filled insight, which enables us to see deeply and wisely.

Although history knows Thomas for his doubts, our salvation will come from imitating his faith each time we are in church when we gratefully make our own his magnificent affirmation, "My Lord and my God!"

July 4 – St. Elizabeth of Portugal (Optional Memorial)

The Lord's words, "Blessed are the peacemakers" certainly apply to Elizabeth of Portugal. One would think that her life in which she was born into nobility and married a king would be perfect. Looks are deceptive. Her life was very far from being ideal.

She was born in Spain in 1271. She was named after Elizabeth of Hungary, her great aunt, and was called in Spanish, Isabella. At the age of twelve, she married the king of Portugal in an arranged marriage. He was an effective king but hardly a family man. He was consistently unfaithful. He had two children with Elizabeth and seven illegitimate children with various other women.

Elizabeth remained faithful and profoundly Christian through this difficult marriage. When her husband's legitimate son grew envious of his illegitimate half-brother and staged a revolt against his father, Elizabeth sought to bring about reconciliation between them. Several times in her life she had to play the role of peacemaker. She was rewarded for her efforts with false accusations and was sent away from the castle.

She was a woman of deep faith and heroic charity. Her husband recognized this toward the end of his life and made her executor of his will. She was at his bedside during his final illness and encouraged all his children, legitimate and illegitimate, to be at his bedside as well. She held no grudges against him, tried to prevent animosity among his children, and tried to live in peace with all people. Though treated badly by a number of people, she never responded in kind. She was a true peacemaker. After a difficult life in a difficult world to which she sought only to bring peace, she died at the age of 65.

It is far easier to start an argument than to end one. Elizabeth of Portugal was one of those precious people that the Lord calls "peacemakers." She is indeed called a "child of God."

JULY 5 – ST. ANTHONY MARY ZACCARIA (OPTIONAL MEMORIAL)

He wanted his followers not to end up as minor saints but to become great saints. St. Anthony Mary Zaccaria never sold people short. He knew that great holiness was available to everyone.

He was born in Italy in 1502. He studied medicine at the prestigious University of Padua but eventually decided to become a priest. There was a deeper healing that the society and the Church needed.

He was ordained a priest at the age of twenty-six and eventually founded the Clerics Regular of St. Paul (the first congregation named after St. Paul) who were popularly known as "Barnabites" because they were given the care of the Church of St. Barnabas in Milan.

The great inspiration of Anthony's life was St. Paul. His congregation of men, to which congregations of women and laity were later added, was to be the vanguard of a spiritual revival in the Church. The Barnabites were a reforming congregation which was established before the Council of Trent ever began.

St. Anthony Mary Zaccaria's program for his followers was a simple but potent one: to advance spiritually daily, never to step back, always to move forward. That is a splendid program for attaining the great holiness envisioned for us. Reflecting each day on how we have advanced spiritually that day can be a powerful tool of grace and growth.

Anthony Mary's devotion to St. Paul was completed by his devotion to the Eucharist where Christ's crucified and redeeming love is linked to us.

The mission of Anthony Mary Zaccaria was to remind us that holiness, great holiness, is not for somebody else. It's for us.

July 6 – St. Maria Goretti (Optional Memorial)

Maria Goretti was a young Italian girl who was murdered and martyred in 1902. She came from a large family and while her mother was gone she took care of the family. One day, a young man from the neighborhood made advances toward her, which we would call "sexual harassment." Then, he attempted to rape her. She refused to surrender and in his rage he stabbed her some fourteen times fatally wounding her. She died in the hospital a few hours later.

We honor the heroism of this young girl who would not let her body be dishonored by sin because it was the Temple of the Holy Spirit, anointed with the holy oil of the catechumens in Baptism.

These events are tragically all too common in our time as we read about the sexual abuse of minors. Maria Goretti's heroism reminds us that we glorify God not only in our hearts but in our bodies as well.

We glorify God in our bodies by taking care of our health, respecting the dignity of our human sexuality and respecting the sexuality of others. There is not only the problem today of physical assault on one's sexuality. There is a cultural assault on human sexuality. The humor of off-color jokes, the eroticism of fashion, advertising, pornography and the sexualization of the very young in magazines all set the scene for a trivialization of sex and the reduction of people to sexual objects defined by sexual attractiveness rather than persons with a purpose and dignity from God.

Chastity is a virtue much needed today. It is a virtue not of weakness but of strength and self-respect. It is a virtue not of repression but one that seeks to integrate our sexuality with our spiritual identity as Christians. It is a virtue that does not degrade but respects the awesome power of sexuality to express marital love and to transmit life.

Through living and promoting the virtue of chastity, we make Jesus Lord of every part of our life. We follow Jesus not only in our mind and heart but also in our bodies.

JULY 9 – ST. AUGUSTINE ZHAO RONG AND COMPANIONS (OPTIONAL MEMORIAL)

Today, as we honor Father Augustine Zhao Rong and his 119 spiritual companions, the 120 martyrs in China, we have an opportunity to look at a difficult, heroic and constantly developing story of the Catholic Church in China.

These 120 "martyrs in China" (87 of them were actually Chinese) were killed in various waves of persecution from 1814 through 1930. Missionary activity in China has been unusually difficult since it was often thought to be aligned with foreign imperialism. Among these martyrs were six bishops, 23 priests, seven nuns and over 70 lay people. During times of Chinese resistance to foreign influence, these martyrs who sought to bring the Gospel of Jesus Christ to the people of China were caught in the crossfire and died for the faith.

Father Augustine had been sent to guard some Catholic prisoners and the example and teaching of one of the imprisoned priests converted him. He was ordained a priest and served the Church until he was imprisoned during the Boxer rebellion and died in prison. These 120 martyrs are really only the tip of the iceberg of an heroic story of massive fidelity to Christ in China that is virtually unknown to Catholics around the world.

The story of the Catholic Church in China today is a mystery to most Catholics. In 1958, the government created its own Patriotic Catholic Church which would have direct allegiance to the government of China rather than to Rome. Today, there is the "official" Church and an "underground" Catholic Church with many of the bishops of the "Patriotic Church" having been now ratified by Rome. The situation is fluid and there are many contacts between the Vatican and the Patriotic Church.

These martyrs that we remember today are that grain of wheat of which the Lord speaks in today's Gospel. They sowed the seeds of a spirituality that is victorious over any persecution. We can only pray that their witness and prayer will eventually lead to a splendid growth of a unified Church in China.

These martyrs remind us that seeds have been planted by

heroic Catholics all over the world of which we are unaware and which are growing without our knowing it. The grace of Christ and the reach of His Church are universal. The work of evangelization will never be over until the Gospel reaches every culture and every heart.

July 11 – St. Benedict (Memorial)

St. Benedict has been called the "founder of Western Monasticism." He developed a rule of life that other congregations of monks through the centuries have used as a model. The monastic tradition in the West flows from his life, his spirituality and his genius.

Born around 480, as a young man, he wanted to leave behind the decadence of the city and the compromised Christianity that he witnessed all around him. He decided to become a hermit and live alone but he attracted many followers to his way of life. He eventually wrote a rule of life, the Rule of St. Benedict, which is known for its balance. The Lord used the dissatisfaction he felt with society in his time to create an institution that could transform culture in all times.

His motto became "Ora et Labora" – pray and work. We need both. His rule has sustained Christian life in difficult and turbulent years. The Benedictine Order has been an enormous blessing to the Church. Although some Benedictines were magnificent missionaries, their primary purpose was to create monasteries as places of renewal for the Church. In a hard and brutal time, Benedictine monasteries were places of civilization and civility. They were islands of prayer, learning, hospitality and faith. They are perhaps models of what parishes can be in our time.

Benedict's monastery of Monte Cassino is located on top of a high mountain. From that height one can see everything in perspective. Benedict wanted every monastery to be a place where people could put things in perspective. There are several dimensions of Benedictine spirituality that apply to all of us.

The first is stability. The monk was to bind himself to a particular abbey and there commit himself to finding the Lord. It challenges us to find God's grace where we are. Wherever we are living can be a place of mission and union with the Lord. The constant quest for "greener grass" seldom creates a solid spirituality.

The second feature of Benedictine spirituality is that of sacred reading or "lectio divina." This is a prayerful reading of Scripture and its application to our lives. In every passage of Scripture we can ask what the Lord is saying to us in those words. Too often, we use an academic approach to studying Scripture that can turn God's Word into an object of analysis rather than His living Word to each of us.

Finally, Benedict balances prayer and work. We need both for a healthy spirituality. The would-be mystic runs the risk of enveloping the self in the self. The activist runs the risk of running on empty. Prayer and work nourish each other. Spirituality is more than prayer. Our spirituality is defined not only by our prayer but by how it shapes our interactions with the world.

A last point: Benedict was not a priest. He was a dedicated Christian who was a true spiritual shepherd to others. With all the discussion in our time of who should or should not be ordained, perhaps his most powerful lesson for us in our time is that we do not have to be ordained to be Christ to others.

JULY 13 – ST. HENRY (OPTIONAL MEMORIAL)

St. Henry is the patron saint of the childless, of the handicapped and of those rejected by religious orders. It does not seem that his life will be the story of what we would call a "winner."

But he was an important figure at the turn of the first millennium. He was born in 972. It is said that he wanted to be a priest at one time but eventually was drawn into politics and administration. He was King of Germany, King of Italy and then Holy Roman Emperor – the classic trifecta of the early Middle Ages.

He was very much a product of his time. Church and State were united. Henry made bishops and crushed bishops. He used the Church to cement his power. He demanded obedience from his client bishops. All this does not mean that he was an evil man because this was not an age of collegiality. It was not a "therapeutic culture" as is our own. Henry was unilateral and demanding for the sake of keeping the Holy Roman Empire unified and to build up the Church as he saw appropriate. The Office of Readings for today records his declaration to establish his own diocese at Bamberg and to build a cathedral there where he is to be buried.

He supported the reform movement that began from the Abbey of Cluny. Whatever reform occurred under Henry would not have happened had he not been insistent and demanding of his bishops. It also held off the Reformation for four centuries.

We know little of his spiritual life except that the Church tells us he is a saint. Despite his imperial administrative style, in his heart he sought, in the words of the prophet Micah, to do what is right and walk humbly before God. His fame in the Church does not rest on his material accomplishments but on the fact that he built his life on the rock of Christ's truth and fidelity to Christ's Church.

He was strong, he was unilateral, he was demanding but he was faithful. He is also the patron saint of the childless, of the handicapped and of those rejected by religious orders.

As with so many people, there was more to him than meets the eye.

July 14 – Bl. Kateri Tekakwitha (Memorial)

Blessed Kateri Tekakwitha lived in the late 1600s. She is known as the "Lily of the Mohawks" because of her complete dedication to Christ. She was an outcast among her own people for several reasons.

She was a convert to Christianity, which led to her being ridiculed among her own people. She was of mixed blood. Her father was Mohawk and her mother was Algonquin which meant that neither tribe fully accepted her. She had a skin disfigurement from smallpox and she did not marry but remained totally faithful to the Lord.

Yet, for all this she became beautiful and accepted in the Lord's sight. These four factors led to her holiness.

As a convert, she came to know Jesus Christ more vividly than many who take their faith for granted. Fully accepted by no one tribe, she came to appreciate the deep humanity behind all our ethnic labels. Her being unmarried enabled her to witness to the transforming love of Jesus Christ as her deepest source of fulfillment. Finally, disfigured on the outside, she grew profoundly beautiful within. She was a contemplative of very deep prayer.

It is to people like her that Jesus speaks His words in today's Gospel of revealing the full depth of the life and love of God. Only the open heart is ready to be filled with the grace of God.

The real truth about each of us is not on the outside but on the inside. We like to dress in a certain way and create an image, a "look," to tell the world who we are or want to be. But the deepest truth about us is within. We will have to live for the rest of eternity with that inner truth.

The life of Kateri Tekakwitha teaches us that the very elements of our lives that we consider to be crosses may turn out to be avenues to Christ. The very things to which many people aspire (appearance, success and prosperity) may be roadblocks to the full embrace of Christ.

Whatever our physical appearance may be, we all can be magnificent within.

JULY 15 – ST. BONAVENTURE (MEMORIAL)

Grasping the full expanse of Christ's love and centering our life on Jesus alone are the twin themes of the life and work of St. Bonaventure. He is a great Doctor of the Church who was born in 1218.

He taught at the University of Paris at the same time as St. Thomas Aquinas. They may have been at different ends of the theological spectrum with Bonaventure representing a more conservative theology and Aquinas the more liberal through his use of Aristotle, but they were friends. That in itself is a huge lesson for us today.

Bonaventure is not appreciated as much as Aquinas for all kinds of reasons. One of them is that his theological work was limited to his early years while Aquinas had a lifetime of writing. Bonaventure was called into administration at the age of 36.

As Superior General of the Franciscan Order, he saved the Franciscan movement. St. Francis was a compelling visionary but not a great administrator. At his death, a split began to form between those who wanted to maintain his vision literally and those who wanted to adapt it to a changing world. Bonaventure reformulated the Franciscan charism in a moderate way and kept the Order from splitting or being suppressed. It was one thing to have five Franciscans come to the town to beg for food each evening. It was something else to have five thousand do so. St. Bonaventure has been called the "Second Founder of the Franciscan Order."

In typical Franciscan fashion, he taught that the love of God should be at the center of our actions. According to Bonaventure, it is not the light of intellect but the fire of love that carries the soul to God. He taught that when we come to see truth, any truth, it is the light of God at work in us. That is a magnificent point for meditation. He also spoke about vices that can affect the Christian. They are the vices of knowledge without devotion, research without wonder, activity without faith, learning without love, intelligence without humility, and thinking without wisdom.

Theologian, teacher, religious superior and cardinal are all roles where people can become contentious, cautious, abrupt or self-absorbed. In all the positions he held, he radiated the love of Christ, the light of Christ and the compassion of Christ.

The office didn't change him, he changed the office.

The memorial of Our Lady of Mount Carmel is a great feast for the members of the Carmelite Order, a revered and growing spiritual family in the Church.

The remote origins of this order go to the mountains of Carmel in the Holy Land, the home of the great prophet Elijah. Later, Christians went there to immerse themselves in prayer, following the example of Elijah discerning God's voice in the small wind and the example of Mary hearing God's Word and keeping it.

Gradually, their numbers grew. In 1250, St. Simon Stock had a vision of Mary in which she gave him the brown scapular for all "Carmelites" to wear. It was a large cloth hanging in front and back that was to be a sign of dedication to Mary and to the Carmelite way of prayer. It carried the promise that whoever wears it and is faithful to all that it means would experience the patronage of Mary and the glory of heaven. Gradually, the scapular became smaller and even made into a medal in our own time.

Whatever its form, its meaning is the same. The scapular is not magic but, like a wedding ring whose power comes from the faithfulness it represents, the scapular symbolizes Mary's special care for the wearer and the loyalty of the one wearing it to the Carmelite way of life.

The emphasis on the life of contemplative prayer is the gift of the Carmelites to the Church. It is no surprise that many great giants of prayer such as Teresa of Avila, John of the Cross, Thérèse of Lisieux, Edith Stein and Elizabeth of the Trinity were all Carmelites.

Sometimes people may think that contemplation is like entering a room. They want the key to go in for a while and then come out. But contemplative prayer is deeper. It is developing our identity in Christ and seeing our life as an expression of Christ's Passion, Death and Resurrection. We find ourselves by losing ourselves in Christ. Contemplation is more than "saying prayers." It is being in prayer before God to speak but largely to listen.

The Carmelite way calls us to the deep prayer that is the life of the soul and teaches us that in filling our soul, nothing can take the place of God.

July 18 – St. Camillus de Lellis (Optional Memorial)

Health care reform is on the minds of many people these days. It was also on the mind of Camillus de Lellis over four hundred years ago. Even though he has not been formally declared as such, he could well be the patron saint of health care reform.

Camillus was born in 1550 during the Italian Renaissance. He came from a military family and was evidently an imposing figure who stood at six and a half feet tall. He also had a gambling addiction that kept him in poverty. He was wounded in the constant interplay of battles that pervaded Italy in those days and went to a hospital where he received horrible care.

Later, he left the Capuchin order three times because of his recurring leg ailment. He returned to a hospital in Rome where the attention he received was not only unprofessional but also abusive. This opened the door to his real vocation in life. He assembled a group of men who would care for the sick and called them the Congregation of the Servants of the Sick. Their insignia was a habit with a bold red cross on it. This red cross was the remote beginning of the formal institution of the "red cross" at the Geneva Convention as the symbol for international health care workers.

The many hospitals in Camillus' time were built more as monuments to the wealthy who, in fact, received their health care at home. These hospitals became warehouses to simply remove the sick from the streets and from sight. It is an irony that the Renaissance that so exalted the human person was interested only in the healthy, athletic and creative person.

Camillus' revolution in health care recognized the sick as worthy of dignity and care since they also carry the image of God within them. The Renaissance exalted the beauty of the human body and form. It also tended to ignore the sick and the disabled. These are the people St. Camillus gathered together. He sought to treat the entire person. The emphasis he gave to physical hygiene was matched by care for their soul and spirit. As a priest, he could tend to their spiritual care as well as their physical condition. His approach was truly "holistic." Finally, he developed in his clergy professionalism and attention to the best medical knowledge available. They not only took care of the sick in hospitals but set up treatment centers in the field of battle, the first "MASH" unit.

Today, his religious congregation, the Camillians as they are called, is found in thirty countries and on five continents tending to the emotional, physical and spiritual ailments of those entrusted to its care.

St. Camillus teaches us an important lesson today. Advanced medical technology is not an asset to a society if it reaches only a few. A health care system is measured not by how it treats the wealthy but by how it treats the poor. The character of a society is not shown by its exalting the bold and the beautiful, as did the Renaissance, but by how it treats the person at the side of the road.

After four centuries, St. Camillus de Lellis still has lots to teach us.

July 20 – St. Apollinarius (Optional Memorial)

"You can't keep a good man down" is a saying we all have heard. That certainly applies to St. Apollinarius who led an extraordinary life that might seem remote from us but is very relevant to our life.

It is said that he was made a bishop by St. Peter himself and sent to bring the Gospel to Ravenna during the reign of Emperor Claudius. Upon his arrival in Ravenna, he sought lodging with a soldier whose blind son he proceeded to heal. This brought about the conversion of the whole family and many others as well. He preached in Ravenna for some twelve years and the number of Christians increased significantly.

Reported by the pagan priests for being a Christian, he was arrested, tried, found guilty and tortured. Thinking he was dead, they threw him into the sea. But he was alive.

A widow nursed him back to health and for six months he preached and gained more converts. He was arrested again and expelled from the city. He continued to heal and preach. He was tried again and banished from the city. He was chained on a ship to go into exile. There was a tremendous storm, a shipwreck and he and a few of his companions survived.

He continued to preach, heal and make converts and found his way back to Ravenna. He was arrested again and beat up. They dragged him into the pagan temple but then the statue collapsed killing the pagan priests but not harming Apollinarius.

The preaching, healing, convert making continued. Finally, he was put to death in the year 75 after being bishop of Ravenna for 28 years.

St. Apollinarius is relevant to our life because, in a way, his life is the story of the Church itself. Over the centuries the Church has been persecuted and left for dead only to rise and increase its membership. The promise of Christ has been with the Church through every kind of travail.

The fact of the Church's survival is Christ's assurance that His love and redemption will have power until the end of time. Only when history closes will the work and the story of the Church be over. Until then, because Christ lives, His Church lives as well.

July 21 – St. Lawrence of Brindisi (Optional Memorial)

It is hard to imagine what Lawrence of Brindisi did not do in his life except get married. He was priest, theologian, preacher, diplomat, administrator and saint.

He was born in 1559 and joined the Capuchin Franciscans. He had a brilliant mind for languages in particular. He taught theology and developed a series of magnificent biblical portraits of Mary, a very personal devotion of his.

His talent at preaching was evident from his earliest years. After he was ordained, he began preaching tours that took him all over Europe. Since he was multilingual, he could reach many more people than most. He was given the special mission of seeking the conversion of Jews in Italy because of his knowledge of Hebrew.

He was sent on a number of diplomatic missions in the course of which he founded Capuchin houses in many sections of Europe and held virtually every office in the Capuchin Order.

Perhaps the most vivid moment of his life was his motivating the German troops to defeat the Turks in their defense of Hungary. It was said that he rode ahead of the army on a stallion while he held high a cross. It was a striking picture that really told the story of his life.

He was a sower of the seed. Whether in the classroom, behind a desk, on a preaching tour or in peace negotiations among princes, he sowed the Word.

Sometimes, we confine the potential of sowing the Word of God to the pulpit or to the classroom. Lawrence of Brindisi shows us that when we try to heal a quarrel, we are sowing. When we administer a program or manage an organization, we are sowing. When we are assisting people in making difficult decisions, we are sowing. When we counsel people who are friends, family or clients we are sowing. In fact, more sowing goes on outside the pulpit and classroom than in them.

We should be careful not to limit the venues where we can profoundly touch people's lives. In everything he did Lawrence of Brindisi was a light and a sower of the seed of God's Word.

Every place he went and everything he did became a place where he generously sowed the Word of God. Even though most of us will never be in a pulpit or teach in a classroom, Lawrence of Brindisi shows us that we too can still be sowers of God's Word everyday.

July 22 – St. Mary Magdalene (Memorial)

Mary Magdalene could well be called the patron saint of sinners, which makes her a patron saint of us all. There is a great deal of speculation about Mary Magdalene today as to which "Mary" in the Gospels refers to her and which does not.

What is profoundly true about Mary Magdalene was that she was converted to Christ. Our first reading from St. Paul's Second Letter to the Corinthians is about conversion. Some people had complained about the kind of people he was bringing into the Church and St. Paul states that in Christ each of us is a new creation. Mary Magdalene became a new creation in Christ whatever the details of her past. That is the most significant truth about her that is firmly rooted in the Gospels.

She then became a witness to the Risen Christ and, as we see in today's Gospel, became an "Apostle to the Apostles," the first to tell them about the Resurrection.

Mary Magdalene's life shows us the truth of an adage that has been around for a few years, "Every saint has a past and every sinner has a future." What we have been or what we are does not decide what we can be.

People of strong virtue and holiness don't just happen. The road to holiness is a difficult one. Saints don't drop out of heaven; they are created here on earth. Every saint has a past.

Whatever our past may be doesn't have to be our future. We can become new in Christ and take a different turn in our life. When we do so, we can become a witness to the power of Christ as Mary Magdalene was. Every sinner has a future.

Mary Magdalene has intrigued generations of Christians. She has been portrayed by many artists and sculptors in an amazing number of ways. Speculation about details of her life is a cottage industry today. But there is one fact about her that has inspired Christians and given each of us hope. She became a new creation in Christ.

If we turn to the Lord, He has a great future in store for each of us. "Every saint has a past and every sinner has a future."

July 23 – St. Bridget of Sweden (Optional Memorial)

The conventional life of a woman of the 14th century was not for St. Bridget. Her life story is remarkable and profoundly moving.

She was born in 1304 in Sweden. Her mother died when she was 12 and at the age of 14 she was married to a young prince. They had eight children in their marriage of over a quarter century. Bridget was a person gifted with mystical tendencies from a very early age. From the age of seven, she had visions of the Crucified Lord.

After her husband died, she dedicated herself to a life of prayer as her visions and mystical experiences continued. She was inspired to establish a monastery for 60 nuns and 13 priests (the numbers were precise and significant). The nuns lived on one side and the men on the other. The men were subject to the nuns in temporal matters and the nuns to the priests in spiritual matters.

During her life, Bridget made the three great pilgrimages of medieval times. She went to St. James at Compostella in Spain with her husband who died shortly thereafter. Then she went to Rome where she remained a very long time never hesitating to share her revelations from the Lord about Church matters and about the conduct of churchmen.

She also had mystical visions and descriptions from Mary of events in the life of Christ. Some of Bridget's most moving revelations are of the birth and passion of Christ. The level of detail, which she provided, fueled many late Renaissance portrayals of these events. Although her revelations are not a matter of faith and any Catholic is completely free in regard to them, still they show the deep emotional bond between herself and the Lord. She could feel every lash of the scourging, every hit of the hammer on the nails, every thorn wound of Christ. She was indeed, as St. Paul says, "crucified with Christ."

Her final pilgrimage to the Holy Land occasioned even more mystical descriptions of events from the life of Christ. She died shortly afterward. In the course of her extraordinary life, she established herself as a very public mystic to be reckoned with, a woman of precise, graphic and deep spiritual identification with Christ as well as a very strong voice for reform in the Church. She drew her wisdom and strength from Christ, the branch from the Vine.

St. Bridget of Sweden illustrates the truth that the more we identify with Christ, the more His life comes to life in us. Jesus will not longer be "out there" but "in here."

July 24 – St. Sharbel Makhluf (Optional Memorial)

Quiet during life, active after death, St. Sharbel has been called the "Hermit of Lebanon." He was born in 1828 in Lebanon of a poor Maronite family. At age 25 he was ordained a priest in the Maronite Rite and then lived as a monk for 16 years. He then became a hermit for the next 23 years.

We tend to think of hermits as a feature of the early Church whose purpose is all but extinct today. Although some hermits exist in the West, they are very numerous in the East. They are the hidden energy cells of prayer that support the Church and give witness on earth to the deep union with God for which we were all created.

Humility has to do less with self-abasement than with honesty and truth. Humility enables us to see the truth that we are earthen vessels, that we are creatures made for God, that our life is not completely in our hands, that our public strengths can often mask our private weakness to others and even to ourselves, and that ultimately our real fulfillment can be nothing less than God. Such humility marked Sharbel's life.

It is said that people never saw his face in life. It was always kept bowed or turned toward the altar. His gaze was on God. For God he gave up everything and was given the life and depth of God in return.

On December 16 in 1898 as he celebrated the Divine Liturgy, he raised the host offering Christ to the Father saying in the words of the ritual, "This is my offering, accept it." At that moment he suffered a stroke. He hovered between life and death for eight days, repeating those words until he finally died on Christmas Eve at the age of 70.

For all his humility in life, the events that followed his death are striking. It is said that a light hovered over his grave for 45 days and nights. Great miracles of healing in the many hundreds occurred through his intercession. He continues to be a powerful intercessor for all who call on him. It may well be that his greatest miracle will be to bring some reconciliation and peace to the Middle East where he lived his life. This "Hermit of Lebanon" may well transform lives and nations.

Quiet in life, active after death. The events following his death show us the power of silence and prayer to create a great saint. His prayer that made him holy can now help us know and follow the Lord Jesus.

July 25 – St. James (Feast)

This James is called "the Greater" because he was older than the other Apostle James who is called "the Less." These titles were not used during their lifetime but were given them by tradition. James was the brother of John and was privileged to be present at the Transfiguration as well as in the garden of Gethsemane. He was the first Apostle to be martyred during a persecution sparked by Herod Agrippa.

His relics found their way to Compostella in Spain. This shrine became one of the three great sites of pilgrimage in the Middle Ages along with Rome and Jerusalem.

In today's Gospel reading, which is special to the feast of St. James, the Lord speaks of martyrdom. Jesus' words not only are prophetic in regard to the Apostles but also are an important teaching about spiritual greatness and power for all of us.

There is no short cut to holiness which is what the mother of James seemed to desire for her sons. There is no express lane to spiritual greatness. We have to experience something of the dying of Jesus to know His Risen life. Some ambitions in us have to die to make room for the Christ life of grace. Like weeding a garden, we have to make room for the healthy growth by eliminating the weeds.

In the Middle Ages, those making the pilgrim journey to Compostella started out with excitement and enthusiasm. Then they may have been met by robbers, bad weather, injuries so that by the time they came to see the towers of Compostella they were different from when they began. Those who arrived were more mature, knowing much more about themselves, the world in which we live and the resilient power of grace.

We all start our adult journey of life with romantic ideas

about our vocation, job, marriage, parenting and our faith. Then, slowly there is a change. There is a dying of our illusions so that a deeper realistic commitment can come forward. When childhood illusions die, some people become cynics. Others become spiritual adults. It is like the pilgrim road to Compostella.

The mother of James imagined the glory; Jesus asked whether they are willing to go through the dying to get there. This dying is not only physical but the more critical dying to self that is the key to heaven. James did die to self and gave his life for the Lord. Today we remember and take strength from the witness of his life and of his death.

Spiritual maturity does not come to us ready made with the pouring of the last drop of baptismal water as though it were like instant coffee. Spiritual adulthood comes to us from dying to self and rising with Christ. That is a project and journey of a lifetime.

Whatever his initial ambitions may have been, St. James was changed by his journey with Christ. His difficult journey on earth brought light and faith to all the people he met along the way. Can we say the same about ourselves?

July 26 – Sts. Joachim and Ann (Memorial)

Joachim and Ann were the parents of Mary, the Mother of Jesus. Their names are not found in the Gospels but in the devotional writings and traditions of the early Church. They used to have separate feasts in the Church calendar but now they have been appropriately joined.

The Old Testament Book of Sirach praises godly men and women. When we reflect on the future of our lives we look to eternal reward, glory with the Risen Christ and eternal happiness. But there is another dimension to the future of our lives, which is commonly found in the Hebrew Scriptures and that is the impact of our lives on others.

The love and faith of Joachim and Ann passed into their daughter Mary. Sometimes we might think that because Mary was born without original sin in the Immaculate Conception that she somehow grew up on "automatic pilot" and it was irrelevant who her parents were because she would have turned out the same. But Mary was human and her parents had a profound impact on her growth and her spirituality. Mary was shaped and influenced by her parents as were each of us.

This memorial is a chance for us to reflect on the effect we have on the lives of others. The good word, the advice, the mentoring, the example we give are all ways we have shaped, influenced and impacted the lives of others.

There are also the harsh words, the insults, the snide comments, the sarcastic remarks, the demeaning and the discouraging words that can deeply harm or even disable others. We all have experienced the helping word as well as the wounding word.

A question for us is whether people are strengthened, inspired, encouraged in their faith and are stronger Christians because of us or in spite of us.

As we hope for eternal life with Christ, let us not forget the impact of our lives here and the influence we have on others. We do not interact with others like billiard balls simply bouncing off others with little personal impact. We deeply influence each other.

Sirach says of the great men and women of the past that their heritage is with their descendants. Our heritage here on earth is the impact of our life and faith on others.

Our life here can be either a burden or a blessing to the faith of others.

JULY 29 – ST. MARTHA (MEMORIAL)

Books and preaching have often presented a classic contrast between Mary and her sister Martha. Mary was listening to the Lord and Martha was doing the work. They have traditionally been used to describe two ways of life in the Church, the contemplative and the active life.

Although both the contemplative and active apostolates are

real, traditional and necessary parts of the Church's life, Martha and Mary can also represent two dimensions of our spiritual life. We need to listen to the Lord as Mary does and we also need to implement the Lord's teaching in everything we do as Martha probably did.

There is more to Martha than is obvious. At the center of the Gospels of Matthew, Mark and Luke is Peter's great affirmation of faith, "You are Christ, the Son of the living God." In St. John's Gospel, however, it is not Peter's affirmation but Martha's act of faith, "You are the Messiah, the Son of God," that stands at the center. That really is the rest of the story. Martha was also a woman of faith and prayer.

Martha and Mary represent not two airtight stereotypes but two aspects of the Christian life. They are models of two dimensions of Christian discipleship that should and need to be part of every life. We need to listen and we need to act. These two aspects of Christian life influence each other.

Martha and Mary were not rivals for Christ's love. Jesus drew comfort from both and loved both. Our prayer and our work need not be rivals for our time. We need both. Prayer is the fuel of our faith and work is the motion it produces.

Martha and Mary can also represent two kinds of prayer in our life. Mary represents the "prayer of listening," simply being with the Lord. There is also the kind of prayer represented by Martha which is the "working prayer" of intercession, petition, adoration or reparation.

Martha and Mary were sisters and both were friends of Jesus. The active and contemplative states of life in the Church help each other. The active and contemplative dimensions of our life complement and strengthen each other. The active and contemplative forms of prayer in our life enrich each other with depth and direction.

Mary represents the Gospel in our heart. Martha represents the Gospel brought to daily life. We need both.

July 30 – St. Peter Chrysologus (Optional Memorial)

Peter Chrysologus was a renowned preacher and bishop of Ravenna, Italy, which was the capital of the Roman Empire at one point. Born in 380, he was an adult convert to the faith. He was engaged as bishop in the dramatic clarification of the person and nature of Christ that went on in those centuries, but is most known to history as a great preacher.

The mother of the Emperor was so impressed with Peter's short, concise and direct sermons that she nicknamed him "Chrysologus" or golden mouthed. His sermons, of which over 170 are still extant, earned him the title of Doctor of the Church.

In an age without any pervasive public media except word of mouth, the sermon was a major event in the life of a congregation or diocese. Through the sermon, events were interpreted, God's Word was taught, and people were warned, corrected, encouraged or mobilized. The giver of good sermons was a major "gatekeeper" in people's lives. One historian remarked on the fact that one cannot underestimate the importance to colonial America of the "sermon" in generating support for independence.

Many people today turn to secular media to learn what to think about issues, but Peter Chrysologus reminds us of the enduring importance of the church sermon today to help us see events in the light of the Word of God.

God's Word is proclaimed from the pulpit in many ways and for many purposes. In the Catholic Church, the Word of God in Scripture is given the same reverence but not the same worship as the Eucharist. It is important to remember that through the Word of God proclaimed and explained in the liturgy, God speaks to us in a special way. Whenever we come to Mass, the Lord has a message for us both as a congregation and as individuals.

The liturgical homily is not the same as ecclesiastical oratory or speeches. It is a transmission and application of the Word of God to us, which can be used with great power by the Holy Spirit. The homilist may be magnificent or mediocre but the Holy Spirit can use "earthen vessels" to carry saving Truth.

St. Peter Chrysologus respected the sermon as the place

where God's Word comes to our life. The homily today, whatever its eloquence or lack of it, is the place where the Holy Spirit speaks to us and to our need.

July 31 – St. Ignatius of Loyola (Memorial)

St. Paul teaches us in today's first reading that whatever we do should be for the glory of God. That became the motto of St. Ignatius, *"Ad Majorem Dei Gloriam"* (AMDG) "For the Greater Glory of God."

Ignatius was born in 1491. He wanted to make a military name for himself but was wounded in battle. During his recovery, he read the lives of the saints and decided to show the same dedication to Christ as soldiers do to battle. Eventually, he established the "company" of Jesus that later became known as the Jesuits.

He wanted to establish a missionary order to preach the Gospel. He was summoned to counteract the Reformation and renew Catholic life. By their special relationship with the Holy Father, the Jesuits were equipped as a kind of theological "special forces" ready to go wherever directed by the Pope. As time went on, the Jesuits indeed became missionaries not only to foreign lands but also to the world of intellect. Through scholarship, study and the schools they established, the members of the Jesuit order bring the truth of Jesus Christ to virtually every culture on earth. There is practically no field of intellectual endeavor where one will not find a Jesuit at work.

The secret of St. Ignatius' success was his fierce focus on Jesus Christ as the center of his life. He himself had a profound experience of the centrality of Christ and the presence of Christ in all events. The Risen Lord is present not only at the right hand of the Father but in events around us. Ignatius was convinced that everything that occurs in our life as well as all our talents and opportunities can and should be used to promote Jesus Christ.

The result of that powerful religious insight was his composition of the "Spiritual Exercises," a handbook to enable us to come to that same "Ignatian indifference" of being ready to use all for

Christ. He taught us how to liberate the soul from sin and self and use everything in our life for the greater glory of God.

Some people today may seek to flee the prevailing culture in order to find salvation. St. Ignatius teaches us that culture is neither a god nor a devil but a tool that can be used to preach Christ. He calls us not to flee from but to engage the culture around us.

Everything we do or are called to do can be a way of glorifying Christ and growing in His grace.

AUGUST 1 – ST. ALPHONSUS LIGUORI (MEMORIAL)

Liguori Publications is a familiar publishing house in Catholic circles. Established by the Redemptorist Fathers, it takes its name and mission from the great saint we remember today, St. Alphonsus Liguori.

A lawyer who became a priest, Alphonsus was born in 1696 and used his intellectual and communication skills to teach and preach the Gospel in rural areas of Italy. He founded the Redemptorist Fathers to continue that work. He wrote a three volume work of moral theology to teach people how to live and apply the Commandments and precepts of the Gospel to modern life.

His writing is so balanced that his works received an unusual blanket Imprimatur from the Holy See for the guidance of Catholics. Today, he is considered the patron saint of moral theologians. Moral theologians are vital teachers in the Church today to guide us through the complex and difficult areas of biomedical ethics, the morality of complex business practices, government behavior and the morals of corporate behavior in Church, business and State.

In addition to his theological work, St. Alphonsus wrote devotional books on the Blessed Sacrament, the *Glories of Mary* and a widely used version of the Stations of the Cross. Through all these efforts, he tried to teach Catholics how to shape their soul around Christ so they can be light in darkness and the city on the hill.

As might be expected, his life was necessarily immersed in church politics especially within the new Redemptorist Congregation. In an odd twist of irony, Alphonsus found himself expelled from the very order he founded! Toward his later years, he suffered from depression. As with many people, the emotional storms that come upon us, the weather of the heart and mind as it were, are not something for which we are responsible. The key is to hold on to right rudder until the storm passes. Alphonsus did precisely this as he remained constant in prayer as he came closer to God.

When he was a young lawyer of nineteen, he could not have foreseen all that would happen to him in his life. If he had seen the difficult road, he might have hesitated to take that first step. But he took that first step and did great things for the Church. He died a saint at the age of 91.

It is probably a good thing that we cannot see the future. But we can handle the problems that come our way one day at a time. That is how we will become saints as well. We can make our own the familiar prayer with which St. Alphonsus concluded each station in his Way of the Cross: "I love you beloved Jesus. Never permit me to separate myself from you. Grant that I may love you always and then do with me what you will."

That is a great prayer for the Way of the Cross and for every day of our life.

AUGUST 2 – ST. EUSEBIUS OF VERCELLI (OPTIONAL MEMORIAL)

Centuries ago, Eusebius of Vercelli was honored as a martyr. Although he was not actually put to death for the Faith, he suffered a great deal for it. In the old days, he would have been called one of the "confessors" who were sometimes known as "white martyrs" in that although they did not shed their blood they were unusually heroic in their fidelity to Christ.

Eusebius lived during the 300's in Italy. He was elected bishop of Vercelli and is said to have been the first bishop to join clerical life with monastic life. Today, we would say that he invented rectory living.

In the dramatic and protracted conflict over Arianism, a heresy that denied the divinity of Jesus by lessening it, Eusebius was on the side of orthodoxy and St. Athanasius. A synod was held in Milan to heal the breach between Arians and Catholics. Eusebius refused to attend knowing that it was a "set up" to condemn Athanasius. He was forced to attend but was allowed in only when the condemnation of Athanasius was about to be voted. He refused and was sent into exile.

He was jailed by an Arian bishop who abused him terribly. He was humiliated and ridiculed while under house arrest. There was even an attempt to brainwash him into Arianism. But he stood firm. Finally, a new emperor, Julian "the Apostate," issued an edict of toleration, which allowed bishops to return to their dioceses.

Eusebius took a long road back to Vercelli winding his way through many dioceses as a roving champion of orthodoxy. Finally, he returned to Vercelli where he died at the age of 88. It is said that he composed the Athanasian Creed from remarks and notes of St. Athanasius.

Eusebius was not a formal martyr, but he was a man of heroic and indomitable faith. Through his effort and that of many others, the apostolic faith that Jesus is the Son of God, fully human and fully divine, was preserved, handed on and lived.

Like him, we too can be links in the chain of the faith that comes to us from the Apostles.

AUGUST 2 – ST. PETER JULIAN EYMARD (OPTIONAL MEMORIAL)

St. Peter Julian Eymard is known as the "Apostle of the Eucharist." The work he promoted has borne extraordinary results in our world today.

He was born in France in 1811. He became a diocesan priest but was soon attracted to the more structured and rigorous life of the Marist Order. Later, his great devotion to the Eucharist caused him to found the Congregation of the Blessed Sacrament. Establishing a congregation of priests was no easy task because it involved him in a host of issues that were canonical, financial, personal and political. Nevertheless, he persevered.

The Congregation of the Blessed Sacrament promoted every aspect of the Eucharistic life of the Church. Peter Eymard emphasized in many different ways that the Eucharist is, in the words of the Second Vatican Council years later, the "summit and source" of Christian spirituality. Eymard did not use those words but their truth pervades everything he spoke and wrote.

The Eucharist for him was not simply an object to be adored but a vital, loving, dynamic presence of Christ that radiates divine life like a vine projecting and thrusting life into its branches, to use the Lord's image in today's Gospel.

In a very graphic and attractive image linking the Eucharist and the contemplative life, Fr. Eymard remarked that a fireplace, the contemplative life, needs a fire, the Eucharist.

He structured the hour we might spend with the Eucharistic Lord as comprising four quarters. The first is adoration, the second is thanking the Lord for the blessings we have received, the third is reparation for people's indifference and seeking the grace of their conversion, and the fourth is petition for all the needs given to us.

As a precursor to the popularity of Eucharistic Adoration today, Peter Eymard spoke years ago about prayer before the tabernacle. There we are in the presence not only of Light but of Flame, there we can receive the grace to change our world, there we have the place where all the lines of Catholic life and Catholic spirituality converge, and there we have the still point for lives spinning in all directions. The site of our Eucharistic devotion is an island of peace in a noisy world, a place of spiritual fire in a world gone cold, and a place of light in the darkness that overshadows so much of our culture.

For our modern growth of devotion to the Eucharist, Peter Julian Eymard is one of the people we have to thank and to follow.

August 4 – St. John Vianney (Memorial)

St. John Vianney was born in France in 1786. In the seminary he was not a great student but was ordained to the priesthood because he was seen as holy. His first assignment lasted two years. He was then appointed pastor of a small parish of about 250 people in Ars, France and he remained there for the next 42 years, the rest of his life.

He lived simply, caring for every aspect of his parish's life. He was particularly concerned with the moral tone of the community where his parishioners lived. He was faithful in teaching and counseling in and out of the confessional. He experienced the power of evil and attacks by the devil but also experienced the power of grace through those moments of renewal that occurred in people's lives through him. It is said that he spent many hours in the confessional always available to his people. He died at the age of 73 and is the patron saint of parish priests.

In an age of specialization even among clergy, this memorial of St. John Vianney emphasizes the importance of the parish priest. The parish is the frontline where all the policies of a chancery and of the Holy See need to be implemented. The parish priest is the one who guides a particular parish on its journey of faith through baptisms, funerals, weddings, confessions and Sunday Masses. When people have an inquiry about any religious or moral issue, they do not go to the experts but to their parish priest.

St. John Vianney also teaches us to "bloom where we are planted." It is always tempting to dream of another place as the paradise where we will become holy. Eden, however, is gone. We are called to follow the Lord wherever we are. Ars was a small town and not a great parish. But John Vianney was a great priest. Our "Ars" is where we are now and that is where we will become a saint.

Finally, although John Vianney experienced extraordinary phenomena both of evil and of grace, that is not why he is a saint. He is a saint because he was the faithful watchman of whom Ezekiel speaks and the long-working laborer bringing in the Lord's harvest.

If we are faithful and caring for the "Ars" we are given, we too will become a saint.

AUGUST 5 – DEDICATION OF THE BASILICA OF ST. MARY MAJOR IN ROME (OPTIONAL MEMORIAL)

Today is the anniversary of the dedication of the church of St. Mary Major, Santa Maria Maggiore, "big St. Mary's," in Rome. It is one of four major basilicas in Rome. The others are St. Peter's, St. Paul's and St. John Lateran. The rest of the basilicas in the world are called "minor basilicas."

This church in honor of Mary was first built after the Council of Ephesus in the 400's that affirmed Mary as the "Mother of God." It is the oldest church in the West in Mary's honor. It is the biggest church in Rome in honor of Mary. Over the years, it has seen many additions and changes just like the Church itself.

St. Mary Major has been a house of prayer, a home for God's people for centuries. This memorial reminds us that Mary herself was the home of God during her pregnancy. Today her love is a home for all Christians, not just Catholics but all Christians. She is a place to find Christ and like her church in Rome she has lived the history of the Church with the Church.

This memorial also reminds us that the church is a sacred place. It is sanctified by the Lord's Eucharistic presence but also by the altar of sacrifice, the baptismal font, the confessional, and the prayers said at Mass, funerals, weddings and in the quiet hours of the afternoon. Each church is a symbol of the New Jerusalem where God will dwell with His people as the Book of Revelation envisions and is also a promise of the full union with Christ that can be ours forever.

This memorial also challenges us to make our life, our work and our family a home for Christ, for His truth, His work. The purpose of any church is to make us a spiritual temple through our hearing of God's Word and keeping it.

Like Mary and like the church of St. Mary Major in Rome, we can be a place where people can find Christ.

August 7 – St. Sixtus II and His Companions (Optional Memorial)

The story of Pope Sixtus and his companions is a story of tragedy and triumph. Sixtus was reputedly a man steeped in the Greek philosophy of his day who became a convert to Christianity. Eventually he became bishop of Rome. He held that position, however, only for one year until he was put to death.

In the year 253 AD, a Roman named Valerian became Emperor. Initially, he was favorably disposed to all religions in the Empire including Christianity. The fortunes of the Roman Empire, however, were on the downswing and people at his court persuaded Valerian that the gods were angry because of his tolerance of the Christians.

Valerian then issued an edict condemning Christianity in the year 257. The persecution lasted over three years. The lands and wealth of upper class Christians were confiscated before they were martyred. During the persecution, Sixtus gathered with fellow Christians in the catacombs. As he was preaching one night, some Roman soldiers entered the catacombs and beheaded him on the spot. They then martyred the deacons and subdeacons that were with him.

Sixtus' body was then reverently buried and given a place of honor in the catacombs of St. Callixtus in an area called the "little Vatican" where several early popes had been buried.

Valerian went on to do battle with the enemies of Rome. He was defeated by Shapur, the King of Persia who humiliated him by using him as a footstool each time he mounted his horse. It is said that after Valerian died, Shapur had his body stuffed with straw and put on display as a trophy in a Persian temple for decades afterwards.

The Book of Wisdom tells us that the souls of the just are in God's hands. Though their lives on earth may know suffering, they shall sit at God's right hand. We call it sharing in Christ's victory. We see the truth of this in the story of Sixtus and Valerian.

Whatever the circumstances of our life here, in God's own time justice will be done.

August 7 – St. Cajetan (Optional Memorial)

How to be faithful in unfaithful times is the lesson for us in the life of St. Cajetan. Cajetan was born in Italy in 1480. He received a law degree from the renowned University of Padua and later became a court clerk for Pope Julius II.

During his early life and his time in Rome, he saw a great deal of the corruption and venality that had seeped into the lives of many churchmen. Cajetan sought a way to initiate reform in the Church. As an individual, he was powerless to transform as huge and gigantic an institution as the Catholic Church. But he could make a beginning in the ways that were available to him.

His first step was to embrace Gospel living as faithfully and profoundly as he was able. He began by giving away his accumulated wealth that could, as the Lord says in today's Gospel reading, distract him from growing spiritually rich.

His second step was to found a small community of like-minded people who also wanted to live the Gospel message. It was called the Oratory of Divine Love and cells of this group began to spread throughout Italy. It was as though he was the "Johnny Appleseed" of a reformed Christianity.

He also took the additional practical steps of founding a hospital for the poor and attacking the systemic causes of alienation from the Church by establishing a bank that gave interest-free loans to the poor rather than charging the outrageous, usurious interest that was the case in his day.

Eventually, together with a bishop who later became Pope Paul IV, he established a congregation of priests who became known as Theatines. Their purpose was to live Catholic life in all its purity and honesty in order to confront the Reformation in a very practical way by the witness of their lives. Cajetan's work took place on the very edge of the Reformation because he was ordained in 1516, one year before Martin Luther nailed his theses to the cathedral door.

Cajetan shows us what a person who loves the Church can do to strengthen her by the personal witness of one's life, gathering in small communities of faith and taking practical steps to implement the Gospel message.

The credibility of the Gospel message depends not only on the hierarchy but also on each one of us.

August 8 – St. Dominic (Memorial)

St. Dominic is the founder of one of the great religious families in the Church, the "Order of Preachers" who were later called "Dominicans" and today are called "Blackfriars" in Europe. The name "Blackfriars" derives from the black mantle that Dominicans wear over their white habit. To be in the path of a formally dressed Dominican is like being in the path of an indomitable Catholic humvee.

So often in the Church's life, when a need arises, the Lord sends someone to help the Church meet that need. The period of the 1200's in which Dominic lived was a time of change. People were moving from the countryside to cities and began the rise of an urban culture which produced a potpourri of ideas and movements. Unlike the traditionally more conservative rural areas, cities are places of intellectual ferment for better or worse.

One group of people that arose in Dominic's time were known as the Albigensians from the town of Albi in France. They taught strange distortions of the Gospel. Until very recently they were sympathetically portrayed as an early version of the Puritans. Recently, however, it has become clear that they dominated their cities with a dictatorial ideology that used Christian language but brutalized people within and outside the movement.

From his passing experience with the Albigensians, Dominic realized that part of the Church's problem is this new era was that the Gospel was not adequately preached and taught. To remedy this, he established a group of priests who would dedicate themselves to preaching and living Gospel truth. They were a group of mobile Catholic "Special Forces" who could be deployed wherever there was a need to defend the Faith. This was an innovation because until this time, monks were usually bound to a monastery.

This was innovative on a second score in that bishops at that time were the only ones who preached. Parish priests did not. That is why Dominic's congregation was called the "Order of Preachers." Several features of their life can apply to us.

They were to be men of learning. Knowing our faith is important because we cannot base our lives on a feeling, an impression or a buzz. We should know what we believe and why. Secondly, they were to be men of prayer. Dominic's motto was *"contemplare et aliis contemplata tradere"* – to contemplate and share the results of our prayer with others. Finally, they were to share their faith by their simple, honest Christian lives which were a contrast to the indulgent clergy of that time.

The Dominican Order has given the Church many great popes, saints, theologians and missionaries. St. Dominic teaches us the importance of learning, prayer and witness. The message we carry is not the slogan of the year, but the wisdom of God that every human being needs. Dominicans communicate that wisdom by learning, prayer and witness. We may not be able or equipped to do all three. Each of us can do at least one.

August 9 – St. Teresa Benedicta of the Cross (Memorial)

Teresa Benedicta of the Cross, known in her earlier life as Edith Stein, is the third of the most widely known "Teresas" of the Carmelite Order in addition to Teresa of Avila and Thérèse of Lisieux.

Her life reflects the passion, beauty and cruelty of the last century. She was born in Germany in 1891 of a prominent Jewish family. Endowed with a strong and restless mind, she abandoned her Jewish faith and entered a period of atheism or agnosticism in her quest for truth. She studied under Edmund Husserl, the founder of phenomenology, and received her doctorate in philosophy. She had a number of teaching positions but one day began to read the life of Teresa of Avila and suddenly discovered, in the words of Pope John Paul, that truth has a name, Jesus Christ.

She was baptized in 1922 and eventually entered the Carmelite order. In Christ, her soul finally found rest. Many of her meditations about Carmel and about the Cross remain with us. In one essay, she reflects on the triple falls of Jesus in the Way of the Cross. They represent the triple fall of humanity in the first sin, then the rejection of Jesus by His own people, and finally the abandonment of Jesus by His disciples then and now. But, she continues, on His Way of the Cross, the Lord also has helpers. After the first fall there were the righteous ones of the Old Testament, then His faithful disciples in His lifetime, and now there are those who embrace the cross to build His Kingdom.

With the Holocaust at its height, she moved to a Carmelite convent in the Netherlands. The bishops there had issued a condemnation of Hitler's treatment of the Jews. In retaliation, Hitler ordered the extermination of all non-Aryan Catholics. Sister Teresa Benedicta was sent to Auschwitz where she died in the gas chamber for being Jewish and Catholic.

Each convent where Carmelite sisters live is called a "Carmel." Auschwitz was her last "Carmel" where she followed Jesus to His cross. Although her death was not with nails but with zyklon gas, it was a kind of crucifixion and a sacrifice.

Her life shows us the drive of the mind toward God, the drama of conversion, and the beauty of sacrifice even in the face of the barbarity of evil. Sister Benedicta referred to her times as engulfed in flames. But, she said, the cross towers over them and cannot be consumed by them. It is the path to heaven and will lift everyone who embraces it into the life of the Trinity. At Auschwitz on August 9, 1942, the cross lifted her into the arms of the Trinity.

Whatever the burning tensions of our time, the cross will lift us above them and lead us into the life of the Trinity.

AUGUST 10 – ST. LAWRENCE (FEAST)

St. Lawrence was a deacon, a permanent deacon, of the Church at Rome. As a deacon, he was involved in the work of administration. During Valerian's persecution in 258, which was begun in part because the government was in debt and needed money, the property of Christians was being confiscated. In anticipation of the officials coming to him as administrator of the Church's goods, Lawrence sold the Church's property and distributed the proceeds to the poor.

When asked to produce the Church's treasures, he pointed to the poor and said that they are the treasures of the Church. It is said he was executed by being burned to death on a griddle. He is often pictured with a griddle and a palm branch of victory.

Today the Church has many magnificent churches and art treasures that have inspired generations of people. But the real assets of the Church, the "wealth" of the Church, is in her members, in changed lives, people committed to Christ, individuals who have been forgiven, healed and made whole – and who themselves become, as St. Paul says in today's first reading, sources of Christ's grace to others.

Everything we do and have as a Church, our schools, churches and organizations are all meant to lead people to Christ because the Church's measure of success is not in the number of buildings built but in the number of souls saved. Everything we have is to help people directly or indirectly to be like that seed in the Gospel that dies to self and emerges with new life.

There are many ways of following Christ. St. Augustine gives a wonderful image in today's Office of Readings when he states that many flowers grow in God's garden. There are the lilies of celibate lives, the ivy of married life and the violets of widows and widowers. But the red rose of martyrdom always stands out. We honor martyrs like Lawrence because their fidelity to Christ and His Church is clear, decisive and dramatic.

Whatever the circumstances of our lives, we can strive to give a witness to Christ that may or may not be as dramatic as that of Lawrence but can be as clear and decisive.

August 11 – St. Clare (Memorial)

There is a well known image of St. Clare standing on a convent balcony, holding high a ciborium that is filled with light while soldiers cower in fear on the ground. It captures an incident from her life that typifies what Clare's mission was all about.

St. Clare was born in 1193 and was a friend of St. Francis. When she was about eighteen years old, she was drawn to Francis' way of life, its simplicity, its strength and its faith. She left her family to join his way of life and others joined her as well.

Francis and Clare established the Second Franciscan Order. Later a group of these became popularly known as the "Poor Clares." She never left her convent yet she inspired a generation.

Towns in Italy in those days were like little states, one attacking the other. One day, Assisi was attacked by an army from a town nearby. Clare took the ciborium with the Eucharist from the chapel, went to the convent porch and raised it high. A magnificent blinding light shone from it that startled the soldiers and caused them to retreat. She saved Assisi that day. On a deeper level, however, she inspired a generation by holding up Jesus Christ.

So deep was her love for the Eucharist that it is said that when she was ill, she had a vision of the Mass that was being celebrated in the chapel. She is known today as the patron of broadcasters.

Her holding up the ciborium as strength against invaders reminds us that the Eucharist is a powerful source of strength in the spiritual assaults we experience in our life.

Her poverty, like that of Francis, was not an indictment of the wealthy but a caution against accumulation of any kind that can distract us from our real fulfillment in Christ, as our readings today teach us. The deepest truth about us derives not from what we have but from what we are.

Her fidelity is a model to us as well. She died at the age of 60 still faithful to the grace of conversion that she received when she was 18.

These virtues of Eucharistic faith, simplicity of life and fidelity to the grace of conversion were powerful virtues in St. Clare in the 1200s. They are as powerful today.

AUGUST 13 – STS. PONTIAN AND HIPPOLYTUS (OPTIONAL MEMORIAL)

The joining of Saints Pontian and Hippolytus in the same memorial reflects a story of conversion and fraternity in suffering.

Hippolytus was a priest in Rome in the third century. He felt that the Pope had been too lenient in allowing certain Christians who had abandoned the faith during a persecution to return. He proceeded to establish his own rival, more rigorous church becoming, in effect the first antipope. He drew up for his followers a book of liturgical directions called the *Apostolic Tradition*. It contains the oldest version of the Eucharistic prayer in use before the 4th century and is the basis of our second Eucharistic prayer today.

The schism lasted about 18 years. Then in 235 a persecution broke out which was aimed at decapitating the Church by exiling her leaders. By this time, the Roman Catholic Pope was Pontian. Pontian and Hippolytus were sent to the salt mines in Sardinia. It is said that Hippolytus was so impressed by Pontian's faith and humility that he abandoned his papal claim and instructed his followers to seek reconciliation with the Church. Because of his return to the Church and his martyrdom, Hippolytus is the only antipope to be honored as a saint.

Before he was sent into exile, Pontian resigned the office of Pope to allow the Church to have a strong and free leader.

Both Pontian and Hippolytus are honored as martyrs today. Persecution can work as a solvent. It can dissolve the petty quarrels that so often divide us. It can be a time of judgment that separates deep faith from its superficial imitations. It can cause the true faith and heroism of individuals to come forth.

It enabled Hippolytus to realize from what he saw in Pontian's example that humility and compassion are deeper reflections of Christ than rigorous justice.

Pontian and Hippolytus remind us that the grace to witness and the grace of conversion can be found anywhere, even in salt mines. There Pontian gave witness and there Hippolytus was saved. God's grace can reach anywhere.

August 14 – St. Maximilian Mary Kolbe (Memorial)

Maximilian Kolbe was a Polish Conventual Franciscan. He was a saint of our time and a martyr of our time. There are still people alive today who knew him. We can divide Maximilian's life into two phases, the days of success and the days of glory.

The days of his success involved his work as a missionary of modern times. He established the Militia of Mary Immaculate. This was a community of faith and evangelization, a little like the "new movements" today. He organized and built the "City of the Immaculate" in Poland which comprised at one point some 800 Franciscans. He later established another one in Japan. Through this "City of the Immaculate" he promoted the Gospel and devotion to Mary through the media of his time which were newspapers and magazines, one of which was entitled "Knight of the Immaculate." Those were the days of his success.

Then came World War II and the Nazi occupation of Poland. Then began his days of glory.

He was sent to Auschwitz for opposing the Nazis. It is a reminder to us of the diverse number of people from many areas of society who became brothers and sisters when confined in that death camp. There, he evangelized, gave comfort and prayed with and for fellow prisoners. In prison, he was a true priest, a bridge to Christ.

The most famous moment of his imprisonment occurred when a crime was committed in the camp. Since nobody came forward to admit the crime, it was decreed that until the perpetrator was found, every tenth prisoner would be executed. A married man and father standing next to Maximilian Kolbe was one of those taken to be executed. Maximilian took that man's place and was killed by lethal injection in 1941. Quite literally, he loved in deed and truth as St. John teaches in today's first reading, giving his life for another as Jesus says in today's Gospel reading.

All the intimidation and machinery of death at Auschwitz could not destroy the strong, uncomplicated faith of Maximilian Kolbe. His last days were his days of glory.

He was truly a "Knight of the Immaculate" That dull, dark, damp prison camp was his place of glory. With all that he achieved in his life, his giving his life for another was his greatest act of glory.

In a scandal soaked society like ours, we should try not to forget the quiet and magnificent acts of sacrifice and heroism going on around us every day. They too are part of our time.

August 16 – St. Stephen of Hungary (Optional Memorial)

"Might makes right." "Winning is everything." "Take all you can get." "Do unto others before they do unto you." These contemporary sayings characterized the life of the peoples along the Danube River about the year 1000. They were divided into violent, warring and superstitious tribes and factions. Wars could ignite in a second.

The saint we honor today, Stephen, was one of those people but became a Christian when very young. He then tried to bring national and spiritual unity to his land. He asked the Holy Father to crown him king which the Pope did in the year 1000. Stephen then became the first Catholic king of Hungary.

Like the men in the Gospel who used their talents in the master's service, Stephen used his position to strengthen faith among his people. He invited the Benedictine monks to establish monasteries as centers for faith and learning. He built churches as places of unity so people could converge to celebrate their faith together. He had the Gospel preached to plant the seeds of Christian morality into their hearts. Through all this, Stephen fused national and spiritual identity. The culture became Christian.

It was a great achievement and a great gift to future generations.

What has happened since then? The people of Hungary have experienced their own national drama of faith, most recently burdened by Communism, and are now slowly restoring their heritage.

We too were given a heritage inspired by biblical faith. We were given something strong and beautiful. What are we doing to protect that culture? That is something we have to do in every generation. We cannot wait for a Stephen to come among us. In a consumer culture, consumers have power to protest about movies, television programs, music and advertising that demean faith in God.

That is one way we can stay faithful to the powerful spiritual heritage we have received. On this memorial of St. Stephen, we can resolve to use our talents to strengthen the spiritual roots of our culture. It is much easier to tear a bridge down than to build it. It is much easier to corrupt a culture than to build one.

We should protect the gift of a spiritually strong heritage we have received.

August 18 – St. Jane Frances de Chantal (Optional Memorial)

The memorial of St. Jane Frances de Chantal is celebrated on December 12. Since, however, December 12th is the feast of Our Lady of Guadalupe, St. Jane's memorial is perpetually "bumped." The bishops of the United States requested the Holy See to transfer this memorial in the United States to August 18.

St. Jane Frances de Chantal could be called the patron saint of the second career or even the patron of those depressed by grief. In the first part of her life, she was a faithful wife and mother. In the second part of her life, after her husband died, she founded a religious congregation. That tragedy of death that brought suffering to her led her to begin a new life of dedication to Christ and His Church.

Jane Frances was born into an upper middle class French family in 1572. She received the proper education of the day and was reputed to be intelligent and beautiful. With her husband, a member of the nobility, their lives took on the beauty and happiness of a fairy tale. It was a good marriage; she cared for her children and for the community around their castle.

One day, her husband was killed in a hunting accident and things fell apart. She became a widow at 28. She lost interest in everything and went into what we would call today a deep depression. She was told to leave the castle by his family and went to manage an estate of her father-in-law who was as neurotic as he was tyrannical. Her depression continued.

Seven years later, she attended some Lenten talks given by a young bishop called Francis de Sales. He showed her how to use the sufferings of her life in a positive way. She impressed him by her deepening spirituality and their spiritual friendship grew. Together, when her children were grown, they eventually founded a religious community of women who would help the city's poor. They were known as the Visitation Sisters imitating Mary's visit of aid to the older Elizabeth. They became her new family founded in faith of which Jesus speaks in today's Gospel reading.

The Holy See insisted that the sisters be cloistered as the Visitation Sisters are to this day. At her death, some 80 Visitation convents existed in France.

Out of the darkness in her life came light not only for herself but also for the Church. Whatever darkness we may experience in our life, it is important that we remain constant in prayer and the fulfillment of our obligations. That is how we will be ready to greet the dawn.

August 19 – St. John Eudes (Optional Memorial)

Reform in the Church has probably been sought by every generation. Just as individuals constantly need to go back to the Gospel and renew their relationship with the Truth of Christ, so the Church needs to constantly renew itself in the Gospel of Christ. Some eras have a more insistent need for reform than others do.

The Church in the 1600's needed reform. One of those who led the way was St. John Eudes. John Eudes was born in France in 1601. He was ordained at twenty-four and began to experience great success as a teacher. A good part of his life was the preaching of missions, short but intense parish retreats, in parishes throughout France as a "home missionary." It is said that in his lifetime he preached over 100 missions.

John Eudes did not call for structural reform in the Church as such. His emphasis was on conversion of heart. This effort to bring people closer to the Lord is the real center of any reform. Without a change of heart, structural reform simply rearranges the chairs. A change of heart can bring new life even to an old way of doing things.

His emphasis on parish missions was one element of his effort at reform. Another was the training of clergy. He organized a group of priests, later known as the Congregation of Jesus and Mary (today the "Eudists"), to teach in seminaries and form future pastors in the love of Jesus Christ.

Popular morality being at an ebb, there were many unmarried and abandoned women who were pregnant. He established a congregation of sisters to care for them with dignity, help them bring their pregnancy to term, and enable them to lead a new life. He also founded a society for widows, which had a form that we would call a "secular institute."

In addition to preaching, staffing seminaries and caring for widows and unwed mothers, he preached devotion to the Sacred Heart and to the Holy Heart of Mary. Through this devotion, he wanted people to appreciate the great love God has for them and their true worth which that love shows. He wanted people to experience, as St. Paul tells the Ephesians, the full breadth and length of Christ's love for them and the appreciation that Christ works and ministers through them. His love is an energy that propels the Christian to do the work of Jesus.

There are always many suggestions for reform on the table. The deepest source of Church renewal will always be in the Truth and love of Jesus Christ. When Jesus touches the heart, true reform of the Church and of our life begins.

AUGUST 20 – ST. BERNARD (MEMORIAL)

Every year, *Time* magazine designates as "person of the year" someone who has had the greatest impact on the world. Various candidates are always suggested beforehand. We could call Bernard of Clairvaux the person of the century, the 12th century. He was a monk of huge influence in his time.

Bernard was born in 1090. As a young man, he decided to become a monk by joining a small monastery at Citeaux. He arrived with 30 friends and relatives and brought that monastery to life. He was then sent to start a monastery on his own in a place called "Valley of Light" or "Clairvaux." There he thrived. Many men came to become monks there. Eventually he founded more than a hundred other daughter monasteries.

Bernard was charismatic, brilliant and thrived on conflict. Many people, including church and civil leaders, came to him for advice. Through his preaching and influence he strode through the 12th century like a colossus. He was an advisor to Popes, helped heal a Papal schism, became an arbitrator between warring states, and was a spellbinding preacher and a reformer. He gave a great new impulse and vigor to monastic life.

Even though he opposed the excessive reliance on reason and dialectic of some of the new philosophers such as Abelard, he used brilliantly the same techniques of argument and logic to emphasize the importance of faith. For St. Bernard, faith is a gift from above rather than a conclusion from below.

He was ordered by the Pope to preach the Second Crusade and recruited thousands of men. Whatever the effect of the Crusades, one incident shows Bernard's truest character. While the Crusade was being preached, a monk in the Rhineland began to incite the people to also kill the Jewish people to save the faith thereby sparking anti-Jewish riots. The local archbishop hid some of the Jewish people to protect them but the situation was volatile. Bernard came to condemn the monk who incited these events, calling him a heretic and liar thereby calming the situation. St. Bernard is remembered among Rhineland Jews to this day as a "righteous Gentile" and many even name their children after him.

In the end, the source of Bernard's influence was more than native intelligence. It was his prayer life where wisdom was born. He once remarked that one must become a reservoir in order to become a river. One result of a life of prayer is developing the spiritual resources to share with others.

Our spiritual life is not just a personal possession. It has a public effect.

AUGUST 21 – ST. PIUS X (MEMORIAL)

Pope Pius X was elected Pope in 1903 by a strange turn of events. After being a parish priest for 17 years, he was made bishop of a diocese that was practically bankrupt. He stabilized the diocese and then became Patriarch of Venice where he was very popular.

When the time came to elect a new Pope, the Austrian Emperor vetoed the candidate elected. So Cardinal Sarto was elected and became Pope Pius X. One of the first things he did was abolish the "right of veto."

He was Pope in a very turbulent time politically and intellectually. All kinds of new and untested ideas were swirling about Europe and through the Church. During his eleven years as Pope, his accomplishments were striking.

He encouraged frequent Holy Communion rather than once a year.

He enabled young children to receive Holy Communion rather than at the age of 13.

He reformed Church music to replace baroque polyphony with simpler chants.

He started a reform of Church Law to create a code of law for the first time.

He reorganized the offices of the Vatican in Rome.

He protected the Church against the excesses of Modernism.

None of this was easy but the times were turbulent. It was by holding the Church on course, securing the center, that Pius X answered Christ's question to him, "Do you love me?" He showed his fidelity to his mission and his love of Christ by stabilizing the Church as he did his first diocese.

There are times when a shepherd must lead the sheep into new pastures. That was not the time of Pius X. There are other times when the shepherd must work to keep the sheep in the fold especially when predators are around. That was the challenge facing Pius X.

When strong winds are blowing, we instinctively need to hold on to something stable. That's what Pius X did for the Church. He held on to the apostolic faith. In that, there is a message for us.

In complex times, we need to hold to the apostolic faith, the Eucharist and the Church. When we are not strong, they will be our strength.

AUGUST 22 – THE QUEENSHIP OF MARY (MEMORIAL)

The feast of the Queenship of Mary was established by Pope Pius XII in 1954 to be celebrated on the last day of May. That was a Marian year in which the Holy Father proclaimed as a dogma of the Faith the long held belief in the Assumption of Mary. When the Church calendar was revised, the Queenship of Mary was transferred to August 22nd, the octave day of the Assumption. This links Mary's queenship to her glorification by Jesus in the Assumption.

The Queenship of Mary is the fifth glorious mystery of the Rosary. It is the crowning mystery of her life and place in the redemption of the world. The mystery of the Queenship of Mary recognizes the bestowal on Mary by Christ of an extraordinary power of intercession, the power to mediate His grace and the power to guide the people of the Church. It is a share in Christ's kingship in heaven because of her closeness to her Son on earth in body and heart. All of this was given to Mary by the Risen Lord.

Mary was raised to this holy authority by Christ and given His graces to bestow on the entire human race, even to those people of good will outside the Church. They may not know her name but they can know her intercession. She is recognized on this feast as Queen of Heaven, the greatest of saints, and Queen of the Earth whose love and intercession embraces the universe. Today is a day to thank the Lord Jesus for the gift of His Mother to us as helper, guide, intercessor, example, companion and queen. This array of titles is hers because of her Son, Jesus.

For our part, we can make Mary a part of our spiritual life not only by seeking her help and intercession but by imitating her fidelity to the Lord and her loyalty to His plan in all the events of our life.

If during our life, we are left alone, when others have abandoned us, Jesus and His Mother are with us. If we are alone at the hour of our death without any caregivers nearby, Jesus and His Mother are with us. If we are alone at the time of our death because it comes to us in an accident or violent human deed, Jesus and His Mother are with us. When we come to face our eternity with the truth of our life, Jesus and His Mother are with us.

The angel's words in today's Gospel reading evoke the first half of the "Hail Mary" and the grand beginning of the great events of our redemption. This memorial of the Queenship of Mary is all about the second half of the "Hail Mary" when we say, "Holy Mary, Mother of God, pray for us sinners now and at the hour of our death." The moment of our death is when the work of our individual redemption is concluded. And Mary is there.

August 23 – St. Rose of Lima (Optional Memorial)

Sometimes it is difficult for us to empathize with a particular saint because of the intensity of his or her life. There are some saints whose lives display in huge capital letters a feature of the Christian life that we should all imitate.

Rose of Lima was one of those saints. She was born in Lima, Peru in 1586. It is said that she was a beautiful baby. Baptized

Isabel, she was nicknamed "Rose" because her cheeks were the color of a red rose. In her very young years, people admired her beauty. She was a very devout girl, perhaps even mystical, and she gave herself completely to Christ.

She did not want any of her natural beauty to distract her or others from Christ. Accordingly, she began a life of intense even excessive penance and mortification. She was so intent on focusing only on Christ that she cut off her beautiful hair and even tried to disfigure her beauty. She lived in a shack on the family property doing embroidery and tending the garden.

She became a member of the third order of St. Dominic and followed its rule thoroughly and precisely. She was a young woman of intense devotion, penance and prayer.

She had found the pearl of great price in Jesus and gave herself completely to Him. She showed in a dramatic way the seriousness of her commitment. Her powerful penances remind us of the need we all have to practice penance as an antidote to self-indulgence.

We are not called to imitate her intensity but to recognize in her a person who was thoroughly devoted to the Lord. The Church would surely encourage us to make our fasting and mortification much more moderate than hers. But we should still practice fasting and mortification. They are powerful antidotes to the self-indulgence that surrounds us every day.

Rose of Lima may not be our role model in every detail. But her life reminds us of the need we all have to sacrifice for Christ. If our faith requires absolutely no change in our lifestyle, we may be deceiving ourselves about the seriousness of our faith.

The more we sacrifice for Christ, the more His life will come to life in us.

AUGUST 24 – ST. BARTHOLOMEW (FEAST)

St. Bartholomew, also known as Nathaniel, was one of the twelve Apostles. It is said that he preached the Gospel in what we know as India and Armenia. He gave his life for Christ, tradition reports, by being skinned alive. Today's Gospel reading captures the moment of his call.

Some disciples heard about Jesus but then the moment came when Jesus Himself touched their life. So it happened with Bartholomew. Philip had told him that they found the Messiah in Jesus of Nazareth. Bartholomew was skeptical since he wondered whether anything good could come from Nazareth.

We can become trapped by stereotypes of all sorts, racial, ethnic and religious. Maybe we tend to label people too quickly until we meet them personally and, suddenly, it's a different story. So, Bartholomew was told to come and see for himself. Then he became a disciple.

This Gospel account warns us against prejudice and pre-judgments about people without meeting them. Beneath every cultural label is a person with individuality, hopes and desires. Our tendency is to think in universals and stereotypes rather than to encounter individuals. Such prejudices can really damage and distort our judgments.

This Gospel also calls us to come and see for ourselves, to come to know the Lord in prayer and in the Sacraments.

Jesus is not just an historical person, a religious icon, or a presence far away. He is a living Lord, calling to us as He did to those first disciples. As with Bartholomew, the Lord has a lot to show us and give us.

We cannot rely on reports from others. We need to come and see for ourselves.

AUGUST 25 – ST. LOUIS OF FRANCE (OPTIONAL MEMORIAL)

King Lear is described in the play by the same name as "every inch a king." We could say of Louis IX of France that he was "every inch a saint." St. Louis was a Christian king in name and in spirit. He ruled France in the 13th century during a time of great cultural achievement. It was a time when cathedrals were being built, universities established, hospitals organized, and an equitable court system established. These are all significant cultural achievements, which Louis not only allowed but also encouraged.

He was raised by his mother to be a thoroughly devoted Catholic with a deep spirituality. He not only surrounded himself with all the externals of Catholic practice but they manifested the deep Catholicism in his soul.

He became king at the age of eleven in 1226. He was guided and protected by his mother until he reached teenage years. At the age of 20, he married his wife Margaret and together they had eleven children.

St. Louis cared about his people and sought to mitigate the harsh life of the feudal system. He encouraged religious orders in France, he forbade usury or excessive interest on loans, and when engaged in various crusades he insisted that the Moslem captives be treated with respect. He built the magnificent Sainte Chapelle in Paris as a shrine for the Crown of Thorns, which he had received and is often portrayed as holding it in his hands. He led crusades to the Holy Land that were not militarily successful and in one of which he was taken prisoner. After his release, he died of typhoid fever at the age of 56.

The life of St. Louis reminds us that power does not have to corrupt. Power can be used to create some measure of justice, lighten the burden of people's lives, exemplify virtue, and strengthen the community of the Church. A position of authority in Church or State becomes a place where one can be a powerful light to others.

The memorial of St. Louis also reminds us to pray for all those in authority on any level that they would be instruments of God's justice and peace.

Power is not a prize but an opportunity.

August 25 – St. Joseph Calasanz (Optional Memorial)

St. Joseph Calasanz (Calasanctius) is the founder of the Piarist Order. Both of today's readings speak to his work with youth and to his own life.

He was born in Spain in 1556. He received a good education, was called to become a priest and was ordained at the age of 26. He spent his early years in the priesthood in various administrative posts without much experience of parish life. After he had been ordained nine years, he moved to Rome where he became an aide to a cardinal and a tutor to his household.

While in Rome, Joseph Calasanz joined the Confraternity of Christian Doctrine to teach young people. The number of poor children who did not receive an education was an eye opener to him. Together with 14 other priests, he opened the first free school in Europe held in various church facilities. The support of the Pope enabled him to have a secure financial base for his school.

He and the other Piarists took the traditional vows of poverty, chastity and obedience and added a fourth vow to educate youth. He showed Christ's love to young people in all the forms described by St. Paul. He accepted poor children to educate them when few others cared. Joseph Calasanz reminds us of the commitment we all should have to give young people an education to become contributing adults. Schools, especially parochial schools and Religious Education programs, deserve our support. Through them we build the future of the Church.

St. Joseph Calasanz' work was under attack on many fronts. He was under suspicion because he was a friend of Galileo. There were two members of his Order who were the cause of scandal because of their behavior with children. Because they were politically well connected inside and outside of the Church, Joseph Calasanz had to choose between expelling them with the consequent loss of his funding and the collapse of his Order's mission, or removing them from contact with children by placing them in administrative positions. He chose the latter and when the perpetrators came to power, they removed him from office. His Order was suppressed during his old age and was only reinstated after his death. Finally, there were members of society's elite who saw

the education of the poor as at best pointless and at worst dangerous. In his elder years, Joseph Calasanz was forced to defend his
work as though he were at the Alamo.

But, he continued to show the many faces of love that Paul
describes even to his accusers and maintained humility before all
the decisions of Church authority.

Both dimensions of Joseph Calasanz' life speak to us: the
importance of educating our young people and obedience to our
calling as well as to Church authority even when under fire. He
died at the age of 92, as faithful to the Lord as he was when ordained 65 years earlier.

His body became worn out but not his commitment to Jesus Christ.

AUGUST 27 – ST. MONICA (MEMORIAL)

We know St. Monica as the mother of St. Augustine, how she followed his travels not only in spirit but also by actually following
him from place to place praying for his conversion. Her prayers
were answered and Augustine was baptized. Her prayers were
like drops of water slowly wearing away at rock. She teaches us
never to give up on anyone. Even when our prayers do not seem
to be answered, slowly they are making an impact. The Lord can
bring anyone back to life as He did the widow's son in today's
Gospel.

Monica herself did not have an easy life. She was born in
Tagaste in 331 in what is now Algeria. Her husband was very difficult; today we might even say "abusive." She was the faithful wife
of the Book of Sirach and won his conversion as well.

There is also a story from the life of Monica that is important
to recall today. As she followed her son about, she encountered
differing liturgical practices. She wrote about this to Ambrose, the
bishop of Milan and her spiritual director. When she followed her
son to Rome, she noted that they stand at a particular point in the
Mass while back in Milan they kneel. She inquired of Ambrose
what she should do. Ambrose wrote back that when in Rome,

she should do as the Romans do. That remains a good principle for us today, to follow the liturgical practices of the parish where we are.

Monica, however, stands most prominently for the power of the prayer of intercession. It can be helpful to us to make a list of people for whom we pray and to keep that list nearby. It reminds us to pray for others and also recalls for us the prayers that have been answered.

Prayer for others is a magnificent way of showing our love for them. Not only do we all need a Monica in our life; we all can be a Monica to others.

AUGUST 28 – ST. AUGUSTINE (MEMORIAL)

St. Augustine was born in 354 in North Africa. He is one of the truly great theologians of the Church. His whole life as bishop was spent in debate with various heresies and through all that he set the terms and definitions that shaped Catholic theology for the next thousand years.

More interesting to most people is his life story before he became a bishop. His life story could be called "The Restless Heart" based on his famous dictum that our hearts are restless until they rest in God.

His very devout mother, Monica, prayed for him constantly. He became a lawyer, studied literature, led a dissolute life and had a child out of wedlock. He went from pleasure to pleasure because he had the money, the looks and the wit. Then came the moment of his conversion. One day, he heard a child in the next yard singing *"Tolle lege"* ("Take and read") over and over. He opened the Scriptures and read St. Paul. Monica's prayers were answered, the Holy Spirit entered his heart, and Augustine was baptized. He was later ordained and became a bishop.

Years later, he wrote the story of his conversion called *The Confessions,* the very first Christian autobiography. As he reflected on his life, he realized that his travelling from fad to fad was really a disguised search for God. He wrote that while he was looking for God "out there" all the while God was "in here," prompting his search. Reflecting on this period of his life, he remarked that all the while God was with him but he was not with God.

The restlessness of the heart is a sign that we were designed for God. As St. John writes in today's first reading, God doesn't love us because we love Him. It's the other way around. God loved us first and therefore we come to love Him.

As the Lord teaches in today's Gospel and as St. Augustine's life confirms, teachers and guides in our life only open to us to God who is the true Father, Teacher and Guide within us.

The message of St. Augustine's life for us is that although we can see evidence of God in the ordered majesty of the universe, there is also the striving of our heart, the searching of our lives, the quest for life, truth and beauty we all experience that can lead us to God as well.

The desire for God is itself a sign that God is with us. He most frequently calls us not from without but from within.

To paraphrase St. Augustine, God is with us. Are we with Him?

AUGUST 29 – THE MARTYRDOM OF ST. JOHN THE BAPTIST (MEMORIAL)

It can happen that we shrink John the Baptist's significance into his being the one who first identified Jesus as the Messiah and who baptized Jesus. John was also a prophet in the classic sense of one who speaks forth God's Word. He was the pillar of iron and wall of brass of which Jeremiah speaks.

We have a wider use of the word "martyr" on this memorial than is usual. We imagine a martyr as one who gives his or her life for Christ. That is the "classical" meaning of the word "martyr." Venerable Bede gives us an important and challenging reflection in today's Office of Readings about the martyrdom of John the Baptist. Bede writes that John's persecutor did not demand that he should deny Christ but only that he should remain quiet about the truth. That truth was the fact of the immorality of Herod's marriage.

John the Baptist was a martyr for the truth. The age of martyrs is not limited to the early centuries of the Church. There are many people today who are put to death for being followers of Christ. There are as many, if not more, who are put to death for speaking out about truth, justice and honesty. There are people slain in the Middle East today because they take the risk of pursuing peace.

We can apply Bede's words to ourselves. Few of us will be called upon to engage in an open denial of Christ. But we are called upon every week to take a stand for the truth, for fairness and for honesty in business, private life and in government. These Gospel values are the truths for which we are called to give witness. They are places where we can take our stand for the Kingdom of Christ.

Today, if we speak the truth we will not have an armed guard beat down our door to arrest us. The persecution today is more subtle through the loss of employment, the disappearance of speaking engagements, loss of elected office or promotion at work, ostracism by friends and partners, the absence of invitations to public events and private dinners, as well as street corner character assassination. These economic impacts can cause suffering as surely as physical assault. There are sectors of our society that love a devotional Catholicism that never leaves the sacristy or the heart. These same forces will violently attack and slander a Church that "gets involved."

There are many ways of being a martyr for Christ. Witness to the truth about Him is one way. There are also the paths of witness to the Gospel values of justice, fairness and peace. Although we may be willing to announce our faith in Christ, are we willing to stand for the Gospel values about which the Lord preached?

September 3 – St. Gregory the Great (Memorial)

Pope Saint Gregory was born around 540. He is called "the Great" because he was a great Pope who faced enormous difficulties in a dramatic time of transition for the Church. He was a true father and Doctor of the Church.

He was a Benedictine monk who wanted to be a missionary. As it turned out, he was elected Pope in 590 and his desire to be a missionary took a different turn. He faced a number of crises that required a missionary mind.

With the decline of the Roman Empire, huge hordes of "barbarians" – European tribal nations – moved into the Empire's former territories. In the middle of this chaos, Gregory initiated a plan to convert the barbarians and introduce Christian morality and law into their lives.

He sent missionaries to Britain encouraging them to connect Christ to the customs of the people in what we call "inculturation." He inspired the musical development of the liturgy in what later became known as "Gregorian Chant." He wrote handbooks for bishops and lives of the saints to inspire the Church. He established the style of direction of the Church in the Middle Ages.

In his 13 years as Pope, he did a great deal politically, administratively, materially and liturgically to build up the Church. He was "great." In all this he was the first to use the title "Servant of the servants of God," a title that alludes to the Lord's command of service.

He was involved with, some might say micromanaged, a great many things in his years as Pope. In today's Office of Readings, he writes about all the pressures put on him, with people coming to him from all sides. He describes how his prayer life and love for the Lord keep him balanced. That is one message we can draw from his life.

In everything we do, a strong prayer life reminds us that in whatever work we are doing, we are still followers of Jesus. Our prayer life opens us to Christ's grace to keep our judgment balanced, reasoned and Christian so that we are not distracted by criticism or by praise.

In the darkness of his times, Gregory's faith was a light for the Church and for Europe. But before that light could shine out to others it had to shine within. God's light must shine in our hearts so we can display Christ to the world.

In the darkness of our time, our faith can be a light to others.

SEPTEMBER 8 – THE NATIVITY OF THE BLESSED VIRGIN MARY (FEAST)

The feast of the Nativity of Mary reminds us that Mary had a family. Sometimes it seems that we imagine Mary to have suddenly appeared on the earth without any ties to the past. But Mary was part of a family.

We like to think of ourselves as self-made men and women. But we are all products of a family and stand on the shoulders of ancestors who transmitted life to us, as Mary's ancestors did to her. We are indebted to family and friends who equipped us for life by word and example as Mary's family equipped her.

We have received the faith and our Catholic traditions from those before us, as Mary received teaching about her Jewish heritage from her parents and larger family.

We inherit a great many things but what happens in our soul is up to us.

Discussion about cloning appears periodically in the media. Apart from the possibility and morality of human cloning, we can ask that if a human being were cloned, what exactly would be replicated? Only the biological makeup of an individual presumably could be cloned. What cannot be duplicated is a person's experience, which is unique to each of us. The experience we have of our families, the encouragement from others, or lack of it, constitute our individual makeup.

Each of us is a unique product of God's action of grace or of the effect of sin. We cannot clone a tyrant and we cannot clone a saint. What happens in our soul is up to us.

The feast of the Nativity of Mary reminds us that Mary, like all of us, was taught a great deal by her parents Joachim and Ann as were we by our parents. But there was the very individual and personal response to God's grace that was entirely her own and for which others could only prepare the way. The same is true of us. Our families can only prepare us to make a very personal and individual response to God's grace. The responding is up to us.

We are all part of a chain of life and part of God's plan as was Mary. Our personal response to God's plan is up to us.

Our eternity is not determined by what we have received from others but what we have done with it. What happens in our soul is up to us.

SEPTEMBER 9 – ST. PETER CLAVER (MEMORIAL)

St. Peter Claver was a missionary in a double sense. He was a missionary of the Gospel not only to non-Christians but to Christians as well.

He was born in 1580 in Spain where he became a Jesuit. He was then sent to Colombia in South America, which was a principal center for the slave trade. In Colombia, he took care of the slaves who were transported from Africa in cargo ships. He brought them medicine and food.

He once remarked that his approach was to speak with his hands before he spoke with his lips. Then, through an interpreter and with pictures, he taught them the essentials of the Gospel. It is said that he baptized over 300,000 individuals in the course of his ministry.

He wanted not only to bring the redeeming grace of Jesus Christ into the lives of these slaves but also to show their masters that as human beings, these slaves had a dignity and value in God's sight. The second direction of his missionary activity was to the slave owners and traders to show them that these people were not property but human beings with a soul from God and a destiny larger than this world.

Predictably, the owners and traders complained about him to his superiors and vilified him. When he died, however, he was buried like a saint. Even those who complained about him mourned his loss because they realized that a man walked among them who brought out a bit more of their humanity.

Peter Claver is revered not only because of his work of conversion but because he helped people realize their own dignity and worth. Although he was reviled in his lifetime, he never responded in kind. The lesson he has for all of us is that whatever our race, sex or ethnic background, we each have a dignity that comes not from ourselves, not from others and not from society but from God.

That is something we can forget about others and about ourselves. In the eyes of the Lord, we count, no matter what others may think. That is the important message from Peter Claver to us in an age of "outer-directed people" who find their worth in what others think of them.

We all have an inherent dignity and value that we ourselves need to respect, even when others don't.

September 12 – Most Holy Name of Mary (Optional Memorial)

This memorial in honor of the Most Holy Name of Mary has been restored to the Church calendar in the most recent revision along with the feast of the Most Holy Name of Jesus.

Years ago, there was a musical called "West Side Story." There is in it a familiar song called "Maria." A young man sings about the girl he loves and how her name evokes everything beautiful that he knows as well as everything about her. Referring to her name, he sings: "Say it loud and there's music playing; say it soft and it's almost like praying."

The name evokes the person. Lovers often write the name of the one they love over and over. The name of Mary brings to mind everything she was to Jesus and everything she is to us. It reminds us of her fidelity to God's Word, her journey with Jesus through the joyful, luminous, suffering and glorious moments of His life. It reminds us of all the ways that Mary has been part of the Church's life throughout history and how she is part of our life as Christians today.

There is a growing practice in the Church of saying the "Jesus prayer." This prayer is of ancient origin and consists in the slow repetition of the name of Jesus and allowing the Holy Spirit to bring forth everything Jesus did for us as it opens our hearts and minds to the gradual influence of grace. Perhaps we can try to say the "Mary prayer." This consists also in slowly repeating the name of Mary and letting her influence, love and faith blend with our hearts and souls to draw us closer to her Son.

Mary is a powerful intercessor. We can entrust to Mary our leaders, our friends, victims of natural and man-made disasters, our relatives and those in need. We know they will find in her a helper and a friend. We can also entrust our hopes and dreams to her as well. If we have the custom of saying the "Jesus prayer": we can also start the "Mary prayer."

As we quietly and slowly repeat her name, we can let Mary touch our hearts and minds through that prayer to make us strong and wise in her Son, Jesus.

Mary's name and the name of her Son have enormous power to bring to our minds and lives Christ's grace, hope and peace. There are many beautiful prayers we can say to Mary. The Church's tradition has gathered thousands. But a prayer we can always say wherever we are, whether we have a prayer book or not, is the "Mary prayer." Her name evokes all that is beautiful, worthy and holy. She is, in a paraphrase of Gerard Manley Hopkins, our atmosphere, our happier world, wherein we meet no sin.

September 13 – St. John Chrysostom (Memorial)

They say you "can't fight city hall." St. John Chrysostom certainly tried and in the long run he won.

John of Antioch (the name Chrysostom or "golden-mouthed" because of his stunning preaching was given posthumously) was born in 349. He was baptized at the age of 23, prepared to be a monk and was ordained to the priesthood at 39. He quickly became known as a great preacher and orator.

There were some tax riots and his sermons managed to calm people down. He was then made Patriarch of Constantinople, which was truly a "bully pulpit" in those days. When he became patriarch he began a crusade against the excesses of the prevailing culture. He was genuinely counter-cultural. He reformed the Church's internal life by bringing discipline into the lives of the clergy. He criticized the extravagant clothing of the day, excessive makeup popularized by the royal court and condemned people for going to the races and games on solemn holy days.

In all this, he made an enemy of the very powerful empress Eudoxia because she wore extravagant clothing, excessive makeup and went to the games on solemn holy days. St. John Chrysostom and the empress Eudoxia were like oil and water. Both were strong personalities but opposites in their commitment to Christ. When the empress had a statue of herself erected outside his cathedral, John responded with a series of not too subtle sermons on the sins of the Old Testament queen Jezebel. That popped the cork on her anger and she sent him into exile.

There followed an earthquake in Constantinople. Because Eudoxia was also superstitious, she had him brought back. He continued his sermons and she had him returned to exile where he died.

John Chrysostom was not only a splendid preacher (his extant Easter sermon remains a model of economy, cadence and depth), he was also a great Doctor of the Church. He diagnosed what was ailing in his diocese and did not hesitate to tell his "patients" the truth. He knew that sometimes radical spiritual surgery is needed. His tools were the Word of God and the words of his sermons. He spoke plainly, courageously and frequently.

Like the sower in Jesus' parable, his words fell in many places, but the Truth of Christ was spoken. He gave an honest diagnosis and the tools for healing. To those who accepted it, he was a true spiritual doctor. To those who refused it, they at least heard what was ailing their souls.

In the end, St. John Chrysostom won. He was faithful to his mission, spoke the truth fearlessly though not cautiously, and became a saint. He didn't care about "city hall." He did care about the Truth.

September 15 – Our Lady of Sorrows (Memorial)

The memorial of Our Lady of Sorrows used to be called the feast of the "Seven Dolors" from the Latin word for "sorrows." This devotion often pictures Mary with seven swords through her heart. The seven traditional sorrows of Mary are the prophecy of Simeon, the flight into Egypt, losing the child Jesus, meeting Jesus on the way to Calvary, standing at the foot of the Cross, taking the body of Jesus down from the Cross, and the burial of Jesus.

When we love someone, we share their joy and their sorrow. When parents watch their child perform some task, every worry and anxiety of the child is inscribed on their faces as well. In the same way, Mary suffered with Jesus. She was a partner in His Passion and now the Risen Lord has imparted to her His glory. Mary continues to bring the grace of Christ's redemption into people's lives. She is part of everything her Son did and does.

The memorial of Our Lady of Sorrows points to the truth that the Kingdom of God is erected in our life and in the world not just in grand triumphant moments but more commonly through suffering.

The great moments that built up our nation, for example, were forged through suffering and were not painless. The same is true of bringing the Kingdom of God into our world.

Suffering for the Kingdom of God has great dignity and spiritual power. Pope Pius IX once remarked that Mary stood at the foot of the Cross in today's Gospel reading. As our sequence says, *"Stabat mater dolorosa juxta crucem lacrimosa."* Mary stood there. She was not swooning, not beating the ground in grief, not collapsed in tears. She stood there trusting that this is how it must be, obedient to the Father's will.

The memorial of Our Lady of Sorrows reminds us that Mary

was part of Jesus' life, both in His suffering and now in His glory. It reminds us of the truth that the Kingdom of God is built up through suffering in union with Christ. Finally, it shows us the immense dignity of those who suffer for the sake of the Kingdom, standing at the Cross.

Mary can help us stand before the crosses in our life with dignity, trust and strength.

September 16 – Sts. Cornelius and Cyprian (Memorial)

The Lord prays to the Father that His Church would be guided and protected by Truth in difficult times to come. Pope Cornelius and Bishop Cyprian witnessed to the faith during one of those difficult times in the middle of the 3rd century.

Persecutions punctuated the life of the early Church. Some persecutions were major, others minor. But the witness of many Christians was always powerful. Pope Cornelius died in 253 in what is called today a "concentration camp" and Cyprian was put to death in the open in 258. We honor them today for their heroic witness.

They also had to deal with conflict within the Church concerning the issue of "traitors," those Christians who in previous persecutions had betrayed their Baptism by worshipping Roman gods and betrayed their fellow Christians as well. Once the persecution had abated, they wanted to return to the Church. Could they?

One very rigorous priest named Novatian taught that they could not be readmitted to full communion with the Church. He taught that the Church did not have the power to forgive the sin of apostasy or public rejection of the Church. Novation was not saying that the Church should not but was teaching that the Church could not apply Christ's forgiveness to apostasy.

Pope Cornelius and Bishop Cyprian both taught that the power of the keys given to the Church by Christ was plenary and complete. If a person genuinely repents of any sin, the Church is empowered to forgive any sin.

It was a difficult struggle but Cornelius and Cyprian won the day and affirmed the teaching of the Church that we take for granted today.

Cornelius and Cyprian both rejoiced in each other's heroism and popularity among the laity. Cyprian once remarked that when Cornelius is honored so is the Church. In this they are examples to us.

When a Christian spreads the light of Christ, the Church is strengthened. When the Gospel is honored, Christ is honored. It matters not who receives the credit. What every Christian should seek is to exalt Jesus Christ and strengthen His Church.

Whenever Christ is exalted, His Kingdom grows. It does not matter who ignites the match, Christ is the flame.

September 17 – St. Robert Bellarmine (Optional Memorial)

St. Robert Bellarmine not only instructed others how to build their lives on the rock of Christ's teaching but did so himself.

Robert Bellarmine was born in 1542 in Tuscany, Italy. He became a Jesuit at 18 and was ordained a priest at 28. This was the time of the Counter-Reformation. He defended the Faith as a teacher at the University of Louvain in Belgium, and then at the Roman College in Rome where he wrote books and catechisms as well.

Perhaps the most famous episode in his life was the Galileo controversy. He had counseled Galileo to be more prudent in how he presented his conclusions about the sun being the center of the solar system because it entailed a radical shift in how the universe was viewed with a whole carload of implications in many areas of life. Galileo would hear none of it and the rest is history. Bellarmine's concern was the impact of a claim that made a sudden shift from all that had been taught until then.

Saint Robert Bellarmine became a bishop and Cardinal. He died at the age of 79. He was small in stature but an intellectual giant. His life exhibited no visions or miracles but was simply and majestically a life of solemn fidelity to the Church.

Most importantly, he blended orthodoxy with charity and kindness to his opponents. He was truly a Catholic gentleman. He had the rare gift of being able to articulate and defend Catholic truth without ridiculing his opponents, without sarcasm toward opposing positions, and without questioning the motives of those who differed from him. He was a splendid Christian in word and deed. That was how he built his own spiritual life on rock.

As the Lord teaches us in today's Gospel reading, salvation is not only a matter of having the right ideas. It is also a matter of living the truth of those ideas. Correct faith must be accompanied by a life shaped by that faith. There should be no place in the life of a Christian, a teacher or even a controversialist like Bellarmine for denigrating others.

The practice of charity does not exempt us from the service of truth. In the same way, the service of truth does not exempt us from the practice of charity. That is one lesson for us from the life of Robert Bellarmine, Jesuit, bishop, cardinal, apologist and saint!

September 19 – St. Januarius (Optional Memorial)

When most people hear about St. Januarius, they think of the vial of his blood that liquefies several times a year in Naples. It is an extraordinary phenomenon about which a great deal has been written over the years. Many articles speak about the biochemistry or the supernatural quality of this phenomenon. Explanations abound, the phenomenon remains.

Whatever its real nature or cause may be, the liquefying of the blood of St. Januarius can have several meanings for us. Januarius was a bishop who heroically gave his life for his faith. The drama and the memory of that witness have been lost over the years. That is enough to make any martyr's blood boil.

The phenomenon of his blood coming alive, as it were, also reminds us that the blood of martyrs is always flowing, that every age has its martyrs. Every era has its heroic Christians who suffer for their faith in many ways. When we tend to become self-satisfied and complacent about our Catholicism, we can read stories from missionary publications that describe the great lengths to which people go in other parts of the world to practice and to defend their faith. Martyrdom is not a Roman relic but a living fact of the Church's life.

Finally, the phenomenon of Januarius' blood becoming liquid can remind us that however stagnant our faith has become, it can come back to life. The fact is that it is not prosperity and happiness that excites a dormant faith. Difficulties and problems do. We can all come to know a deeper embrace of Christ. However far we may drift from the Lord we can always come back.

Scientists may discuss this extraordinary occurrence of Januarius' blood in the cathedral at Naples for generations to come. Far more impressive is the renewal in grace, the coming alive of a soul dead to sin, that happens all the time in our churches.

The bubbling of Januarius' blood is not just a story for supermarket tabloids. It should be a reminder of the revival and resurgence of spiritual life that can always be ours. The revival of spiritual life and grace in our soul is not just a two hour phenomenon like that of Januarius' blood. It can last a lifetime on earth and an eternity in heaven.

Grace brings people back to life every day.

September 20 – Sts. Andrew Kim, Paul Chong and Companions (Memorial)

Today we remember and honor Andrew Kim, Paul Chong and their companions. They are Korean martyrs, 103 of them, who were put to death for the faith at different times over a thirty-year period in the late 19th century. Today, we honor them together.

Andrew Kim was the first Korean priest and pastor and Paul Chong was a lay leader.

Discussion continues in the Church today about the role of women and of the laity in general. As the conversation goes on, we should not forget that the most important category or role in the Church that is open to everyone is that of "disciple." That is our most fundamental identity. If people are saved it is not because of their position within the Church but because they were faithful disciples.

As the Lord implies in today's Gospel reading, the life of a disciple is not to be a secret but a light to others. We are not to be ashamed of being Christian but glory in it and display it for others to see.

The title of "martyr" is especially honored in the Church's life and history because the martyrs were all heroic and public disciples of the Lord. They were men and women, clergy and laity, young and old. The martyrs of ancient Rome or of Korea in the 19th century are examples to us of the power of Christ's grace to make strong the weakest heart that is open to Him. They are also examples of the potency of public witness to show the truth of Christ and give encouragement to others.

We may not be called to be martyrs in our lifetime but we are all called to be disciples who show the effect of Jesus Christ on our lives to others.

The role we all have in common and the role that will be our salvation is that of a disciple of the Lord, a faithful disciple of Jesus.

That is something we all can be.

September 21 – St. Matthew (Feast)

In this Gospel reading, we have the account of Matthew's conversion when Jesus called him. It was a powerful moment of grace for Matthew and a moment of grace for many others.

It was a moment of grace for other tax collectors. They were shunned by fellow Jews as traitors because they collected taxes for the Romans. Through Matthew, they had a chance to meet Jesus. What they did with that meeting, we don't know. But they were given an opportunity to meet the Lord.

His conversion was a moment of grace for his fellow Jews

because Matthew's Gospel was written for Jewish-Christians to show them that Jesus is the fulfillment of the Hebrew prophecies. Matthew's Gospel, more than any other, is a bridge between Judaism and Jesus Christ.

His conversion was a moment of grace for all of us because for centuries Matthew's Gospel was the great teaching book of the Church, the first catechism. The Church used Matthew's Gospel because it incorporates five huge blocks of teaching material from Jesus which remain a guide to Christian living and a challenge to us today.

Finally, his conversion was a moment of grace for the people in Ethiopia where tradition says he preached the Gospel and was put to death. They received the Gospel for the first time from him.

Matthew was an ordinary tax collector who was turned into a great Apostle by Jesus. The Lord turned the circumstances of Matthew's life into instruments of the Gospel.

The same can happen in our life. The Lord can take what seem to be negatives in our life and make them places of grace but first we have to invite Christ inside. As St. Bede says in today's Office of Readings, we need to invite Christ not into our earthly residence as Matthew did but into our lives as Matthew also did.

As with St. Matthew, our turning to Christ can also be a moment of grace for others.

September 23 – St. Pio of Pietrelcina (Memorial)

Few saints in our calendar have had as controversial and extraordinary a life as St. Pio of Pietrelcina known as "Padre Pio." He was born in 1887 in Pietrelcina in Southern Italy of a poor family. He showed profound devotion as a child and his family knew that he would someday become a priest.

He entered the Capuchin Order in 1903 and was ordained seven years later. In 1918, he had a profound experience of Christ in which he received the stigmata or wounds of Christ in his own body. Those wounds lasted until his death a half century later. He quickly became known throughout Italy not only for the stigmata but also for healings that occurred through his prayer, his ability to read consciences in the confessional, and his very prayerful Masses. News about Padre Pio was spread outside Italy by American soldiers who returned home after World War II with accounts of events associated with Padre Pio.

Padre Pio preached Christ crucified not only by carrying Christ's wounds in his body but also in his soul by patiently enduring calumny, detraction, false accusations and even the suspension of his priestly ministry by Church officials. Eventually, he was cleared of all charges and allowed to resume his full priestly ministry.

It is estimated that he heard some 25,000 confessions a year, supported a massive correspondence with Catholics in several countries and initiated prayer groups around the world. Over the years, he collected funds to found at his monastery of San Giovanni Rotondo a 1200 bed "state of the art" hospital.

A number of extraordinary phenomena, many similar to those described by Jesus in today's Gospel, accompanied his work as a priest to lead people in a world grown cold and cynical to sorrow for sin, conversion of life and the embrace of Christ crucified. To focus on anything else in the life of Padre Pio than the redeeming Cross of Christ is to miss the purpose of his extraordinary life.

His life is evidence in our time of the unfailing presence of Christ's forgiveness and mercy that we all deeply need and can all deeply receive.

September 26 – Sts. Cosmas and Damian (Optional Memorial)

There are some saints about whom we know very little. People all over the world may honor them. Churches may be named after them. Their names may be repeatedly mentioned in Church records and even in the liturgy. But the facts and details of their lives may have faded from memory.

Cosmas and Damian are saints like these. We know only a few facts about them. We know that they suffered martyrdom for their faith around the year 300. Their witness to Christ was so strong that after their death people instinctively turned to them for the power of their intercession and their names were even included in the Roman Canon of the Mass.

There are traditions about Cosmas and Damian that have come to us. It is said that they were twins who were also physicians. They brought their belief in God to the art of healing. It is said that they did a great deal of their medical work for free. Today, they are the patron saints of physicians, surgeons and pharmacists.

This memorial in honor of Cosmas and Damian is an opportunity for us to reflect on the medical profession. The Old Testament Book of Sirach has a splendid meditation on the healing art of the doctor as coming from God (Sirach 38:1-14). There are many medical professionals today who donate their services to bring help to the poor here and abroad. The high and generous esteem in which the medical profession is held in our society entails a responsibility to provide some service free of charge to those in need.

This day also reminds us to care for our health. It is no act of faith and may even be presumption to delay seeking the help of a physician in our physical ailments. We have a responsibility to care for our health and to seek assistance when it is in distress.

Cosmas and Damian also remind us that in an age like ours that has seen so many new medical breakthroughs, technologies and drugs, nothing can replace the human touch, the presence at the bedside and the prayer of faith to give strength and support to those who are ill. Illness is a difficult time. Knowing that others are raising us up to the Lord in prayer can give great strength to the soul and maybe even to the body.

This day in honor of Cosmas and Damian teaches us that although we may not be physicians, we can bring to those who are hurting on the inside or the outside the healing touch of compassion and the power of our prayer.

September 27 – St. Vincent de Paul (Memorial)

St. Vincent de Paul is the patron saint of organized charities. Vincent de Paul societies are groups that give assistance with food and clothing. He didn't found them but inspired their purpose, which is why they are named after him.

Vincent de Paul was born in France in 1581. He was ordained a priest at the early age of 19 but didn't plan a life of service. In fact, it was just the other way around. He didn't become a priest to serve but to be served. He was ambitious for power and prestige and so became chaplain to the rich and famous.

One day, he met a priest who introduced him to the care of the poor. Vincent went to work in a very poor area of France and then began to organize groups of people to bring food and clothing to the poor. He organized groups of priests to minister to the poor in rural areas and they later became known as "Vincentians."

Charity has always been a part of the Church's life but Vincent de Paul gave it an organized form. The transformation in his life that working with the poor effected became a blessing to the poor and also to the wealthy.

He labored for the Kingdom as the Lord mandates in today's Gospel by bringing in the harvest of souls, especially the poor into the Church. Even though the traditional emphasis has been on Vincent de Paul's assistance to those in need, he also helped the rich.

He enabled them to see that every human being has an inherent dignity. Our true worth is determined not by the goods we have but by our having an immortal soul and an eternal destiny with God. Though people may look lowly in the eyes of the world, as St. Paul reminds us, they are precious in God's sight and therefore should also be in the eyes of a Christian.

Vincent also enabled people with means to realize that we show our true dignity not by accumulating goods but by helping people who cross our path. The world we inhabit is wider than ourselves. We are part of a community of souls. By giving, we receive the grace of releasing the potential of our deepest humanity.

Our prosperity is not only a blessing but also an opportunity to advance the Kingdom of God.

SEPTEMBER 28 – ST. LAWRENCE RUIZ AND HIS COMPANIONS (OPTIONAL MEMORIAL)

St. Lawrence Ruiz is the first canonized Filipino saint and martyr. His companions were clerical and lay missionaries from various countries who were put to death in Nagasaki, Japan between 1633 and 1637.

Lawrence had a Chinese father and a Filipino mother who were both Christian. He married a Filipino girl and together they had three children. He was an educated man who served as a kind of calligrapher or archivist for a friary of Dominican priests.

It seems that he was accused of being an accessory to a crime and, fearing wrongful arrest, the Dominican Fathers allowed him to go on a missionary journey to Japan where, unknown to them, a persecution of Christians was commencing. He and his fifteen companions were arrested in Japan for being Christian.

He was subjected to a torture in which huge amounts of water were forced into his stomach forcing him to expel the water and blood. He was then hung upside down for three days; his temples were slit open to allow the blood to flow out slowly as the force of his weight caused asphyxiation. His body was then burned and his ashes scattered in the ocean.

His martyrdom is described here in such graphic detail because it shows how much one man suffered for his loyalty to Jesus Christ. He received the gift of endurance described by the Letter to the Hebrews to remain faithful to Christ.

In contrast, we know how relatively little we have to suffer for being a Christian. The occasional quizzical stare cannot be compared with the great sufferings he endured.

Lawrence Ruiz reminds us that for the martyrs suffering for Christ has entailed much more than hurt feelings. People have given their blood and their lives for the faith. Their example reminds us that the grace of God is available to give us strength to bear witness in our life.

Sometimes when we are ashamed to make the sign of the Cross in public before a meal or to acknowledge our Catholicism to others or to admit that we go to church on Sunday, perhaps the example of Lawrence Ruiz suspended from his feet with his blood flooding his brain will come to mind. We can ask God to give us a little bit of the enormous courage he showed.

The stories of the martyrs help place into perspective both our tribulations and our fidelity to Christ.

SEPTEMBER 28 – ST. WENCESLAUS (OPTIONAL MEMORIAL)

Jesus' words in today's Gospel reading about families divided because of one's commitment to Christ certainly came true in the life of St. Wenceslaus. He is a martyr and the patron saint of Bohemia (today's Czech Republic).

Wenceslaus lived in the early 900's. His father was Christian but his mother was not. His grandmother, however, raised him in the knowledge and love of Christ. The land was divided by conflict between Christians and non-Christians. After Wenceslaus' father died, he succeeded as king but, because of his youth, his mother was made regent.

She began to obstruct the work and the life of the Church. When Wenceslaus was in his teenage years, several nobles urged him to take control and become king. He was a friend of the Church. Through an alliance with the German king, which was unpopular among some interest groups, he brought German missionaries to Bohemia, built churches and he himself lived an exemplary life.

The relatively recent Christmas carol "Good King Wenceslaus" tries to capture his care for the poor and needy. Still, despite his best efforts, the kingdom was still wracked by religious warfare and competing interest groups. Finally, in 935 his brother Boleslaus was persuaded to assassinate him. While Wenceslaus was on his way to Mass, he was attacked and literally hacked to pieces. On hearing the news, the people spontaneously acclaimed him as a martyr.

Boleslaus repented and had his brother's relics transferred with great solemnity to the cathedral. Perhaps we will never know the mix of motives in Boleslaus' actions, which may have included religion, ambition, sibling rivalry, politics or wealth.

We do know the clear motive of Wenceslaus, which was fidelity to Jesus Christ and His Gospel in everything he did. Sometimes even today in an age of compromises, such clarity of motive may separate us from others, but it doesn't separate us from Christ.

The life of Wencesalus reminds not to compartmentalize our life. If our purpose, motives and actions are all unified around Christ, whatever the turmoil and confusion around us, we will have peace within.

September 29 – Sts. Michael, Gabriel and Raphael (Feast)

Today, we celebrate the feast of the three great archangels in Scripture: Michael, the great defender in the battles of the soul, Gabriel, the messenger of God's Word to us, and Raphael, the instrument of healing.

There is a way of trivializing angels into the childish beings painted by Renaissance artists but in the Scriptures they are more awesome than that. They are pure spirits, part of God's creation, which are given a mission to bring God's protection (Michael) or God's inspiration (Gabriel) or God's healing (Raphael) into our life.

This feast of the archangels should remind us of God's concern about our life. These messengers of God are found throughout the Old and New Testaments as well as in the teaching of the Church. Their presence teaches us several things.

First, there is a great interest in the demonic these days. The angels remind us of a benign presence, a holy spiritual presence in our life as well. They come as messengers of God's love and care.

Secondly, when we conclude that we have understood the universe, the angels remind us that God's creation is larger, more magnificent and more mysterious than we ever imagined.

Thirdly, they remind us that we are not left alone to fend for ourselves after we are born, like dice thrown on a table. Here on earth, God has given us these magnificent spiritual presences to be with us for healing, for battle and for right judgment.

If in our life we have experienced extraordinary healing in body or soul, known a dramatic and life-changing inspiration or experienced God's protection, then we have known His angels in our life. We are never as alone as we might think.

Devotion to the archangels opens our life to their presence so they can bring us strength, comfort and wisdom.

These awesome spiritual presences remind us that God is on our side.

September 30 – St. Jerome (Memorial)

He was brilliant, irascible, acid tongued, devout and one of the great treasures of the Church.

Jerome was born around 340. He had received a splendid education that helped hone his brilliant mind. He had been a nominal Christian and then had a dream in which Christ told him that he was a Christian in name and a pagan at heart. This moved Jerome to go on a retreat to the desert.

There it seems he was ordained a priest though there is no evidence that he ever publicly celebrated the liturgy. He wanted to be a recluse and focus more on study than on service. He traveled to Rome and met Pope Damasus who was impressed by his brilliance and made him his secretary.

He translated the Bible from Hebrew and Greek into popular Latin so that his translation was called the popular or "Vulgate" translation. It was his great gift to the Church and remained the official translation of the Scriptures for the next twelve centuries. Jerome was far from being a politically correct person. In fact, he had the knack for saying the wrong thing to the wrong person at the wrong time. He sarcastically criticized the habits and lifestyles of the lay and clerical elite of Rome. He was attacked by gossip, which is the artillery of cowards, and was viciously caricatured. Not surprisingly, his stay in Rome lasted only three years.

He then moved to the Holy Land and set up a kind of retreat center where he continued writing commentaries on the Scriptures. Jerome's holiness came not from his scholarship but from his penitential life in which he genuinely struggled to come closer to Christ and to follow the Lord.

This memorial in honor of St. Jerome reminds us, first of all, of the great gift we have of today of many splendid translations of the Bible. We have an access to Scripture unparalleled in Christian history. The challenge today is to use that access to study God's Word which St. Paul describes so masterfully in today's first reading.

Jerome also teaches us that we can become saints despite the personality burdens we may have. We can be saints in spite of ourselves.

Jerome's holiness came toward the end of his life as he moved from intellectual arrogance to humility, from knowing all about God's Word to keeping it, when the Word of God filled not only his mind but his heart.

The same can be true of us.

OCTOBER 1 – ST. THÉRÈSE OF THE CHILD JESUS (MEMORIAL)

In the Gospels, Jesus took a little child who had no social standing in those days and taught us that whoever welcomes one such child is welcoming Him. The least among us, the Lord says, has great value in His sight.

That is certainly true of St. Thérèse of the Child Jesus. She was born in France in 1873. She followed her siblings into the Carmelite convent. During her time there, she didn't achieve anything extraordinary as far as the world was concerned but simply followed the way, her "little way," of fidelity to routine. She contracted tuberculosis at the age of 22 and died two years later.

When she was sick, she wrote her autobiography called *Story of a Soul* that became a sensation after her death. It sold like wildfire as devotion to her spread all over the globe. One reason for this is that her "little way" was something with which everyone could identify.

She emphasized simple obedience rather than exterior mortification of the body. She showed respect to people around her especially to the many difficult personalities in the convent. She showed the dignity and power of daily life to create a spiritual giant. In 1997, she was made a Doctor of the Church.

In one of her reflections, she considered what her mission in life might be. While reading St. Paul's First Letter to the Corinthians, she realized that if the place where she was did not manifest Christian love, her call was to put it there. That is an important lesson for us. So often we look for the perfect parish. If there are deficiencies in our parish, our calling might be to supply what is missing rather than hunt for the pluperfect community.

Thérèse is often showed holding a bouquet of roses that derives from her remark that when she is with the Lord she will ask for a shower of roses or graces to fall onto people.

When we read about the great saints of the Church, its martyrs, those who founded religious orders, established great institutions or led crusades of different kinds, we might admire them but perhaps not identify with them.

We can identify with Thérèse who showed that fidelity to our daily responsibilities is the "little way" to huge holiness and it is wide open to every one of us wherever we are.

OCTOBER 2 – THE GUARDIAN ANGELS (MEMORIAL)

Today, we celebrate a day in honor of the guardian angels. Last week, we celebrated the archangels Michael, Gabriel and Raphael. Michael brings protection in spiritual battle. Gabriel brings messages of spiritual import. Raphael brings healing.

Today, we honor the guardian angels, the helpers God gives to each of us. The *Catechism of the Catholic Church* presents three major points about the angels.

First, they are spiritual beings that inhabit God's creation. They are not simply symbols but real beings whose comings and goings we cannot diagram. Still, Scripture is replete with their presence.

Secondly, Christ is the center and head of the angelic world. They are His agents and instruments. The angels are not free-floating, independent beings. They were created for a purpose and a mission. The word "angel" signifies their office as messenger rather than their nature.

Finally, they are given to us as helpers and guides so that in this life we are already in contact with the heavenly host as they join us in prayer at every Mass. Just as God gave a guiding angel to Israel, so we all are within His protecting grace.

St. Bernard's homily in today's Office of Readings remarks that the memorial of the guardian angels should inspire us with respect, devotion and confidence. We should respect their presence among us, imitate their faithful service, and have confidence because of their protection.

The guardian angels are signs of God's love and care for us. We are given good spirits, guarding spirits and caring spirits from God. Their purpose is to help us on our way to God. The Church teaches that every human being is given a guardian angel. The presence of a guardian angel does not depend on our having faith or being in a state of grace. We are given a guide simply because we were created in the image and likeness of God.

The presence and teaching about the guardian angels is not to increase our knowledge about the spiritual population of the universe but to show forth the great and unique dignity of every human person in being given such a glorious creature as a lifelong companion. In living our life none of us is completely alone.

There exists a guardian angel whose purpose is to be with us on our pilgrim way. That is a truth of great comfort and power.

October 4 – St. Francis of Assisi (Memorial)

These readings are appropriate for this memorial of St. Francis of Assisi, arguably the most popular saint of the Church's calendar.

The first reading contains St. Paul's remark about his carrying the "marks of Christ" because St. Francis is the first saint who it is said carried the stigmata or wounds of Christ. In fact, one major Franciscan symbol is that of two arms crossed, one of Christ and the other of Francis each showing its wounds. St. Francis, however, reproduced Christ in ways more important than the stigmata. He reproduced the spirit and love of Christ in his own time. For all the supposed charm of medieval Italy which we romanticize, it was a difficult time. Town fought against town and human life was cheap. Into this world, Francis brought simplicity and Christian love.

Born in 1182, he came from an upper middle class family, was somewhat of a dilettante, and enjoyed a very privileged world until he was hurt in battle and began to reassess his life. In prayer, he heard the Lord say, "Rebuild my Church." He thought the Lord was referring to a dilapidated chapel in the neighborhood. Later, it became clear that the Lord wanted him to renew the people and life of the Church.

He gave up everything for Christ with the surrender of a child described by Jesus in today's Gospel reading. Francis gave up his father's business and began to live a life of Gospel simplicity. That was a spark that lit a spiritual fire throughout Italy and Europe.

Unfortunately, St. Francis has been caricatured these days as the "Francis of the birdbath." He certainly loved all God's creatures but there was much more to him than that. He was a man of deep prayer and penance. His life of poverty showed that the things of this world were to be used, not worshipped. He showed that we fulfill our vocation from God as human beings not by accumulation but by liberating ourselves from the assumption that more is better.

The call of St. Francis to us today is not necessarily to embrace voluntary poverty but simplicity of life. Simplicity of life frees us to become spiritually wealthy in spiritual goods. The great gift of St. Francis to our world is the insight that who we are is more important than what we have. In a world trapped by accumulation, materialism and consumerism, Francis brings us liberation through simplicity of life to be free for the things of God. That is a profound liberation that every age desperately needs.

It is said that at the moment of Francis' death there was silence. Only the birds sang.

OCTOBER 6 – ST. BRUNO (OPTIONAL MEMORIAL)

When we see corruption around us, we can either engage the problems and seek to correct them or withdraw and take care that they do not infect us. St. Bruno's course was the latter one.

Bruno was a German monk, born around 1035. He received an excellent education and after his ordination became a professor of theology. At the age of 43 he was made chancellor of the diocese of Rheims. Together with a few other priests, he denounced the bishop as unfit for the office. This placed him in danger on many levels and so he left the area. When a new bishop was put in place, Bruno requested permission to become a hermit.

He and six others were given an area where he established the beginnings of the Carthusian Order with the first "charterhouse" called Le Grand Chartreuse. It was a way of life based on the life of the Egyptian desert monks. Each monk was a hermit and gathered with the others only for liturgy and meals. This remains the life of Carthusians today. There were no written constitutions at first because the others simply followed Bruno's example.

He was called to Rome by the Pope to assist in the reform on the clergy but Bruno only stayed there a short while and established another charterhouse in Italy where he died at the age of 70.

The constitutions of the Carthusians, one of the most austere orders in the Church, were not changed for a thousand years. Several centuries ago, a Pope remarked that the Carthusians were never reformed because they had never been deformed. They seek to keep their charterhouses small and obscure. They have distaste for publicity and do not seek the canonization of any of their members. It is remarked that they seek to make saints not publicize them. St. Bruno, in fact, was never formally canonized. The Carthusians were given verbal permission to celebrate his feast and it was later added to the Roman calendar.

Bruno's response to the corruption of his time was not simply to leave it behind but to embrace Christ more fully and establish an alternative community. Like St. Paul, he wanted to be taken possession of by Jesus Christ and to that end, he left everything behind.

We are not called to become Carthusians but to recognize the truth of their way of life. When scandals abound, we might not be able to do much about them except to embrace Jesus Christ more fully and faithfully.

If we are not in a position to save others, we can try to save ourselves.

October 6 – Bl. Marie-Rose Durocher (Optional Memorial)

Turning on a light transforms a room. In an area that may have looked forbidding, we notice new features that we had not appreciated before, we can find our way around the room, and even rearrange it to make it safer or to enhance its beauty. There are programs on cable television these days that show how a discerning and artistic eye can transform a bland area into a place of beauty.

Education is like turning on a light in a darkened room. Through education, we see aspects of our world that we had not noticed before, we can find our way around our world, become aware of its beauty and its dangers, and even find ways to protect and enhance its beauty.

Blessed Marie-Rose Durocher established a congregation of sisters dedicated to the great work of education. She was born in Canada in 1811. In her very early years, she served as the housekeeper for her priest brother and worked in his parish. Back in those days, it may be hard to believe that Canada was one big (very big!) diocese. To help minister to the needs of the people, the bishop in Montreal sought to recruit religious orders from Europe to work in various apostolates. None were interested.

He began to establish his own congregations. When she was 32, Marie Rose and the bishop established the Sisters of the Holy Names of Jesus and Mary, one of the great religious congregations of Canada. Their purpose was to educate not the children of the wealthy but of the poor.

Their work was to turn on the light in young minds and souls to truth and to Jesus Christ. Their work enabled many young people to find their way around the world, see the truths of its darkness and light, embrace Jesus Christ, and discover the mission of their life.

Blessed Marie-Rose Durocher lived only six years after the Congregation was formed. By the time of her death the Congregation had spread to several locations in Canada and later to the United States.

Education of the minds and souls of young people is a magnificent apostolate. It releases the powers of an individual's mind and brings them into contact with Christ. A teacher can never know the full growth that will come from the seeds that he or she plants. But even in the middle of children's classroom antics, a teacher is planting, turning on a light, touching tumblers that will release a child's God-given talents and powers. Blessed Marie-Rose realized the power and impact of a teacher. Her influence endures in the Congregation she founded.

Teachers deserve our prayer. They are sowers of seed, carriers of light and instruments of grace.

OCTOBER 7 – OUR LADY OF THE ROSARY (MEMORIAL)

The memorial of Our Lady of the Rosary began as a festival to commemorate the victory of the Christian forces over Islam in the Battle of Lepanto in 1571. G.K. Chesterton recounts this victory in the rhythmically stunning poem, "Lepanto." His poem is a series of verbal snapshots that capture the actors and events leading up to this great Christian victory to save Europe.

Pope Pius V originally established this feast as Our Lady of Victory but it was later changed to Our Lady of the Rosary to recall the prayer through which victory came to the Christian world. It is a chance for us to reflect on this ancient and powerful prayer in the Church.

The Rosary is a simple but potent prayer that enables us to review the great moments in the redemption of the world as we proceed through the joyful, luminous, sorrowful and glorious mysteries. In the Rosary, we travel through the entire Paschal Mystery of Christ from the announcement of His birth to the crowning of Mary as Queen of heaven and earth, and our powerful helper on earth.

We journey through the Paschal Mystery in the company of Mary and see the drama of these moments through her eyes. The original Rosary of fifteen decades was based on the Old Testament Book of Psalms with its 150 psalms. The recitation of the prayers was imagined as a necklace of roses or "rosary."

The Rosary is not magic. Like anything else, it can become mechanical. When, however, we say it prayerfully, thoughtfully and reflectively it becomes a magnificent way of joining our life's moments of joy, light, sorrow and glory to the mystery of Jesus Christ.

Many Catholic prisoners of war have remarked that they had prayed the rosary in their cells by using the fingers of their hands. It helped them maintain sanity and hope. The beauty of the Rosary is that it is a prayer for all people of every culture. It is a prayer for all ages, for the young who cannot yet read or the old who can no longer read and everyone in between. It is also a prayer for spiritual victory over all the temptations in our life and the evils of our time.

The Rosary is one more way that the Lord teaches us to pray. Through the Rosary, Mary continues to be in prayer with the Church as she was with the Apostles in today's first reading. Through the Rosary, we open ourselves to God's will as Mary did in today's Gospel.

It is a way of bringing healing, grace and spiritual victory to the lives of others and to our world. It is a prayer everyone can say.

OCTOBER 9 – ST. DENIS AND HIS COMPANIONS (OPTIONAL MEMORIAL)

There is a famous Benedictine abbey and basilica of St. Denis on the outskirts of Paris. Some consider the architecture of this basilica to outshine the cathedral of Notre Dame. Its origins take us to the life and intriguing death of St. Denis and his companions.

St. Denis lived in the 3rd century in Italy. He was sent by the Pope to revivify the Christian communities of Gaul (modern day France) which had been decimated and demoralized during a recent persecution. He established a small church in Paris and began to preach the Gospel. As might be expected, his success angered some opponents. He was arrested, tortured and then beheaded along with his companions on a hill in modern day Paris.

The place of his martyrdom is called "Mount of Martyrs" or Montmartre. The legend is told that after he was beheaded, he stood up, took his head in his arms and walked a distance away where he eventually fell. There a Christian built a church to honor his mortal remains. Eventually, bigger churches were built on that site until finally a great Benedictine abbey was constructed that popularized the style of architecture we know as French Gothic. Many kings and nobles of Paris sought burial in the Abbey of St. Denis. It became the place to be.

Part of St. Denis' popularity arose from the confusion of his name with that of Dionysius in the Acts of the Apostles and a philosopher from years later called Pseudo-Dionysius. The lives, adventures and teachings of all three were blended in popular understanding.

Still, the bare facts of the life and death of St. Denis and his companions were the basis for his designation as a patron saint of France. If we know little about his life, it was the fact of his death that captured popular piety.

His death was the light that illuminated the failing faith of the people of Gaul. His death gave the Church new life in the ancient lands of France. His death showed the people the power of grace in one person's life.

Whatever the facts of the story of his carrying his decapitated head, it gives vivid illustration to St. Paul's teaching that though the Christian seems to be dying, we live; though chastised, we are not yet put to final death. The power of St. Denis' faith and example was not something that could be extinguished by his execution.

The message for us from the death of St. Denis is that although our lives on earth come to an end, the power of our example continues... for better or worse.

OCTOBER 9 – ST. JOHN LEONARDI (OPTIONAL MEMORIAL)

St. John Leonardi was born in the beautiful Italian town of Lucca in 1541. He worked for a while as a pharmacist but realized that people needed a deeper healing than the medical. He began to visit hospitals and prisons. He was ordained a priest when he was twenty years old and began to teach catechism to young people.

These were the difficult days of the Reformation. People were not sure what to believe or who to believe. As he taught the Faith, John Leonardi realized that handing on the Faith required some organization. He was one of the forefathers of the Confraternity of Christian Doctrine or CCD as we sometimes call it today.

John Leonardi met with some criticism in his hometown, as all pioneers do, and so he moved to Rome. There he was instrumental in founding the College for the Propagation of the Faith to train missionaries.

This memorial of John Leonardi reminds us to thank God and to pray for all the volunteers in every parish who are involved in the religious education program. They may not realize it, but by virtue of teaching they are members of the worldwide Confraternity of Christian Doctrine. Perhaps we should not only thank the many volunteers who make this program of handing on the Faith work but it may be helpful to try to revive the organizational potential of an actual Confraternity of Christian Doctrine for mutual information and support.

We all hand on the Faith in many informal ways, but the CCD teacher does so in a systematic, instructional way. Every parish has some version of John Leonardi's Confraternity in its midst.

The people who teach in our religious education programs are missionaries of Christ's truth to children today who are the adults of tomorrow. We should thank God for them, ask the Holy Spirit to guide them, and assist them in any way we can.

The Faith is too precious a gift to be handed on in a hit or miss fashion. Those who do so in a structured way are a vital arm of the Church's mission today. They are possibly providing the only structured presentation of the Faith their students will ever hear. They need our help. They deserve our help.

OCTOBER 14 – ST. CALLISTUS I (OPTIONAL MEMORIAL)

We do not know much about the personality of Pope Callistus but the facts of his life are fascinating. He was born some time in the late 2nd century. He was a slave in a Roman household and seems to have been put in charge of a local bank. Somehow, funds disappeared. He fled but was apprehended and sent to prison.

Later, he tried to retrieve the missing funds but entered an altercation with the bank's creditors who wouldn't pay and Callistus was sent to the salt mines. After he was freed, he was put in charge of a cemetery that later became a revered burial area for Popes. That cemetery is called to this day the "Cemetery of St. Callistus."

Later, he was ordained a priest and became advisor to the Pope. Eventually, he was himself elected Pope and rose to the dignity and demands of that office. He defended the apostolic faith and made some changes in Church Law.

He knew human weakness from his own experience so in a very controversial decision he allowed those who had done public penance for leaving the Church during persecution to come back to full membership. He knew how difficult it was for free Christian women to find a Christian husband. Not wanting them to put their faith in jeopardy, he allowed a variance from Roman law and allowed free Christian women to marry Christian men who were slaves. He also allowed men who had been married more than once to be ordained to the priesthood.

Finally, after five years as Pope he was martyred for the Faith in 222.

A slave, banker, fugitive, cemetery keeper, priest and Pope – that is some life! All of us take twists and turns in our life that go in directions which we least expect. The question for each of us is whether the story of our life is leading us closer to Christ or drawing us away from the Lord. In Callistus' case, the drama of his life led him closer to Christ until finally he gave his life for the Lord in his greatest act of witness to the honesty of his faith.

Whatever the turns our own life has taken, Christ's grace is present at every juncture to enable us to follow Him more closely. Despite his past and perhaps because of it, Callistus tended the flock of God faithfully and received something greater than a papal throne; he received a throne in heaven.

However winding the path of our life may be, it can always lead to Christ.

OCTOBER 15 – ST. TERESA OF JESUS (MEMORIAL)

Teresa of Jesus, from Avila, is one of the great mystics, doctors and women of the Church. She initiated a reform of the Carmelite Order in the 1500's when the Order was losing its spirit of penance and prayer. In fact, the Convent of the Incarnation where she spent her early years as a nun was more like a sorority house than a convent.

Reform was difficult work because it opposed many entrenched interests. There was opposition from Carmelites, bishops and townspeople but she stayed firm in her purpose.

Born in 1515, Teresa was a very practical woman. Many letters of hers survive in which she negotiated about property purchases, dealt with bishops, gave advice to the other sisters, and decided construction details of new convents. She was what we would call today a "Type A" personality, very much a "hands on" individual.

But, she was also a mystic of deep prayer. She had a conversion experience at the age of 39 and realized that religious life and Catholic life generally had to be deeper than outward gestures and observances. It had to be an opening to and transformation by the Spirit of God. She was a woman of deep wisdom born of her union with Christ.

One result of her profound mystical journey was a kind of "road map" of the spiritual life. Her most famous work is called the *Interior Castle* in which she pictures a person going in their spiritual life from room to room, each with its own furniture and obstacles, finally coming to the Throne Room of the King which is deep union with God. We can arrive at that Throne Room only by going through the other rooms first. There is no secret elevator to deep spirituality. Spiritual growth is real but gradual. Teresa was cautious about instant transformations.

We tend to imagine mystics as being disconnected from the world as though people of deep prayer cannot be people of practical judgment as well. Teresa shows us that we can combine love of God and mission in our world. The Holy Spirit helps us not only in our weakness in praying but also in our weakness in living.

Teresa of Avila not only reminds us that by Baptism the way to deep holiness is open to all of us but also that as a branch of Jesus' vine, we glorify the Lord by how we pray, by what we do with our life, and also by what we are.

Teresa once remarked that if we remember that we have only one soul, only one death to die and only one life to live, everything falls into perspective.

October 16 – St. Hedwig (Optional Memorial)

We all have a prejudice about the rich and famous. We assume that their lives are filled with luxury, good fortune, constant success and happiness. One would think that would be the case with St. Hedwig. But it was not.

She was born around 1174. She was the daughter of a duke and an aunt of a queen. She married a prince when she was twelve and he was eighteen. Two of her brothers became bishops and two of her sisters became queens. She became Queen of Poland and the mother of seven. It seems to be a storybook life.

Yet, Hedwig outlived six of her seven children. When enemy forces kidnapped her husband, she went into the enemy camp to negotiate both his release and an armistice between the warring family members. Two of her sons were in constant battle with each other.

In a royal court that was filled with ambition and intrigue, she strove mightily to live an honest Christian life. In a court where fidelity was not a common virtue, she was the good wife whose praises are sung by the Book of Sirach in today's first reading. In an environment of conspicuous consumption and wealth, she and her husband used their money to endow convents and monasteries throughout their country. Cistercian convents, Augustinian and Franciscan monasteries, and Dominican houses all became places from which the Faith could spread throughout the land.

She was herself a woman of extraordinary penance and prayer. She gave personal service to the poor and to lepers. After her husband had died, she went to live with the Cistercian nuns at a convent she had founded. She wore their habit and followed their way of life but did not take the vow of poverty so that she could continue to show generosity to individuals and religious communities in need.

Although we picture the rich and famous as occupying a world of privilege different from ours, they do not. Like Hedwig, they live in a world of human frailty, violence, rivalry among children and illness. It is a world whose vices are often made worse because of the resources available to indulge them. It is very easy to become hardened by such a world, but Hedwig was not. She worked to remain profoundly Christian, going to penitential extremes on occasion to retain her calling as a follower of Christ and doing the will of God as Jesus calls us to do in today's Gospel.

Hedwig was Queen of Poland. But her real crown came from Christ who made her part of the royal company of saints. That is a group of which we all can be a part.

OCTOBER 16 – ST. MARGARET MARY ALACOQUE (OPTIONAL MEMORIAL)

St. Margaret Mary Alacoque was a Visitation sister in the 1600's in France. She had a deep experience and vision of the Sacred Heart of Jesus. Devotion to the Sacred Heart had been growing in the Church and it was from her vision that we have the familiar image of Jesus in a white garment with a red cloak, pointing to His exposed heart.

From her experience of the Lord came the practice of First Fridays, the Holy Hour of Reparation and the Feast of the Sacred Heart. The Lord revealed Himself to her in such a vivid way to remind us of His love which is ignored by many but still there for all of us. It is a love that redeems, transforms and strengthens.

It would be a wonderful corollary of her visions to say that Saint Margaret Mary had a happy life but she didn't. Born in 1647, she was one of seven children. Her father died when she was young and other family members treated her and her mother badly. When she joined the Visitation Sisters, one of the nuns in charge made life very difficult for her. When she experienced her visions of Christ, her superior didn't believe her and several sisters became hostile to her. When she was placed in charge of novices, one family sued her and denounced her to the bishop as unorthodox. She died at the age of 43.

These facts are important because people often speak about the lack of love from others and the resulting impact it has had on their lives. St. Margaret Mary experienced the same lack of love but she found her strength, her balance and her fulfillment in the love of Jesus Christ.

We all need love. Human beings are made to love and to be loved. It may not come from people around us for all kinds of reasons but Christ's love abides.

Every Mass is a chance for us to experience Christ's love for each of us and then reflect it to others, enabling people who have known relationships that are only utilitarian, manipulative, commercial or purely physical to know something of the breadth, height and depth of Christ's love.

The life of St. Margaret Mary encourages us to experience the "rest" that flows from Christ's love for us and reflect it to others.

In a world of so much superficial love, Christ's genuine love for each of us lasts.

OCTOBER 17 – ST. IGNATIUS OF ANTIOCH (MEMORIAL)

Pilgrimages are a great tradition that we have inherited from the Middle Ages. A group of people set out for a shrine and in the course of their travels they interact, share various experiences, come to like or dislike one another, and mature in various ways. Then, one day the goal of their travel is in sight. Arrival usually comes as a thrill and makes the entire journey worthwhile.

Spiritual writers since the Middle Ages have seen the pilgrimage as a model for the Christian life. Our life is filled with a menu of experiences. There comes a moment when we come to our goal and may be caught off guard. Ignatius of Antioch had a grand pilgrimage at the end of his life.

He was a bishop and martyr of the early Church. In 107, he was arrested during a persecution and was transported to Rome to be put to death. En route, he wrote letters to seven church communities along the way. These letters are valuable, revealing and splendid testimonies to the life and faith of the early Church. In fact, they were treated almost with the reverence given to Scripture.

The themes of his letters were the power of Christ's Death and Resurrection, the unity of the Church around the Eucharist and the bishop, the Church at Rome as deserving special regard because it was the church of Sts. Peter and Paul. Ignatius was one of many martyrs whose number we can not even guess. Ignatius never minced words in his letters. In one letter, he wrote a warning that could apply to the political spin doctors of today. Ignatius cautioned those who call evil good and call good evil, who call darkness as light and light as darkness, those who call bitter what is sweet and call what is sweet bitter that a severe judgment awaits them not only for deception but for the coarsening of society.

What is most striking about Ignatius was this "procession" to Rome to meet the end of his life. He was taken in chains to be executed and one would expect a somber and grim march to death. Instead, it became a virtually grand parade as Christians came out to greet him and hear him address them along the way. His transport to Rome became a march to meet Christ.

Maybe we can see our life like that. Just as our biological life is never static, so our spiritual life is never at rest. We are either moving toward or away from the Lord. The various stages of our life comprise a pilgrimage, a procession to meet Christ face to face. The Lord tells us that where He is, there will His servants be.

We do not know how death will come to us. But we can see the life we are given not as a grim procession toward death but as a great journey on our way to meet the Lord. Our death is not an end but an arrival.

October 18 – St. Luke (Feast)

St. Luke is the author of the third Gospel, a companion of St. Paul as we see in today's first reading and some say a doctor, the "dear physician" to whom St. Paul refers at the conclusion of his Letter to the Colossians. It does appear that Luke gives more physical details about the illnesses cured by Jesus than do the other Gospel writers.

In his Gospel, Luke recorded for all time elements of Jesus' teaching that are important for every generation to remember.

In Luke's Gospel, we see how Jesus embraces all people, rich and poor, Jew and Gentile, male and female.

In Luke's Gospel, we see Jesus calling people to repentance and the rehabilitating gift of forgiveness exemplified in the parable of the Prodigal Son.

In Luke's Gospel, Jesus calls us to show compassion to all who cross our path as does the Good Samaritan in Jesus' parable recorded only by Luke.

These are Gospel truths that can get lost today as we tend to make Jesus exclusive rather than inclusive, as though the Lord likes only "our kind" of people. We can make Jesus' forgiveness as restricted as our own tends to be. We can make Jesus' compassion as limited as ours tends to be, given only to the chic minority of the hour rather than to every need we meet.

St. Luke gave his life for Christ and that is his greatest act of witness to the Lord. But the Gospel he wrote is also a great act of witness that has nourished and challenged Christians for centuries.

In St. Luke's Gospel, Jesus calls us to leave behind narrowness, self-absorption, a compassion constricted only to those who think as we do, and invites us to enter a larger world of His own heart and love. His is a world where compassion is free to all in need, where our vision of the future embraces all people, and where we respect people who think and believe differently than we do.

This is not an easy world to construct but it is a world where the spirit of Christ is set free. Luke shows us Jesus Christ as the person we are all called to be.

OCTOBER 19 – STS. JOHN DE BREBEUF, ISAAC JOGUES AND THEIR COMPANIONS (MEMORIAL)

The passage from the salons of 17th century France to the wilds of North America must have been shocking and harrowing for the Jesuit missionaries we honor today. They are the protomartyrs or "first martyrs" of North America. Their names deserve to be read in every Catholic church in our land today: Fathers John de Brebeuf, Anthony Daniel, Charles Garnier, Isaac Jogues, Gabriel Lalemant, Noel Chabanel and two Jesuit lay brothers, Rene Goupil and John de La Lande.

They were not the first missionaries to North America but they were the Church's first martyrs here. They came to Quebec, then known as "New France," to do missionary work. They sent back to France narratives of their work called the "Jesuit Relations" which made their trials and tribulations widely known.

They worked among the nomadic Algonquin, the more settled Hurons and attempted to reach the warlike Iroquois. In addition to the barriers of language and culture, they came to a land unknown to them and to a people where promiscuity, violence and cannibalism were common.

Whenever the Indians encountered catastrophe through influenza or drought, the medicine men were quick to blame the "blackrobes." The world they entered to preach the Gospel was racked by violent tribal conflicts among the Huron, Mohawk and Iroquois Indians. The stories of each of these Jesuits are truly heroic. Finally, blamed for all sorts of disasters and incited by the medicine men, the Native Americans put them to death in a period from 1642 to 1649 in ways that are too gruesome and horrible to recount in public.

On this memorial of our North American martyrs, we should thank God, first of all, for the devotion and heroism of these men and of the missionaries to our land after them who sought to follow Christ's mandate in today's Gospel to take the Gospel to all the nations and so brought the Gospel to us.

Secondly, their story should deflate the myth of the "noble savage" whose vices were all European imports. On their own, the Native Americans could be as brutal, violent and hate-filled as Europeans and as some people are today. Original sin is a universal phenomenon and Christ is the universal Redeemer.

Finally, we should continue their work in our country by strengthening the Church which we have inherited. These first martyrs left us a splendid legacy. We respect it by building on it and leaving an even stronger Church to the next generation. That is a magnificent way to continue the work which the courageous North American martyrs began.

OCTOBER 20 – ST. PAUL OF THE CROSS (OPTIONAL MEMORIAL)

St. Paul of the Cross was born Paul Francis Danei in Genoa, Italy in 1694. Later in religious life he was appropriately given the name "Paul of the Cross." He not only preached the power of the cross in his priestly life but also experienced the drama of the cross in his own life.

As a young child, his mother's great devotion to the Passion of Jesus touched him deeply. In his teenage years, he went to Venice to fight the Turks but realized that military life was not for him. He had a profound conversion experience and was called to preach the Passion of Jesus.

He was invested as a layman with a habit that he had seen in a vision. The habit was black with the insignia of the Passion on it. After several men joined him, the bishop allowed him to draw up some rules for this new religious family called the Passionists today.

After he was ordained a priest, he and his fellow Passionists went throughout Italy preaching parish missions and turning people's attention to the power of Christ's cross. There was the temptation back then as there is today to expect life to be filled with joy, health and prosperity only interrupted by sickness and tragedy. The truth is that the road of life is difficult and is graced only now and then by moments of joy, health and prosperity. Rather than calling God to account for evil in the world, we should thank the Lord for the times of grace and peace we are given.

Reflection on the Passion enables us to realize that suffering, a component of every life, has genuine power when united with Christ. The suffering of Christ on Calvary was sufficient to redeem the world. The suffering of Christ today in His Body the Church is still necessary to bring Christ's redemption to people today. That missionary struggle at home and abroad is the ongoing Passion of Jesus. St. Paul wrote that the seeming weakness of Christ on the cross had hidden power to redeem the world. The same is true of our suffering for Christ.

Paul of the Cross also experienced his own personal crosses. He had difficult acquiring recognition of his congregation. It is very painful to face constant delay from others concerning your life's work. It is also said that he experienced periods of desolation in his adult life. The cross was for him more than a religious symbol. It was a deep personal experience.

St. Paul of the Cross teaches us that the cross of Christ is not something at which we gaze but a truth that we live. Carrying our cross with Christ will lead us to Resurrection with Him as well.

October 23 – St. John of Capistrano (Optional Memorial)

When we think of St. John of Capistrano, we usually think of the popular song of years ago, "When the swallows come back to Capistrano" referring to the mission of San Juan Capistrano in California. The real St. John of Capistrano had nothing to do with swallows, California or love songs. He was a man on fire for Catholicism.

He was born in 1386 at Capistrano near Abruzzi in Italy. He became a lawyer and as governor at Perugia he was a crime-buster and zealous prosecutor. At that time, towns battled with each other and John was taken prisoner.

While he was in prison, it is said that St. Francis called him in a dream to become a Franciscan priest. Because his marriage had never been consummated, it was annulled with his wife's consent. At the age of 30 he received his first Holy Communion. After ordination, John of Capistrano became a great preacher throughout Italy, Germany, Austria, Hungary, Poland and Russia during his 30-year ministry. He followed Jesus' mandate in today's Gospel and never looked back from the plow. He did not simply lament the times, which is easy to do, but worked to rebuild the Church, which is hard to do.

He sought reform and reunion among the branches of the Franciscans with marginal success. The Pope also entrusted him with various diplomatic missions. His methods in dealing with heretics and enemies of the Church were severe by today's standards. But it is important to remember that his was not an ecumenical age. The Catholic Church was fighting for its survival. It was the age of three claimants to the Papacy, the Black Death, recurrent wars and pre-Reformation violence. The benign ecumenical environment of our time did not grace his age.

He followed the model of St. Paul in being an ambassador for truth. He was fiercely committed to the truth, fiercely lived that truth, and fiercely defended that truth. He was a man aflame for Christ and the Church.

His spiritual campaign was followed toward the end of his life with a military campaign. The Turks were fighting to take over Europe and John of Capistrano led 70,000 men in a crusade to defend Belgrade, one of the vital European fortress cities. He succeeded and saved Europe for Christianity. He died in Austria shortly thereafter from a plague.

Although we may be drawn to the benign picture of the gathering swallows in the California mission named after him, John of Capistrano teaches us to be strong and unrelenting in defending our Faith and our Church. After all, if we aren't who will be?

October 24 – St. Anthony Mary Claret
(Optional Memorial)

The lives of some saints are prophetic because they stand for truths that have been forgotten or meet a need that has not been addressed. Other saints absorb and reflect all the tensions of faith within the Church at their time. St. Anthony Mary Claret was the latter kind of saint. His life reflects in a deeply personal way the crises of Christ's Church in the 19th century.

Born in Spain in 1807 at the dawn of the industrial revolution, he wanted to be a weaver. His extraordinary intelligence soon drew him to seek the priesthood. He served as a priest in his hometown but was attracted to becoming a missionary in the great wave of missionary activity that was gathering in the Church at that time. After making the Spiritual Exercises of St. Ignatius, he entered the Jesuit novitiate but an illness caused him to see that the life of a Jesuit was not where he was being called.

He returned to Spain and became a missionary to the people of his own country. The mid 1800's was the heyday of parish missions, an apostolate at which he excelled. This was also the time when Spain was experiencing a revolutionary period and the Church was caught up in the rancor.

When the Church and a particular regime or administration become too close, the Church loses its power to become an "honest broker" in political conflicts. Churchmen might see a political party as useful to promoting the Church's goal but the opposite happens because the Church is almost always used by political parties for their goals. The Church becomes identified with their policies and is then swept aside with them when they lose power. Although Anthony Mary Claret did not fuse Church and State in Spain, he was caught in the "blowback" of popular reaction against one claimant to the throne.

Targeted for assassination by opponents of the Queen, he was sent as a missionary to the Canary Islands off the coast of West Africa. He did extraordinary work there, wrote books for a publishing house he had begun, and established a religious congregation to continue his missionary work, a group we know today as the Claretians.

The Queen of Spain encouraged his appointment as archbishop of Santiago in Cuba. He committed himself to reform of the Church there, visiting parishes, preaching enthusiastically, renewing the spiritual life of the people, and trying to bring about better living conditions for the workers. His work of reform may have earned him merit in heaven but it also created enemies on earth. There were several attempts on his life, one of which ended with his face being slashed with a knife, a very visible scar that he carried for the rest of his life.

The Queen then called him back to Spain to become her personal chaplain. Although he avoided life at the royal court, he was identified with the regime with more attempts on his life. Later, he went to Rome to participate in the First Vatican Council. He had a stroke during the Council and was taken to a French Cistercian community where he died at the age of 63.

The guiding thread woven through the twists and turns of his life was fidelity to the Word of God as priest, missionary, bishop, publisher, preacher, reformer, royal chaplain and Council father. When he was a boy, he wanted to be a weaver. God wove a tapestry of his life that Anthony Claret could never have imagined. God can do and is doing the same with our life.

OCTOBER 28 – STS. SIMON AND JUDE (FEAST)

Today, we honor Sts. Simon and Jude who were among the twelve Apostles sent by Jesus into the world to continue His work.

Neither Simon nor Jude is well known. Simon is not given much attention because the spotlight is often on Simon Peter. Jude was not given much notice because he was often confused with Judas Iscariot. One story from our Catholic tradition indicated that Jude was given impossible cases because he was so infrequently petitioned. As patron of impossible cases, however, he has been a magnificent intercessor.

It is said that they suffered martyrdom together in Persia, modern day Iran.

Although the circumstances of their lives after Pentecost are not well known to us, they were just as indispensable to the success of the mission as the other Apostles. Jesus chose them to be the foundation stones of the Church. Although Peter was given the specific ministry of strengthening the brethren, still in God's mysterious plan and in a way unknown to us, they were all important.

Simon and Jude deserve honor because our faith is built on the witness and work of the Twelve. Only the Lord knows the full scope of the work they did. Importance is not a function of publicity. People no one knows do a great deal of important work in business and in the Church. Parents, for example, quietly hand on the faith by word and example in a myriad of ways quietly creating the future of the Church.

People we do not know and probably will never know do so much of what makes the world work. Only when there is a strike, for example, by some public employees do we realize how much we take their work for granted.

Simon and Jude can be our helpers. If we become zealous in a particular cause and do not see immediate results, we can turn to Simon the Zealot to give us patience. If at other times we feel that our burdens are impossible, we can turn to Jude to ask the Lord to give us strength. The Letter to the Ephesians reminds us that we are members of the same household with Simon and Jude.

Simon and Jude remind us that the work we do, even when not acknowledged by others, is important in God's sight. After all, each of us has been called to be a Christian for a reason.

November 3 – St. Martin de Porres (Optional Memorial)

The twin commandments that Jesus teaches us marked the life of St. Martin de Porres. He was a Dominican friar in Peru in the 17th century. He was a humble man who dedicated much of his life to the Lord's work of caring for and curing the sick.

It is said that he had the gift of physical healing. Rich and poor came to him for his combination of medicine and miracle. They say he could heal with a handshake. When you think about it, that is a method of healing open to all of us.

That concern for hurting people came from his own life experience. He was a mulatto, part white and part black. His father was a Spanish army officer and his mother was a freed black slave from Panama. When Martin was born in 1579, his father wanted nothing to do with him although he did acknowledge him later in life.

Martin knew what discrimination was. Although he may not have known the word, he certainly had the experience. That may have led him to become an instrument of God's healing. His was the intuitive understanding that whatever the color of our skin or our ethnic background we all need healing inside and out. That experience of discrimination left no room for arrogance in the life of Martin de Porres. Rather, it opened him to God's call and God's will in his life.

The truth of Martin de Porres' life for us is that his experience of pain and rejection led him not to bitterness or anger but to deep concern and care for those who experienced the same in their life.

In our life, our pains can lead us to become hardened and bitter or they can deepen us and open us to God's grace and to a concern for people in pain that others may overlook. Whenever painful events occur in our life, with God's grace they can bring us to a spiritually higher place than where we were before.

Tragically, there remains discrimination of all sorts in our society. We can try to be instruments of God's peace and healing today as Martin de Porres was so many centuries ago. If we have experienced discrimination for any reason, that experience need not make us bitter but can motivate us to become healers in our world today.

Medical researchers will continue to make breakthroughs to alleviate physical pain. We can all work to alleviate the spiritual pain of discrimination in our society.

NOVEMBER 4 – ST. CHARLES BORROMEO (MEMORIAL)

Today, we remember a great man of the Church, a great churchman, St. Charles Borromeo. He was born in Italy in 1538. His life spanned two eras in the Church's life, before the Council of Trent and afterwards. He was raised in an aristocratic family that was very wealthy and very powerful.

A number of honors were heaped on him in his early years. He was made a cardinal before he was ordained a priest because his uncle was Pope in an era of rampant nepotism. That was one age in the life of the Church.

The Council of Trent was a reforming council, which Charles Borromeo helped bring to a successful conclusion. He was among the first to implement its decrees and embody its teachings in a catechism. He was made a bishop after he was ordained a priest and brought the Council's directives to life in his diocese of Milan. He was dedicated to reform on every level, institutional and personal.

Many people at that time called for reform which generally meant implementing their own ideas. Charles Borromeo was scrupulous in following the Council. Charles Borromeo was the first to put most elements of diocesan structure that we recognize today into place.

Some people attacked him and his reputation. One group even attempted to assassinate him but he stayed faithful to his mission and to the Council. During a plague, he helped care for the sick, contracted the disease and died at the early age of 46.

The Office of Readings for today contains an instruction from Charles Borromeo to his priests that can be applied to all of us. In encouraging them to teach and preach, St. Charles says that they must first preach by how they live, otherwise people will notice the difference. He then admonishes those who are in charge of a parish not to neglect the "parish of their soul" and to be sure to meditate each day.

The parish of our soul or of our family is an image that can apply to all of us. We can try to be good shepherds to those around us. Prayer is how we can take care that we are promoting the Lord and not ourselves.

The world does not need more of our self. It needs more of Christ.

November 10 – St. Leo the Great (Memorial)

There are two Popes who are called "great" in our liturgical calendar. The first is Pope Gregory the Great and the second is the saint we celebrate today, Pope St. Leo the Great.

He lived in Italy in the 5th century. He was a deacon of the Church with many responsibilities. Because he was a natural mediator, many church leaders looked to him for advice and counsel. He was an arbitrator between political factions as well.

He was elected Pope in 440 while still a deacon and a great deal of work awaited him in his new position. The Church was divided politically and theologically. He kept the Church united by standing for the apostolic faith against various heresies. He gave precise expression to the truth that Jesus Christ was a divine Person with a human nature and a divine nature. The voice of Peter from today's Gospel echoed through Leo to a divided Church bringing it together in the apostolic faith.

When the center of the Empire moved to Constantinople, Leo alone kept the city of Rome together and protected it. Perhaps the most famous painting of Leo depicts the scene from his life where he goes out of the city to meet Attila the Hun to persuade him not to destroy the city of Rome.

Pope St. Leo was a genuine leader in every sense, in his teaching, service and unifying of the Church during his 21-year pontificate.

Most importantly, however, he was a saint. He was a man of a wisdom that was born in prayer and meditation and he used that wisdom to protect and defend the Church.

Power can be intoxicating. Pope St. Leo in his exercise of authority knew that he was standing in the place of Peter. All his judgments and decisions were made in that light. Everything he did was not for personal gain but for the good of the Church, her truth, her unity and her fidelity to Christ's mission.

We do not have the great position Pope Leo had but, as followers of Christ, we too can work to promote the unity of the Church and fidelity to her.

November 11 – St. Martin of Tours (Memorial)

Martin of Tours (a town in France, not a travel agency) and Veterans Day go together. He was one of the most popular saints in the Middle Ages with many churches throughout Europe named after him.

He was born in what is now Hungary around 316. He was an officer in the Roman army. One event from his life has been remembered in tradition and image. He saw a beggar one cold night who had no outer garment. Martin cut his military cloak in half and gave it to the beggar. Later, the Lord Jesus came to him in a dream to tell him that He had been disguised as that beggar. For that reason, today's Gospel reading recounts the corporal works of mercy as actions done for Christ.

He left the military, was baptized and went from being a monk to being ordained a priest and later a bishop. As bishop, his goal was the conversion of people in the countryside. People in rural areas were called in Latin the "pagani" or people who lived in the countryside and that word has become synonymous with unbelief.

He established parishes as centers of faith outside the cathedral and made the effort to visit each parish once a year. He left the Roman army for the army of Christ. The Office of Readings today says of him that he was not afraid to die for Christ nor was he afraid to live for Christ. He dedicated himself to the great mission of Christ and became a leader in the Lord's army.

Today we remember those who gave their lives in the service of our country. This Veterans Day used to be called "Armistice Day" to recall the armistice of World War I that took effect on the "eleventh hour of the eleventh day of the eleventh month." That day was later expanded to honor all veterans who died in our country's service.

We may disagree with the politics or wisdom of certain wars, police actions or battles. What we cannot deny is the heroism of the men and women who died in our nation's service. We honor their memory by praying for them and respecting the freedoms they died to preserve. We have many choices today because they made one great choice to serve their country.

We also honor their memory by living out the corporal and spiritual works of mercy. That is a way of serving our country as well, making us a nation strong not only militarily but also in spirit and in compassion.

St. Martin's day and Veterans Day remind us that living the Gospel not only benefits our soul but it serves our nation.

November 12 – St. Josaphat (Memorial)

St. Josaphat was an archbishop and martyr in the 17th century in Ukraine where the Orthodox Church was strong. He worked to re-establish unity of Orthodox Christians with the Pope in Rome while keeping their own linguistic and liturgical traditions. He strove to implement in a concrete way St. Paul's call in today's first reading to unity in one Lord, one faith and one baptism.

He was so successful that he was called the "thief of souls." Predictably, he was opposed by many vested interests and was finally killed in 1623 by being stabbed to death and then shot. He spent his adult life working for unity and peace and has been called the "first martyr of ecumenism."

We might wonder how people could be against unity and peace.

The power of vested interests can be immense. There are people who have a vested interest in maintaining conflict, division and tension. It sells subscriptions and memberships.

We wonder how someone can be for pornography. Yet there is a mountain of money to be made in demeaning human dignity and appealing to people's basest instincts.

We wonder how someone can be in favor of abortion. Yet, the abortion industry is very profitable and very influential.

There are organizations, magazines and even cable television stations that thrive on division, disunity and scandal. If peace should break out, they would have to go out of business.

The battle for unity and for what is moral is not simply intellectual. It is a conflict not of ideas but a veritable "war of the worlds." It is an ancient struggle that takes new forms today. Technology can expand our power for good but it can also expand our power to do evil.

St. Josaphat came into conflict with huge vested interests who were not interested in unity or peace. This struggle will continue to the end of human history.

Pope John Paul II canonized many saints during his pontificate. It is a reminder to us in these difficult times when evil seems to have the upper hand and can be so relentless in its attraction, that holiness is more a part of our landscape than we realize.

The life and death of St. Josaphat reminds us that peace and unity are not givens. They must be won, cherished and protected in any age.

NOVEMBER 13 – ST. FRANCES XAVIER CABRINI (MEMORIAL)

Faith expressed in works surely defines the saint we honor today. Sister Frances Xavier Cabrini, known as Mother Cabrini, is the first naturalized American citizen to become a saint. She was a great and strong woman of great and strong faith. She died in 1917.

She was born in 1850 in Italy where she worked in an orphanage. Eventually, she founded a congregation of sisters, the Missionary Sisters of the Sacred Heart who operated an orphanage in Italy. Deep within, she wanted to be a missionary to China like her namesake Francis Xavier. The Pope encouraged her instead to go to the United States and take care of the Italian immigrants who were arriving in great numbers.

Mother Cabrini and six other sisters arrived in New York City in 1889 to staff an orphanage. Upon her arrival, the archbishop told her that the arrangement had fallen through and that she should return to Italy.

She indicated that she would remain and within a few months had established a school in "Little Italy." A few months later she had convinced the Jesuits to sell her some 450 acres along the Hudson River for an orphanage.

Once she was established and her work thriving, she began to crisscross the country setting up institutions such as schools and orphanages (initially for Italian immigrants but later open to all) in New Orleans, Chicago, Denver, Seattle and even Nicaragua. In 35 years of active work she established over sixty institutions. In her, the Beatitudes that Jesus teaches in today's Gospel came to life in a very concrete way.

Mother Cabrini did not ration her care only to practicing Catholics. She helped all and by doing so she provided an opening for God's grace to work in their lives. Our care for someone is not a reward to him or her but it may be the start of their road to the Lord.

She was a faithful disciple, a strong woman of faith who met the needs she saw. Her faith spread faith.

No great miracles or visions are recorded in her life. Perhaps the most important and greatest miracle in her time on earth was that of a faithful life. She was faithful to the Lord until the end.

In an unfaithful world, that is a great miracle and one we can all try to imitate.

NOVEMBER 15 – ST. ALBERT THE GREAT (OPTIONAL MEMORIAL)

There was a television series in the 1950's called "I Led Three Lives." It was about a certain Herbert Philbrick who was a husband, a spy for the Soviet Union, and a counterspy for the United States.

Albert the Great (Albertus Magnus) could say that he led three lives. He was an administrator, a teacher, and an explorer of God's majesty.

Born in 1206, he was a Dominican friar who became Master General of the Dominican Order. In that position he created structures that helped the Order become better organized than it was, which is hard to imagine since St. Dominic was an organizational genius. Later, Albert was made a bishop. His first life was as an administrator and bishop of the Church.

His second life was as a teacher, most famously as the teacher of Thomas Aquinas. He introduced Aquinas to the Greek philosopher Aristotle, recognized Aquinas' genius and was the spark that lit the flame that illumined the world.

His third life was as a researcher, scientist, and theologian of God's majesty. Everything in creation fascinated him. He brought his faith to his natural curiosity. Although the sciences were not compartmentalized in his time, chemistry, physics, biology, metallurgy and astronomy were all areas where he saw a reflection of God. To study them was to study the work of the Creator. Science brought him closer to God.

Faith is a magnificent gift. Some look up at the stars and see only stars. The person of faith sees the work of a magnificent Creator. Some look at the intricacy and beauty of the earth and see only the beauty of the earth. The person of faith can see in them reflections of God's majesty and power. Some look at difficult situations or difficult people and see only difficult situations and people. The person of faith can see a world aching for redemption and an opportunity for evangelization.

Albert the Great could make the phrase of Gerard Manley Hopkins his own, "the world is charged with the grandeur of God" if we only have the faith to see it.

November 16 – St. Margaret of Scotland (Optional Memorial)

The Lord's promise of faith bearing fruit and bringing results in the lives of others certainly is true of Margaret of Scotland. Margaret of Scotland was not born in Scotland but in Hungary. The king of Scotland fell in love with her around 1066.

King Malcolm deeply loved Margaret but he was also harsh, unkempt and a warrior. He reflected the contours of the country of which he was king. Margaret shared with him her love and her faith. She helped build up the Church in Scotland by establishing convents and monasteries thereby renewing the internal life of the Church. As importantly, she brought out the best in Malcolm. She made him more Christian than he had been before he knew her. Her effect on him was truly transformational. She became the instrument of his deep conversion.

We can ask ourselves whether we bring out the best in people or the worst. Are people's relationship with Christ stronger because they have known us or is it weaker? This is a profound way of being a missionary today. Our task in the "first world," the industrialized world, is not necessarily to bring the Gospel to people who have never heard it before. It is to awaken a latent or sleeping faith, to excite the grace of God that may dwell within people's hearts and minds. There is a saying that we have to take people as they are. But we do not have to leave them that way.

St. Margaret of Scotland was a true missionary. She did not travel to foreign lands but she did deepen people's faith where she lived. She was not only a role model of a faithful Christian, but she awakened faith in others and enabled them to become the disciples the Lord intended them to be.

We cannot single-handedly transform a nation, its institutions and policies by ourselves. But we can motivate others to do so. We can try to create coalitions not for war but for peace and motivate people to become places of light and respect for human life. There are many ways of being a missionary. Some missionaries heroically plow the soil. Others courageously sow the seeds. Others, like Margaret of Scotland, faithfully water the seed that is there.

Are we bringing out the best in people or their worst? Are people better Christians because they know us or not?

NOVEMBER 16 – ST. GERTRUDE (OPTIONAL MEMORIAL)

The great abbey of Helfta in Germany is gone now. Founded in the early 13th century, it was pillaged, damaged, rebuilt and ultimately closed after three centuries of life. In its great days, it saw the flowering of a magnificent school of mysticism that thrived for several decades to enrich the Church. It gave birth to several major women mystics among whom was Gertrude the Great.

She was given to the abbey when she was five years old and remained there for the rest of her life. At the age of 25 on January 27, 1281 (she recorded the date), Gertrude had a conversion experience that changed her life. Hers was not a conversion from sinner to saint but from a lukewarm spirituality to an intense love of God.

Her spiritual experiences were gathered into a book called *Herald of Divine Love* in which we see the dynamics of a deep relationship of one human being with the three Persons of the Trinity. Gertrude was a spiritual advisor to many people inside and outside the abbey and it is said that her prayers of intercession were especially potent.

Several aspects of Gertrude the Great are notable. First, her deep experiences of God never caused any hostility from others in the abbey because they knew her spiritual wisdom enriched them. Secondly, her writings do not evidence any titanic spiritual struggle as we see in Ignatius of Loyola, no great spiritual journey as in Augustine, nor any intense introspective analysis of spiritual states as in Teresa of Avila.

What is characteristic of Gertrude's mystical life is that it was framed by, immersed in and nourished through the liturgy of the Church. The liturgy was not simply a duty she fulfilled or a rule she obeyed but truly how the mystery of Christ enveloped her daily. The rhythms, language and images of the liturgy shaped her mystical experiences. She is a precursor of the Second Vatican Council's call to make the liturgy the summit and source of our spiritual life.

This is an important lesson for us today since our private devotional life can easily become divorced from the liturgy of the Church, producing a "two track" spirituality. In her Spiritual Exercises for nuns, for example, Gertrude presents reflections on Baptism, a nun's "rite of clothing," her "spiritual marriage" at the rite of profession, the following of Christ in the Liturgy of the Hours, and concluding with a preparation for our final passage to Christ at death.

Gertrude the Great shows us how the sacred rhythms, rituals and symbols of our liturgy can inspire and enrich our personal spiritual life as it did hers.

November 17 – St. Elizabeth of Hungary (Memorial)

Her life began as something out of a storybook. Elizabeth of Hungary was born in 1207. She married a handsome prince, had three beautiful children, and cared for the poor. She and her husband had a very happy life together.

After a few years, he died of an illness and everything fell apart. His family turned against her; they turned her out of the castle and abused her in many ways. She was even given a spiritual director who was terrible to her.

Still, she continued to care for the poor and live a simple life. She was a Third Order Franciscan and lived in her last years both by circumstance and by choice a thoroughly Franciscan life. She died at the age of 24!

In her own gentle way, Elizabeth of Hungary's life was one of quiet spiritual heroism. She was faithful to the graces given her and she rose above the pettiness, abuse and greed of people around her. She never responded in kind. Every response of hers was guided by her faith in Christ. She truly followed Jesus' admonition in today's Gospel reading to love our enemies and to do good to those who hate us.

This is genuine spiritual victory. Among all the people in her life, this gentle young woman was the strongest. The rest surrendered to their darkest impulses. She rose above it all and did not become like the people who hated her.

True spiritual victory, true spiritual strength, and true holiness mean not to be absorbed by the times in which we live but to rise above them and keep our eyes on the things of Christ. Whether that happens dramatically as with many of the great hero saints in history or quietly in a small corner of the world as with Elizabeth of Hungary, it is still a sign of enormous spiritual stamina and strength.

As it turned out, the common people recognized her holiness and she was regarded and buried as a saint. In the end, the common people recognized something that the nobility in her life could not see. She had become like Christ. She loved others not only with words but also in deed and in truth.

November 18 – Dedication of the Basilicas of Sts. Peter and Paul (Optional Memorial)

This memorial of the dedication of the basilicas of Saints Peter and Paul is about churches and the Church. The Basilica of St. Peter, the "old St. Peter's" was built by Constantine over the tomb of St. Peter and was dedicated on November 18 in the year 350. The Basilica of St. Paul "outside the walls" was built over the remains of St. Paul and was dedicated forty years later in 390. Neither church exists today.

The old St. Peter's was torn down and replaced by the present St. Peter's Basilica which was dedicated on November 18 in 1626. The old St. Paul's was destroyed by fire and rebuilt and dedicated in 1854. Both churches are metaphors of the ability of the Church with Christ's grace to renew and rebuild itself.

Both of these grand churches have housed many great Church events throughout their history. They have witnessed the storms of politics, persecution and attempted domination by secular powers, but Christ has always come to the Church as He did to Peter in today's Gospel. Even when the Church has been under constraint, the Church has always spoken the Word of God to its opponents.

Church buildings are sacred places to us and we are shocked when we hear about someone defacing a church. Yet, we frequently deface ourselves by sin. People have many opinions these days about church architecture with many opinions about what is traditional and what is modern and what is in between. Most important, of course, is what occurs inside the church namely the celebration of Mass and the Sacraments.

In the same way, our bodies and our lives have different

shapes. Most important is whether we are allowing the light of Christ to shine within our life or whether we are defacing the dignity given us in Baptism.

The true and abiding temple of the Holy Spirit is made up of the lives of Christ's followers. We are the living stones of the living temple called the Church. In that temple of the Church, each of us is important, each of us has a place and a dignity and each of us is called to reflect some facet of Christ to others.

Both of these basilicas see many tourists within their walls. We are not called to be religious "tourists" but the place where Christ's Spirit dwells and abides.

November 18 – St. Rose Philippine Duchesne (Optional Memorial)

From Paris to Missouri, from the French Revolution to the settling of the American West, from wealth to poverty, from administrator to missionary, from ambition to obedience – these are the dramatic transitions that marked the life of Rose Duchesne.

She was born to wealth in France in 1769. Her family had the means to send her to the Visitation Sisters convent school. She was drawn to their way of life and joined the Visitation Sisters against her parents' will. In fact, they refused to attend her profession of vows in 1788 although they reconciled later. This was the time of the "Reign of Terror" in the French Revolution and religious orders were being disbanded.

When the Visitation convent closed, Rose returned to live with her parents for the next ten years where she spent her life in prayer and works of charity following the Visitation rule privately as best she could. After the excesses of the revolution had subsided, she heard of a new order, the Society of the Sacred Heart, which had been established. She joined the Society and became a close friend and collaborator of the foundress Sophie Barat. Although she spent some time in administration, she was drawn to missionary work.

She was sent with four other sisters to establish a convent

in America. She arrived in New Orleans in the Louisiana territory after a perilous 70-day voyage from France. This was followed by another 40-day trip up the Mississippi River to St. Charles, Missouri. There she established a school. Eventually, she would establish six other schools and orphanages along with several convents.

The story of the Wild West is usually a tale of ranchers, rustlers, outlaws, gold miners and marshals galore. What is often missed is the heroism of Catholic sisters and priests who brought stability, education and the Church to the settlement of the West. Rose Duchesne was one of those heroic women who helped settle the "Wild West."

She retired from administrative duties and at the age of 71 went to teach the Potowatamy Indians in Kansas where she became known as the "woman who always prays." She was there only a year when her health forced her into full retirement. She spent the last decade of her life in a convent in St. Charles, Missouri always in prayer. She died in 1852.

From Paris to Missouri, from the French Revolution to the settling of the American West, from wealth to poverty, from administrator to missionary, from ambition to obedience: in Rose Duchesne, these transitions mark the making of a saint, someone who lost her life for Christ and found new life in abundance. So can we.

NOVEMBER 21 – THE PRESENTATION OF THE BLESSED VIRGIN MARY (MEMORIAL)

The Presentation of Mary remembers the moment when Mary was brought to the Temple by her parents to be formally dedicated to the Lord. This moment is not found in Scripture but comes to us from devotional writings of the early Church.

The Temple was a sacred place for the Jewish people. It was where the God of creation, of the Exodus deliverance, of the Sinai covenant and of the Mosaic Law was present with special power. The Temple was so sacred and central to Jewish identity that defiling the Temple triggered the Maccabean revolt.

Mary's being brought to the Temple is a kind of prophetic drama of the temple that she would become. In fact, she would be a temple greater than the one in Jerusalem because God would dwell within her in the flesh for nine months and by grace for the rest of her life. This truth is captured by the titles given Mary as "House of Gold," "Ark of the Covenant," "Tower of David," "Tower of Ivory," "Vessel of Honor" and "Spiritual Vessel."

We cannot repeat or imitate God's dwelling according to the flesh in Mary for nine months. That is unique and unrepeatable. We can, however, imitate God's dwelling in her by grace.

As deeply as the Jewish people revered the Temple, we also revere our churches as places dedicated to God's presence. We find the desecration of a church, any church, as particularly appalling. Yet, we are temples of the Holy Spirit. We should show the same respect for our dignity and our vocation.

When the prophet Zechariah looks to a time when the Lord would again possess Judah and would dwell in Jerusalem, the reference is not to the political entity we know today as Israel. Transporting ancient prophecies into today's political context can distort the Scriptures, and give contemporary politics a virtually divine status. Zechariah looks to the Lord dwelling with His people. We believe this prophecy to have been fulfilled not only in Mary but in Christ's Church.

It speaks to our dignity as people baptized into the Lord. Perhaps we too easily surrender that dignity to the demands of the marketplace and contemporary culture. We follow the call of society rather than the call of the Lord. When we cease following Christ, we distort our discipleship and degrade our dignity. It is like a church being changed into an Internet café.

This memorial of the Presentation of Mary highlights Mary's magnificent role in the work of redemption that was given her from the start. It reminds us that we are also given a part to play in bringing Christ's saving work to others. We are the living, working temples from which the Holy Spirit reaches and teaches people today.

St. Cecilia became the patron saint of church musicians by accident. She was a Roman martyr about the year 250. She had come from a wealthy family and gave her life to Christ. Her promise of virginity and total dedication to Christ was a strong statement against the licentiousness of the times.

Her parents insisted that she marry a Roman named Valerius. She shared her faith with him and he and his brother were converted to Christianity. One of the great secrets of the Church's life is the frequency with which Catholics and non-Catholics marry and how often the non-Catholic party joins the Church. That is a tribute to the Catholic party's faith.

Cecilia's husband and his brother took care to bury the Christian martyrs whose number grew during a persecution. Both of them were arrested and later martyred themselves. Shortly after, Cecilia was arrested. The government made a botched attempt to put her to death through suffocation in her sauna and then tried to behead her. It is said that three swings of the axe failed to completely decapitate her and she lived for three days.

Centuries later, an antiphon associated with her memorial stated that there was music during her wedding but she sang in her heart to God. Slowly her patronage of Church musicians grew from that antiphon and by the 14th century, she was considered the patron saint of church musicians and was frequently pictured playing an organ.

Although she acquired that status accidentally, the surrender of her life to Christ was not accidental. The witness of her life and death deeply impressed the early Church so that there was a memorial in her honor as early as the 4th century.

This is also a day to remember the great gift that musicians have been to the Church over the centuries as they show how God can be praised in a variety of musical styles. Music is intrinsic to human life and it is no surprise that it should be part of every expression of faith that ever existed.

Whether we are musically inclined or not, however, we can admire Cecilia's commitment to Christ. In a culture that is suspicious of serious commitment to anything and seeks to keep all options perpetually open, Cecilia reminds us that commitment brings definition and maturity to our life and commitment to Christ gives our life healing, direction, strength and grace.

Cecilia is an example of that for us.

November 23 – St. Clement (Optional Memorial)

St. Clement is called Clement of Rome to distinguish him from Clement of Alexandria. He is listed as the fourth Pope (Peter, Linus, Cletus, Clement…). He was Pope in the last decade of the 1st century and died a martyr's death during the persecution by the Emperor Domitian.

What remains for us from Pope Clement is a letter he wrote to the Corinthian church when some members of that church rose up against their leaders. His letter is important because it shows the bishop of the church at Rome intervening in a crisis in another church. Although it is said that John the Apostle was still alive at this time, the bishop of Rome is the one who speaks with authority to another church.

He begins with the magnificent salutation, "the Church of God which sojourns at Rome to the Church of God which sojourns at Corinth." That greeting reminds us that every diocese and every parish has a distinctive journey of faith to make. Histories may differ because local dynamics are never identical. But the Holy Spirit is present in each Church guiding it to be faithful to Christ.

Clement praises the Corinthians for their venerable history and calls them to return to obedience to the successors of the Apostles in their midst. Already in the first century of the Church's life we can see an established hierarchy and a structured authority which speaks in the name of Christ, which articulates the apostolic faith, and which derives legitimacy not from personal charisma but from apostolic succession. It is a magnificent letter that reflects the faith of the apostolic age as well as the grandeur of Rome that is now finding Christian expression in the Church.

Clement was successful in tending the flock and bringing peace to the Corinthian church.

Clement died shortly after writing this letter. Apart from guiding the Church, his letter is a magnificent legacy that helps us appreciate the great gift of having an ordered community where the apostolic faith lives and where authority is not attained in a "free for all" but through the "laying on of hands" by successors of the Apostles with the "power of binding and loosening" which comes from Christ.

A crisis came after Clement's time when self-appointed charismatic leaders claimed to speak in the name of Christ. Clement's emphasis on apostolic succession was a valuable tool to guide the faithful back to authentic faith.

We live in a time when the airwaves are filled with self-appointed spokespersons for Catholicism. Our strength as a Church lies in the authority of our bishop.

NOVEMBER 23 – ST. COLUMBAN (OPTIONAL MEMORIAL)

St. Columban (not to be confused with the somewhat erratic St. Columba) was a great abbot missionary of the 6th century. He was born in Ireland and received a splendid education in various monastic schools.

At the age of thirty, he was sent with twelve other monks, called the "twelve apostles of Erin" to evangelize Gaul or modern day France. The damage done by the barbarian invasions had been massive. He entered Gaul and slowly made his way to the interior. His intelligence impressed the king who gave him an old fort for a monastery. In his life Columban himself founded several monasteries that became centers of faith and learning. His followers established many more.

Columban was drawn into the lose-lose politics of royal succession in the course of which he attracted the opposition and hatred of the Queen mother who was arguably the most vicious woman in Europe. Columban also irritated the local French bishops since he had arrived without their knowledge or permission and introduced some Irish ecclesiastical practices such as private confession and a different date for Easter (which was always sure to start a fight in those days).

The result of the opposition of the Queen and the local bishops caused him to be expelled from Gaul. He then began a long wandering journey through Europe setting up monasteries in his multi-year journey. Eventually, he arrived at Bobbio in Italy to establish a magnificent center of learning where he eventually died at the age of 72 in 615.

He followed the Lord's admonition to set our hand to the plow and never look back. Columban was a man intent on bringing the Gospel to everyone he met. He was indeed Isaiah's herald of good tidings and of learning as well. He was one of the great leaders in civilizing Europe. Appropriately, a great missionary family in the Church, the Columban Fathers, is named after him.

This memorial of St. Columban is a moment for us to remember the many missionaries working in foreign lands today. We might consider finding the name of one of them and holding him or her up to the Lord in prayer and perhaps even communicating words of encouragement. That is one way we can take part in the worldwide missionary activity of the Church.

St. Columban teaches us that the Gospel is not something to keep but to share.

NOVEMBER 23 – BL. MIGUEL AGUSTIN PRO (OPTIONAL MEMORIAL)

The Lord's promise of giving His disciples what to say when handed over to persecutors came true at the death of Blessed Miguel Pro. His last words on earth were "Viva Cristo Rey!" (Long Live Christ the King).

Miguel Pro was born in Mexico in 1891. He was born to privilege and had a home life that nurtured faith, individuality and family. He decided to become a Jesuit. When he was a novice, the Mexican revolution rocked the land of Mexico with a virulent persecution of the Church. The novitiate was closed and Miguel and his fellow novices went to Texas, New Mexico and finally came to the Jesuit House in Los Gatos, California.

He studied for the priesthood in Spain and was ordained to the priesthood in Belgium in 1925. When he returned to Mexico, he found that Church institutions had been virtually shut down. Now only were churches closed, but priests were in hiding. Then began a two-year "cat and mouse" game with the government as Miguel wore various disguises to be able to minister to the people.

He used the imagination he had developed in his youth to dress as a beggar, a wealthy businessman, or a dockworker to avoid detection by the police. Once allowed entry into a Catholic home, he would baptize, hear confessions, bless marriages and celebrate the Mass. He was a priest in the underground Church.

After an assassination attempt on a political figure from an auto that had been previously owned by his family, the Pro brothers were arrested. They were falsely accused of the bombing attempt. Finally, Miguel Pro was shot by a firing squad as he said those famous words, "Viva Cristo Rey!" He was 36 years old. It is the only martyrdom of which we have an actual photograph.

This terrible persecution of the Church took place in a country that was 97% Catholic. Whatever the complicated circumstances that enabled this to happen, it reminds us that we can never take the freedom and peace of the Church for granted. Persecution can begin in many subtle ways as the Church is satirized, ridiculed, questioned, marginalized and then restricted. We must keep constant watch to defend our faith and our Church.

Miguel Pro reminds us of the truth of the words of St. Peter in today's first reading that it is better to suffer for doing good than for doing evil. Far better than suffering from the consequences of sin is to suffer in the defense of Christ and His Church.

November 24 – St. Andrew Dung-Lac and His Companions (Optional Memorial)

Today we honor and remember the fidelity and witness of Father Andrew Dung-Lac and his companions who were martyred in Vietnam. They were tortured and killed in various persecutions in the 18th and 19th centuries. Andrew himself was martyred in Hanoi. They were beatified at different times but canonized together by Pope John Paul II in 1988.

There were 117 martyrs in all. Close to a hundred were Vietnamese, some were Spaniards and others were French. They included bishops, priests, laity, parents and seminarians. They represent not only the universal call to holiness but also the universal call to witness that flows from our Baptism. The spiritual descendants of these heroic martyrs are the Vietnamese Catholics today, a dedicated, venerable and growing family within the universal Church.

Andrew Dung-Lac and his companions are reminders of three truths.

They remind us that the Church will always need strong and heroic souls. It will never be easy to be Christian whether in prosperity or persecution. Living a moral life is never easy. These witnesses show us the power of the Holy Spirit to take an earthen vessel and fill it with the strength of God. The Church will always need heroic souls to show us that fidelity to Christ is always possible.

They also remind us that the Church will always have strong and heroic souls. Martyrs were not born strong but they became strong through prayer and the sacramental life of the Church. The Church will always be able to produce heroic souls. An essential part of her holiness is that she can produce holiness in people.

The third truth that these great martyrs teach us is that we are all faced with the choice of whether we will be one of these heroic souls today. Whether we will simply drift along with events as observers of the encroachments of evil, or whether we will stand strong and tall for Christ and His Gospel is up to us.

Father Andrew Dung-Lac and his companions remind us

that the grace of Christ will always be there for us if we are willing to accept its power into our life. That grace comes to us in Baptism, is deepened in Confirmation and is invigorated through the Eucharist and restored in Confession. The Church is the place where these moments happen.

Every church building we see reminds us that they can happen to us.

November 25 – St. Catherine of Alexandria (Optional Memorial)

Sometimes there are certain people on whom we project our deepest hopes and dreams. Catherine of Alexandria is such a person. She was born from a noble family around the year 300 in Alexandria, Egypt. She was a highly educated, strong and articulate Christian woman. For her forthright faith, she was martyred.

A generous weave of story and legend have grown up around her. It is said that when asked when she would marry, she replied that she would only marry someone as intelligent and worthy as she was. She had a vision of Jesus Christ and decided to give her life completely to the Lord.

After converting to Christianity, she forcefully condemned the Emperor for persecuting Christians. In response, he had about fifty of her converts put to death. Later, while he was away, she introduced his wife and some two hundred of his soldiers to the Christian faith. On his return, the Emperor was furious. He ordered her to be put to death on a spiked wheel. In this horrible torture, the victim's limbs were crushed and threaded through the spokes of a huge wheel. The wheel was lifted on a pole where vultures would pick at the body. It was a slow and agonizing death. In Catherine's case, the wheel unexpectedly broke and so she was beheaded.

Her popularity spread through the Middle Ages. In some countries, her feast even became a holy day of obligation. She was one of the voices heard by St. Joan of Arc. Catherine is also numbered among the "fourteen holy helpers." (Her intercession was sought against sudden death.) The famous monastery of Catherine of Alexandria at Mount Sinai claimed to have her relics and became a very popular place of pilgrimage. The spinning wheel of fireworks that is sometimes used today is called a "Catherine wheel."

This enchanting weave of story and legend around St. Catherine expresses the deep aspirations within the Christian soul of what a Christian woman can be. She is portrayed as strong, vigorous, articulate and courageous in her confession of Christ. Today, she is the patron saint of lawyers, teachers, women students, wheel makers, librarians, philosophers, preachers, theologians, the University of Paris and aristocratic women. She was smart, strong, faithful and holy. She embodied the ideal of a strong Christian woman both in the Middle Ages and today.

NOVEMBER 30 – ST. ANDREW (FEAST)

Andrew, the brother of Peter, has been called the "protokleitos" or "first-called" because he introduced Peter to Jesus. In fact, Andrew can also be known as the "repeatedly-called" because his life shows us the deepening of God's grace that can happen in every life. He was a man of many graces.

The first grace was to be a follower of John the Baptist and his call to repentance. Andrew was blessed to see that his life and the world could be different than it was.

His second grace was to meet Jesus as recounted in John's Gospel and to be given the opportunity to bring his brother Peter to Christ. Later, Peter is central to the life of the Church but it was Andrew who was instrumental in Peter's first turning to the Lord.

His third grace was to leave everything to become a disciple as described in today's Gospel reading. There is a seismic difference between familiarity with Christ and His Gospel and the following of Christ. Andrew left his nets behind and followed.

His next grace was the call to become an Apostle, an eyewitness to the events of our redemption and one of those first authorized by Christ Himself to bring His grace and truth to the ends of the earth. It is said that Andrew preached in Greece and is today honored as the founder of the Church at Constantinople, a revered center of the Eastern Church. What Peter was to Rome, Andrew was to Constantinople.

His last grace was to die heroically for Christ. He was attached "spread-eagle" on a cross in the shape of an "X" as that cross became the altar of his own sacrifice.

To use St. Paul's words in today's first reading, Andrew believed in his heart and confessed Christ with his lips. Many of us do one or the other. Some believe in Christ but keep it private. Others support the Church and its causes but have no personal relationship with the Lord.

That new life that the young Andrew sought in following John the Baptist became real for him in Christ. Andrew shows us the unfolding drama of a life that is open to the graces and the calls that come from the Lord.

It is a drama to which we are called every Advent.

DECEMBER 3 – ST. FRANCIS XAVIER (MEMORIAL)

Francis Xavier was a great Jesuit missionary in the 1500's. Anyone who went to a Jesuit school will remember his huge popularity which was often greater than that of Ignatius of Loyola.

Francis Xavier was born in 1506 and came from a noble family in Spain. While studying at the University of Paris, where he was an excellent student and teacher, he met Ignatius of Loyola. That relationship changed Xavier's life.

He was part of the first group of Jesuits. As a Jesuit, he gave his life, his mind, his talents and energies to the Lord through the Order. St. Ignatius sent him to be a missionary to the Far East, to India and then to Japan.

His missionary methods became classic. He learned the language and culture of the people and became all things to all people, finding that personal point of contact with each person to create an avenue for Christ.

In India, he has been described as walking the streets ringing a bell which drew the children and many others to follow him. Then, he would stop and teach them the basic prayers and truths of the Gospel. Through the children he reached the adults. It was like home schooling in reverse.

As the Society of Jesus grew, he became regional provincial, a delegate of the Pope and a diplomat but always a missionary. In his life, he reached thousands of people.

His last earthly goal was to go to China. By now, he was ill and waited on the island of Sancian for a boat to take him there. From that island, he could see China in the distance. He died alone, before the boat came, without the last rites of the Church but strengthened by Christ who was always his real strength. He died at the age of 46 in 1552.

His mission was to bring sight and light to the spiritually blind. During Advent, we can honor this great missionary by trying to share our faith with one person, to help one individual see Christ in a new light through us.

Like Francis Xavier, we can bring someone to Christ by bringing Christ to them at their point of real need.

DECEMBER 4 – ST. JOHN OF DAMASCUS (OPTIONAL MEMORIAL)

John of Damascus (Damascene) was a monk who lived around the 700's. He is considered to be the last of the ancient Greek Fathers of the Church and was proclaimed a Doctor of the Church in 1890. He was drawn into an intense conflict in the Church called the "iconoclast crisis."

The issue centered on whether the Lord Jesus ought to be portrayed in images or not. The iconoclasts (literally "image-smashers") said that to do so was idolatry. Because God is invisible, any claim to portray divinity is sinful arrogance since nothing on earth (except the Eucharist) can convey divinity. Because an icon cannot depict Jesus' divinity, it is bound to be a partial and deceptive portrayal of the full Christ.

John of Damascus and others recognized that this attack on images was really an attack on the truth of the Incarnation. They affirmed that the Incarnation is the bridge between divinity and humanity and legitimizes the use of icons. God became created flesh and blood. To deny that we can portray Christ is to deny the truth of His humanity that became the "sacrament" of His divinity.

It was a multi-generational controversy that was fueled by devotional excesses in the use of icons, influenced by Islam, driven by pre-existing intramural conflicts within the Church with a little bit of theology added.

When the dust settled, this controversy affirmed a great axiom of Christian spirituality. We respect sacred images not because of their intrinsic value but because of what they represent. The art, music, wood and stone of our world can give color, melody and expression to our faith on levels where words fail. In today's first reading, for example, Isaiah uses the images of a fortified city and in the Gospel reading the Lord uses rock to give graphic expression to the power and reliability of God's redeeming grace.

Because truth is deeper than the conceptual, the artist is able to give visible expression to invisible truth. Through the images and sacred art that we see, we can be drawn into communion with the God we cannot see. Works of paint, metal and stone can become "windows" for God's grace.

We can meet the living God not only in what is true and good, but also in what is beautiful.

December 6 – St. Nicholas (Optional Memorial)

The graciousness and abundant blessing of the Kingdom proclaimed by Isaiah in today's first reading and shown by the Lord in today's Gospel reading certainly came to life in the ministry of St. Nicholas.

Nicholas is a great and venerable bishop from the early Church whose image has been tragically twisted out of shape by modern advertising.

He was a bishop in modern-day Turkey who died around the year 350. Nicholas was a man of deep concern for his people in every area of their lives. His compassion quickly became legendary.

One of the many classic stories from his remarkable life involves three poor girls who could not marry because they lacked a dowry. On successive nights, he threw a bag of money sufficient for a dowry into their rooms thus enabling them to wed. By a very complicated cultural route in history, those three bags became the triple globe symbol of pawnbrokers.

St. Nicholas is a wonderful saint for this time of year because he is an example of the Christian charity we should have for others. Regrettably, he has become for many younger people a vehicle to satisfy their own acquisitiveness rather than a person whose kindness to others we should imitate.

His image at this time of year has come to instill not generosity but greed, what we can get rather than what we should give.

Maybe it is time to refurbish the image of St. Nicholas and the truth that his life embodies – in giving, we receive.

December 7 – St. Ambrose (Memorial)

St. Ambrose was a great bishop because he was a great Christian. He was born in 340 from a distinguished family of converts to Christianity. He studied law and was eventually made governor of the area around Milan. The Church at that time was split between "red" and "blue" Christians, between Arians and Catholics. The Arian bishop of Milan had died and the people gathered to elect a new bishop.

The tension in the city was great as was the potential for violence. Ambrose arrived to keep peace between the factions. Soon, a voice was heard from the crowd calling for Ambrose to be made bishop. He was unanimously elected and after being baptized (he was a catechumen), he was ordained to the priesthood and then consecrated bishop on December 7th at the age of 35. In his quarter century as bishop of Milan, Ambrose was the model of a Catholic bishop. He studied the Faith, became its eloquent teacher and defended the Church against political and physical assault.

Ambrose was drawn into controversies with the Emperor and royal court over the rights of the Church and the morality of the Emperor's official actions. After the Emperor had ordered a particularly heinous massacre of his opponents, for example, Ambrose refused him entry into the cathedral until he publicly repented.

Parallel with this public life of Ambrose was another side to his ministry. He instructed converts, gave spiritual direction, carried on a huge correspondence, and celebrated the Sacraments for a great number of average Catholics.

The public issues of his day did not distract him from the care of individual souls. That is one strength of Ambrose we can imitate today. There are many great public moral issues that face our nation today. In some way, we all need to be involved with them. But there are also the individual personal needs of people that surround us. We need to be present not only in the great public square but also in the side streets of the city where life goes on as well.

In this Advent season, Ambrose reminds us that our mission is not only to speak about the redeeming power of Christ on the housetops but also to individuals who need to hear that saving Word. Not only must our voice be heard in the public square but our compassion must be present in the neighborhoods of our time as well.

DECEMBER 9 – ST. JUAN DIEGO (OPTIONAL MEMORIAL)

The "catalyst for new Mexican identity," a "bridge between the two worlds of Indian and Spanish cultures" and a prophet of a "new humanity that recognizes all people as children of God." These are the majestic descriptions given by Pope John Paul II to Juan Diego in his canonization homily.

It is doubtful that this humble widower would have seen himself in such extraordinary terms. Yet, maybe we are more than we imagine ourselves to be. We all tend to underestimate our role in God's plan.

Juan Diego was born in 1474 about twenty miles north of Mexico City. He had converted to Christianity at the age of fifty. He and his wife had no children and after her death, he devoted himself to caring for family members and to prayer.

It was during one of his three hour trips to church, that Mary appeared to him as Our Lady of Guadalupe. She asked that a great church be built on Tepeyac Hill. To convince the bishop of the truth of her appearance, she asked Juan Diego to gather roses in his pancho, or tilma and then to spread them before the bishop. When Juan Diego opened his tilma in front of the bishop, the image of Our Lady of Guadalupe that we all know was miraculously impressed upon it. This happened in 1531.

This miracle sparked a wave of conversions to Christianity as a new Mexican identity coalesced around this sacred image. The native Mexicans came to see that they too were loved by God and were included within the circle of Christ's redeeming love. Through this great act of God's grace, a bridge was built between the peoples of the Americas and Spain, creating the Hispanic culture that is so much a part of our life in North America.

It all goes back to the simple, honest and perhaps mystical widower, Juan Diego. The simplicity and strength of his faith made him an instrument of divine intervention. Simplicity and strength of faith often go together. Simplicity here means clarity and strength means fidelity.

Clarity and fidelity in faith are powerful goals for Advent. They create a heart empty of self and open to God as they did for Juan Diego. They can do so for us.

December 11 – St. Damasus (Optional Memorial)

Renewal to those who have fallen and strength in the struggle to bring forth the Kingdom are the call of every generation.

That effort is required not only of individuals but of the Church as well and it comes in many sizes and shapes. We see an example of that in the saint we remember today.

St. Damasus was born in 305 and was elected Pope in 366. He is probably best remembered as the Pope who appointed St. Jerome as his secretary. Jerome was a disaster as a church official but as a Scripture scholar he was a true benediction to the Church. Pope Damasus commissioned him to make an official translation of the Bible in the popular language of the people that became known as the Latin Vulgate. Damasus also ordered the liturgy to be translated into a language people could understand, which meant from Greek to Latin.

Damasus lived in a brutal era. The office of Bishop of Rome had become highly politicized, a political football in effect, but Damasus' strong character revitalized the office as he also renewed the city of Rome into the beginnings of a truly Christian capital.

Damasus was the first to describe the Church of Rome consistently as the "apostolic see" whose special place in the life of the Church was not due to decisions of councils, historical accident, power politics, church law, or the personality of its bishop but to the very words of Christ to Peter and his successors.

Each generation has its own challenges and opportunities for grace. Every pastor, bishop and Pope brings us a chance to deepen and clarify our commitment to Christ and His Church. They challenge us, provoke us, energize us and inevitably display some aspect of Gospel truth that we may have neglected.

We can't relive the life and times of Damasus and probably would not want to. We have our own era in which to live. But his life reminds us that the Lord is always with us and can always bring new life as He refreshes the old.

Times may change; the love of the Lord is always present and at work among us.

December 12 – Our Lady of Guadalupe (Feast)

Our Lady of Guadalupe is the patroness of the Americas. Her shrine in Mexico City is one of the most popular in the world.

Over four centuries ago, when the Aztec people were being oppressed and their native culture virtually dismantled, a wonderful supernatural intervention occurred in their lives.

On December 9, 1531, Mary appeared to a worker, an Aztec convert to Christianity, named Juan Diego on a place called Tepeyac Hill. She spoke with him in his native tongue asking that a church be built on the site so people could gather to worship her Son.

The Spanish bishop wanted proof that it was indeed Mary who spoke. On December 12, Mary appeared again to Juan Diego and directed him to gather roses into his pancho. When he later opened his mantle in front of the bishop, the flowers fell out and in their place was the wonderful image we know as Our Lady of Guadalupe.

With that gesture, Mary adopted the native people of Mexico as her own. Her countenance, language and dress all spoke to the culture of the native Indians. Her love and compassion became a sign of hope to these dispirited people that God indeed cared for them. The decade after these events witnessed millions of converts to the Faith, and Our Lady of Guadalupe became the bridge that joined the cultures of the Indian and Spanish peoples.

This is yet another instance of Mary with her children on their pilgrimage of faith. Every nation has its own journey to make. As a mother, Mary embraces the culture of every people. She speaks our language, is part of our life, shares our joy and knows our pain. No generation has been without its special care from Mary.

Mary remains with her people. At times, we know her as Madonna, Queen, Woman of Sorrows, Intercessor, Handmaid of the Lord – many grand and beautiful titles, but always, always a Mother leading us to her Son.

Make Mary a deeper part of your life this Advent.

DECEMBER 13 – St. Lucy (Memorial)

We associate St. Lucy today with intercession for ailments of the eyes. Devotion to her was popularized by the location of her feast in the old pre-Gregorian calendar. The facts of her life are sketchy although they have been enhanced over the years by a great deal of devotional material. She lived around the year 300.

She was a young girl from a wealthy family in Sicily. She had become a Christian and decided to give her life completely to Christ. The man wanting to be her husband was enraged and reported her to the authorities during a persecution. She was tortured and then put to death after having her eyes plucked out. Veneration of St. Lucy spread throughout the early Church and was so strong that her name was placed within the canon of the Mass.

Her feast was celebrated before the Gregorian reform on the shortest day of the year. With her feast, daylight grew longer. This led to many celebrations associating her with the return of light. "Lucy candles" were placed in windows. "Lucy bonfires" were set and sprinkled with incense to celebrate the beginning of longer periods of daylight. People in the Scandinavian countries observed her feast as a celebration of the end of the long and dreary winter darkness. She is appropriately the patron saint of lamplighters. When her remains were translated or "stolen" from Constantinople and "relocated" to Venice, she became the patron saint of gondoliers.

After the introduction of the Gregorian calendar, the date of the shortest day shifted from December 13 but the festivities remained. Now, Lucy is mainly invoked by those who suffer from eye ailments. Still, she remains a symbol of the light of faith. It is a light whose presence enabled Balaam to see the glory that Israel would one day have. It is a light whose absence in the Pharisees prevented them from seeing the truth of what the Lord was teaching.

We all remember the injunction of our parents to take care of our eyes. Just as we can lose eyesight, we can also lose the gift of faith. Lucy represents all the people of faith in our world today, young and old, whose faith is a light in darkness.

Advent invites us to join their number.

December 14 – St. John of the Cross (Memorial)

"Light in the darkness" describes the life and times of John of the Cross as well as his spirituality.

John of the Cross is known as the partner of Teresa of Avila in seeking to establish an austere branch of the Carmelite Order that would observe the rigor of its primitive rule. These efforts at reform were met with opposition and personal attack. In one of many episodes of hostility toward his effort, John was placed under house arrest by some fellow Carmelites who wanted to retain a more moderate rule. Eventually, John escaped and pursued the cause of reform and enabled it to take root. He died in 1591.

His life shows us that making reform more than rhetoric entails sacrifice, work and hostility. People do not easily surrender their investment in the status quo.

John is also known as the great geographer of the dark night of the soul. This was territory in which he had become an expert and of whose contours he has provided a map.

We have all experienced dark nights that may come from job loss, family problems, the death of a loved one, protracted illness or a change of circumstance. John speaks, however, of a deeper darkness called the dark night of our very soul, when we feel that even God had left us adrift.

He calls this dark night a purgation or cleansing that takes us into spiritual maturity as we learn not to take faith for granted, to look beyond emotion as a sign of God's presence and to become deeply one with God. He used a striking analogy of wood being consumed by fire. Initially, fire dries out the wood, evaporating and expelling everything resistant to fire. Finally, the wood becomes as beautiful as the fire itself. In the same way, the dark night burns out egoism and leaves us open to God.

John teaches us that the dark night is a difficult but transforming grace. Some see the dark night only as the loss of light and nothing more. John shows us that the dark night is the period before a great spiritual morning.

We can certainly be a Christian without the dark night. The dark night can also make us a saint.

365

December 21 – St. Peter Canisius (Optional Memorial)

The Song of Songs, the Hebrew love song embraced by so many mystics as capturing the drama of a human being embraced by God's love, begins with the moment of romance. As we all know, romance is only the beginning of a relationship, not its substance. Romance has to deepen into a commitment based on knowledge of the other person.

This is true not only of human relationships but is also true of faith. This is something Peter Canisius knew instinctively. Faith cannot remain only an emotional and romantic relationship. Unless grounded in knowledge of the Lord, it can be swept away into a generic or distorted religiosity.

Peter Canisius has been called the Second Apostle of Germany. He was a Jesuit born in 1521 and probably the most important figure in the Catholic Counter-Reformation in Germany. Peter Canisius was present at the Council of Trent and saw his mission as making its clear teaching of Catholic doctrine known throughout Europe. His tools for renewing Catholic identity were not penalties and punishments but education, preaching and writing.

His great claim to fame is the publication of a catechism about ten years before the Catechism of the Council of Trent. He actually wrote three catechisms for different age levels. They went through a staggering number of editions and translations. It is no surprise that Peter Canisius should be designated as the Doctor of Catechetical Studies.

His life reminds us that our faith must move beyond romance to knowledge of the Lord and the truth He teaches in His Church. It is important that we know why we believe what we believe. We need to embrace with our head what we love with our heart.

This does not mean that each believer must become a theologian. It does mean that we need to know that our faith is not an expression of generic religious ideas but is rooted in the Passion, Death and Resurrection of Jesus Christ.

Our faith is not only meant to warm the heart but to enlighten our mind and guide our life.

DECEMBER 23 – ST. JOHN OF KANTY (OPTIONAL MEMORIAL)

"What has Athens to do with Jerusalem?" was a question asked by an early Christian writer, Tertullian. His point was that too much analysis can cloud faith. That certainly was not true for John of Kanty who was a scholar and a saint.

John of Kanty was born in Poland in 1390. He was a gifted boy who received a splendid education. After his priestly ordination, he taught theology and Scripture for several years at the University of Cracow and was later assigned to a parish. He experienced the shadows of both the academic and pastoral life. He wrote the lesson of these difficult experiences on the wall of his room, "Conturbare cave, non est placare suave; diffamare cave, nam revocare grave." ("Don't cause conflict, it's hard to make peace; don't slander others, its harm will not easily cease.")

Eventually he went back to the university to teach. He was known for his personal holiness, his care for the poor, and his fidelity to truth. His memory was so revered at the University of Cracow that his doctoral garment was symbolically placed on successful doctoral candidates for many years after his death.

John of Kanty was a bridge between Athens and Jerusalem. The bright lights of "Athens" can always dazzle people. Scholarship, critique, analysis and discussion, however, can easily become substitutes for faith. Greater value can be placed on critiquing faith than believing it. That is a constant temptation of Athens.

In more recent years, "Jerusalem" has held more attraction for some as theology and analysis are treated as virtual enemies of faith. An uncritical devotionalism (different from devotion) becomes a sign of orthodoxy. Trusting feeling over thinking is the temptation of Jerusalem.

Athens and Jerusalem need each other. Without Athens (or theology), faith can become gullible, taken in by any claim. Without Jerusalem (or faith), theology can become analysis without commitment to Christ.

John of Kanty was a citizen of both great cities, Athens and Jerusalem, and he was a man of prayer. His prayer centered all the areas of his life on Christ. Ours can too.

December 26 – St. Stephen (Feast)

This Gospel reading seems to fracture the mood of the Christmas season. For the past few weeks, we have heard heartwarming music and read pleasant messages of Christmas cheer.

In contrast to that, the Lord here draws a terrifying picture of split families, the betrayal of children by parents and vice versa. But isn't all this really "the rest of the story"?

Jesus came, after all, as a sign of contradiction. The Gospel's proclamation of forgiveness and eternal life requires a separation from our self-centered past. All the wonderful things about which we sang at Christmas begin to take place when we take a serious turn to the Lord.

That implies a break from a pattern of past behaviors. It can quite possibly mean a distance from those friends and even family members who would trivialize and even seek to reverse our conversion. The action of becoming a disciple can be a lonely, even an heroic act. But with it comes everlasting life.

If we honestly want to break with our past, the Lord will help us. He will give us, as He gave Stephen, supernatural strength.

Stephen, after all, was just a human being like us. He was not supernaturally conceived. No angels heralded his coming. No Magi came to acknowledge his birth. He was a convert to the Gospel. But with his baptism, he was filled with the Holy Spirit, as were we.

Here we can see the real and personal significance of the Incarnation. God embraced our weak human nature so we might know the power of His divine Spirit. Our liturgy calls the surrender of our will and the reception of God's grace a "holy exchange" of gifts.

Stephen's heroism was not unique to him. It continues to be repeated by many hundreds of thousands of martyrs and millions of other Christians every day. That same Holy Spirit can fill us if we give our lives fully to the Lord Jesus.

Then, the promise of Christmas peace and power will come true in our lives.

DECEMBER 27 – ST. JOHN, APOSTLE, EVANGELIST (FEAST)

St. John, Apostle and author of the Fourth Gospel, is the only Apostle who did not die a martyr's death. Because he was the last of the Apostles to die, many stories have been handed down about his work and ministry.

It is said that he was given a cup of poisoned wine to drink that he rendered harmless by blessing it. From this story came the old practice years ago of blessing wine on the feast of St. John and allowing people after Mass to drink some of the unconsecrated but blessed wine from the chalice, a practice which had more significance before Communion under both forms became available.

The Gospel of John has been seen as the most sublime portrayal of Jesus and the most evocative in its use of symbols to convey Jesus' teaching. Yet, his Gospel is the most "earthy" in his unrelenting emphasis that the Word became flesh and blood. He is the premier teacher of the power of the Incarnation. The Truth became flesh; the Light became flesh; the Life became flesh. We see this point in today's first reading as St. John emphasizes that they had touched, handled, gazed into the eyes of Truth itself, Life itself, Light itself, the Word itself.

Through faith, people today can have a real relationship with Christ. Faith for St. John is not a mental attitude, a frame of mind or wishful thinking. It is an active relationship with the Risen Christ.

The same Christ who became flesh at Christmas now comes to us in the rituals of the Church. The liturgy is not just a set of devotional ceremonies to remind us of Jesus. It is the place where we make real contact with the real Christ.

St. John teaches us that because of the Incarnation, we can not only have belief about God but can share the very life of God in our souls.

This is the full drama of the Incarnation that goes way beyond the Christmas season.

December 28 – The Holy Innocents (Feast)

The clash of darkness and light is one of the great themes in the writings of St. John and through all of Scripture. Isaiah wrote that people who walked in darkness saw a great light. John today writes that God is light and there is no darkness in Him. Darkness can take many forms.

There is the darkness in Herod's heart. It is the darkness of blind power and cold fear that somebody would take his throne. This is the darkness of someone who would do anything to cling to power, even to kill the innocents we remember today. The desire for power can be morally blinding.

There is the darkness in the lives of people who abuse innocent children. We all know how widespread that seems to be. The natural instinct of an adult is to protect a child, but there are people in darkness who inflict tremendous injury on children. That is another shape to the darkness.

There is the darkness of abortion that kills 1.5 million babies in this country. This is an especially insidious darkness because it intentionally attacks human life at its most vulnerable. There are many antiseptic, well-lit abortion clinics today that are places of darkness.

There is the darkness that kills children in war. These are children caught in the crossfire who have done nothing wrong but are deprived of life or family. War around the world is a part of the darkness today.

The good news is that there is light in Jesus Christ and His disciples who are called to be people of light. If darkness has many shapes and intensities, so does the light. There is the light of personal witness against the evils of abortion and abuse. There is the light of people who care about young life, handicapped life, elderly life and their number is growing.

People who are light not only show the darkness for what it is but can cause the darkness to recede. They remind us that even in the darkness there is the healing light of forgiveness and conversion.

The good news of Christmas is that in the middle of the darkness, there is light... today!

December 29 – St. Thomas Becket (Optional Memorial)

Many people know the story of Thomas Becket from the famous movie "Becket" based on the play by Jean Anouilh. It is the story of an ambitious young man, friend of a king, who became chancellor of England in the 1100's. King Henry II then made him archbishop of Canterbury in 1162 for the most cynical of reasons, to make the Church an arm of the king.

To everyone's surprise, perhaps even to his own, Becket took the role of bishop seriously. He exchanged loyalty to the king for loyalty to Christ and His Church. He stood for the rights of the Church and fearlessly spoke Christ's truth to power. In a moment of apparent exasperation, the king asked whether anyone would "rid him of this turbulent priest." Several knights took this as a command and proceeded to the cathedral to hack Becket to death. He was revered as a martyr immediately and was canonized within three years of his death.

St. Thomas Becket reminds us that the Church is at its strongest when it is a "community of conscience" that is aligned with no political party, when its only commitment is to Gospel truth. Association with people in power can be an intoxicating narcotic. Perhaps in our own time we have seen how the Church can be used for narrow partisan purposes. The alliance the Church has with a political party on a few issues cannot blind it to the differences that may exist in many other areas of policy.

"Let the Church be the Church" is the title of a contemporary religious song. When the Church tries to be disingenuous and clever in its political alliances, it can betray its people who expect Gospel fidelity from their Church. It can betray the very politicians it courts who need a moral watchman to speak the truth. It can betray its Lord Who called the Church into being to be His presence in our world.

Too close a blend of the Church with secular politics can lead to a politicizing of the Gospel where Scripture is made to justify every policy decision by an administration. It can also lead to sacralizing politics by raising a particular administration's policies to the level of Gospel truth.

St. Thomas Becket remains a magnificent example of someone who was a man of the Church first and then a servant of the king. Sometimes those can become reversed.

"Let the Church be the Church" captures the truth of Becket's life and hopefully of our own.

December 31 – St. Sylvester (Optional Memorial)

The First Letter of Saint John was written during a time of great tension in the early Church. This small community experienced a split among its members. This letter was written to strengthen those remaining by encouraging them to stay faithful to the Truth and to the community of Christ's Church.

St. John characterizes the false teachers who occasioned the schism as "anti-Christs." They presented a vision of Jesus that somehow distorted the apostolic faith.

During times of crisis, lines are starkly drawn and people are called to battle. That's how the final days are envisioned: a great battle between Christ and anti-Christ, black hats and white hats, good vs. evil.

Pope St. Sylvester lived in a different kind of time. After years of intermittent persecution, the Church was finally at peace. He became the bishop of Rome in 314, when Constantine was Emperor. Pope Sylvester was the first Pope not to die as a martyr. During his lifetime, the Church acquired a public profile.

There was an explosion of church building, an elaboration of liturgical ritual and the development of rules to govern internal ecclesiastical affairs. Civil power began to be invested in the clergy.

But this time of peace was also a time of a different kind of crisis. The lines between good and evil became blurred by compromise. The Church not only entered the public arena; the public arena entered the Church. The drama of Christian discipleship became domesticated. Christians became comfortable.

It is a great challenge to live the Gospel in times of prosperity. The attractions of status, wealth and power are formidable and more dangerous than persecution because they destroy faith not by opposition but by enticement and by the subtle rationalization of departure from Gospel living they encourage.

This was the challenge that began during the time of Pope Sylvester and remains with us now: how to be faithful in times of prosperity and peace.

Heroism in the Church is not confined to times of persecution. Times of affluence and wealth also need defenders of Faith.

ST PAULS

This book was produced by ST PAULS/Alba House, the Society of St. Paul, an international religious congregation of priests and brothers dedicated to serving the Church through the communications media.

For information regarding this and associated ministries of the Pauline Family of Congregations, write to the Vocation Director, Society of St. Paul, 2187 Victory Blvd., Staten Island, New York 10314-6603. Phone (718) 982-5709; or E-mail: vocation@stpauls.us or check our internet site, www.vocationoffice.org